Stamp Duty Land Tax

Stamp duty on land and buildings has been abolished and replaced with a new tax, stamp duty land tax (SDLT). SDLT will raise in excess of £4 billion, more than inheritance tax and capital gains tax put together.

Stamp Duty Land Tax provides a detailed overview of SDLT and makes a comparison with the old stamp duty provisions, highlighting all the major substantive changes introduced. It gives a detailed discussion of the legislation and puts forward suggested interpretations and planning opportunities.

The author, MICHAEL THOMAS, is a barrister specialising in revenue law at Gray's Inn Tax Chambers. This book has been written in collaboration with the KPMG Stamp Taxes Group. David Goy QC is Consultant Editor. This combination of expertise has resulted in an unrivalled publication which offers comprehensive coverage of practitioner and structuring issues and which will appeal both to property lawyers and to all other professionals involved in land transactions.

Stamp Duty Land Tax

MICHAEL THOMAS

BA (Oxon), BCL (Oxon), Barrister of Gray's Inn

with contributions from KPMG Stamp Taxes Group

Steven McGrady

BA (Oxon), BCL (Oxon), sometime Lecturer in Law at
Christ Church, Oxford and non-practising Solicitor

Gordon Keenay MA

(Cantab), Dip. Stat., PhD

Consultant Editor DAVID GOY QC
LLM, Barrister of the Middle Temple

CAMBRIDGE
UNIVERSITY PRESS

PUBLISHED BY THE PRESS SYNDICATE OF THE UNIVERSITY OF CAMBRIDGE
The Pitt Building, Trumpington Street, Cambridge CB2 1RP, United Kingdom

CAMBRIDGE UNIVERSITY PRESS
The Edinburgh Building, Cambridge, CB2 2RU, UK
40 West 20th Street, New York, NY 10011–4211, USA
477 Williamstown Road, Port Melbourne, VIC 3207, Australia
Ruiz de Alarcón 13, 28014 Madrid, Spain
Dock House, The Waterfront, Cape Town 8001, South Africa

http://www.cambridge.org

First published 2003

Printed in the United Kingdom at the University Press, Cambridge

Typefaces Times 10/12 pt. and Formata Condensed   *System* LATEX 2$_\varepsilon$ [TB]

A catalogue record for this book is available from the British Library

ISBN 0 521 54515 3 paperback

Contents

Preface

Stamp duty land tax (SDLT) is a very important new tax. Although there are many similarities with its predecessor, stamp duty, SDLT is founded upon an entirely different set of concepts. Moreover, the new tax is enforceable through a tough compliance regime which requires taxpayers to self-assess. SDLT is intended to raise in excess of £4 billion per year: more than inheritance tax and capital gains tax combined. Up until quite recently, stamp duty was often something of an afterthought when advising on land transactions; now SDLT is a priority. The importance of the new tax cannot be overstated.

My aim has been to write a detailed commentary on the new SDLT code contained in the Finance Act 2003. This is a forward-facing book and my first priority has been to state the law as it will be after the new regime takes effect on 1 December 2003. Where it is necessary to refer back to the stamp duty position in order to understand the new SDLT provisions that apply to a particular area then I have done so. I have also tried to summarise in Chapter 1 the major changes, both procedural and substantive, brought about by SDLT. Although stamp duty continues to apply to sales of shares and even some land transactions, I have referred to it throughout in the past tense both because the general rule is that it will no longer apply to land transactions and in order to make the discussion easier to follow.

The structure of the material is, I hope, self-explanatory from the Contents. For each area I have tried to set out the law and then to explain how it will apply in practice. My aim has been to focus on areas where the law is likely to cause difficulties. I have tried to express myself in a style that is readily accessible to both non-tax specialists and non-lawyers; although of course I have been hindered in this both by the nature of the material and by my own ability.

I have been very fortunate that the KPMG Stamp Taxes Group, led by Steven McGrady, have lent their vast expertise to this project. Steven McGrady and Gordon Keenay have had considerable input into the book at every stage from the planning to the proof-reading. KPMG's assistance has been especially valuable in addressing the areas where the law runs into practical difficulties and in writing Chapter 7 ('Structuring transactions and planning'). This book is much better as a result of KPMG's input, and I am very grateful to both Steven McGrady and Gordon Keenay in particular for the huge contributions which they have made and for giving their time so freely.

I would also like to thank the following members of KPMG's team: Alan Cook of McGrigor Donald in Glasgow not only contributed the passages on Scots law (with additional input from Ian Gordon, also of McGrigor Donald) and the Table of Scottish property deeds but also proof-read the drafts of several chapters, saving me from several mistakes and adding some important improvements. Alan McAlister of McGrigor Donald in Belfast contributed the references to Northern Ireland law. Sean Randall made contributions to the discussion of group relief in Chapter 5 and drew up the Table of cases and the Table of statutes with Tina Thorogood. Simon Yeo made important contributions to the material on partnerships in Chapter 3 and his proof-reading of the draft of Chapter 3 resulted in a number of improvements to the text. Gordon Keenay has been participating in the ongoing consultations on leases and complex commercial transactions which resulted in his making large contributions to both Chapter 6, including the comparative table, and the section on the likely future developments in Chapter 9. Gordon also drew up the Practitioner checklist and the Table of exemptions and reliefs and, together with Alan Cook, the Glossary. Steven McGrady wrote the section on PFI transactions in Chapter 3 and also made a big contribution to Chapter 9. Finally, Tina Thorogood compiled the index with Gordon Keenay, prepared the List of abbreviations and helped prepare the final manuscript for submission.

I would also like to thank my colleagues in Gray's Inn Tax Chambers for their support in the writing of this book. Patrick Soares and Patrick Way both lent me copies of their own articles on SDLT. I am especially grateful to Stephanie Talbot who typed the manuscript while at home convalescing after an operation and to Elizabeth Allen, Dawn Anderson and Jane Fullbrook who covered for her absence. Most importantly, I would like to thank David Goy QC for guiding me through this project and doing his best to keep me from falling into error. This book has benefited greatly both from David's wealth of expertise on property taxation and his experience of writing practitioner textbooks. The remaining errors are, of course, all my own.

The timetable for writing this book has been extremely tight. I would like to thank my publisher, Kim Hughes, at Cambridge University Press for her assistance in this project and for remaining calm as the deadline for the manuscript slowly receded. I would also like to thank the team at Cambridge University Press and, in particular, Martin Gleeson and Neil de Cort for their efforts in rushing through the manuscript for publication in order to compensate for the missed deadlines.

Finally, I would like to thank Pippa for her encouragement and patience.

I have stated the law as at 8 September 2003. The latest developments can be accessed from the online bulletin board for this book at www.cambridge.org/sdlt/.

Michael Thomas
Gray's Inn Tax Chambers
8 September 2003

The application of SDLT to Scotland and Northern Ireland

The SDLT provisions in the Finance Act 2003 apply to the whole of the United Kingdom, including Scotland and Northern Ireland, both of which have their own legal systems over which the common UK tax system is spread.

Scots property law is very different to English property law – for example, there is no concept of equity, and (until the appointed day under the Abolition of Feudal Tenure etc. (Scotland) Act 2000 which is due on 28 November 2004) the land system is feudal with separate superiority and ownership interests in respect of the same land. This book aims to highlight the principal differences between English and Scots law as they impact on SDLT, the intention being to flag any peculiarly Scottish aspects in order to assist the typical Scottish practitioner. However, it must be emphasised that a detailed treatment of the differences between the two legal systems is outside the scope of this book.

Northern Irish property law is much closer to English law. The Act contains specific references to technical legal terms and statutory provisions which relate purely to Northern Ireland but to all intents and purposes these equate to the like interest and equivalent provisions in the legislation applicable in England and Wales. In that context it is hoped that Northern Irish practitioners will take this into account when reading the text and find the information herein of considerable assistance in understanding the new tax regime. Again, it should be emphasised that this book is not intended to be a definitive statement of Northern Irish law.

Tables

Table of cases

Table of statutes

Table of rates of tax

Rates of SDLT on land transactions (other than leases) for residential property

Relevant consideration	Percentage
Not more than £60,000	0 per cent
More than £60,000 but not more than £250,000	1 per cent
More than £250,000 but not more than £500,000	3 per cent
More than £500,000	4 per cent

Rates of SDLT on land transactions (other than leases) for non-residential or mixed-use property

Relevant consideration	Percentage
Not more than £150,000	0 per cent
More than £150,000 but not more than £250,000	1 per cent
More than £250,000 but not more than £500,000	3 per cent
More than £500,000	4 per cent

Rates of SDLT on leases of residential property

Relevant rental value	Percentage
Not more than £60,000	0 per cent
More than £60,000	1 per cent

Rates of SDLT on leases of non-residential or mixed-use property

Relevant rental value	Percentage
Not more than £150,000	0 per cent
More than £150,000	1 per cent

Glossary

Term	Definition	Relevant paragraph of this book	Relevant statutory provision (FA 2003 unless stated otherwise)
acquisition	• A transfer of an existing chargeable interest. • A creation of a new interest. • The surrender or release of an interest. • The variation of an interest.	2.20	section 43
annuity (as consideration)	An agreement to pay periodical sums, whether for life, or in perpetuity, or for an indefinite period, or for a definite period exceeding twelve years, is taken into account as chargeable consideration only to the extent of twelve annual payments.	4.67	section 52
average annual rent	• The average annual rent over the term of the lease. • If different amounts of rent are payable for different parts of the term, any of which are ascertainable at the effective date, the average annual rent is taken over the period for which the highest ascertainable rent is payable.	6.34	Schedule 5, paragraph 9(3)
building works	Works of construction, improvement or repair of a building or other works to enhance the value of land.	4.42	Schedule 4, paragraph 10
certificate	Either a Revenue certificate or a self-certificate – required to be submitted to the Land Registry or the	8.45	section 79

Term	Definition	Relevant paragraph of this book	Relevant statutory provision (FA 2003 unless stated otherwise)
	Registers of Scotland along with most documents which evidence a land transaction.		
chargeable consideration	• Money or money's worth given directly or indirectly by the purchaser or a person connected with him. • VAT chargeable in respect of the transaction (unless by virtue of a VAT election made after the effective date). • Existing debt assumed by the purchaser. • The release of debt due to the purchaser or owed by the vendor. • The value of building works (though not where the works are carried out after the effective date on land held by the purchaser or a person connected with him and it is not a condition of the transaction that the works are carried out by the vendor or a person connected with him). • The value of the provision of services. • Special rules for leases (including the cash equivalent of rent for accommodation provided to an employee in the course of employment).	4.5	section 50 and Schedule 4
chargeable interest	An interest in land in the United Kingdom or the benefit of a condition, etc. affecting the value of any such interest, but not an exempt interest.	2.6	section 48(1)
chargeable transaction	A land transaction that is not exempt from charge under Schedule 3 or otherwise.	2.2	section 49
clawback	A charge to tax following the withdrawal, triggered by a change in	5.45, 5.62, 5.82, 5.96	Schedule 7, paragraphs 3

Term	Definition	Relevant paragraph of this book	Relevant statutory provision (FA 2003 unless stated otherwise)
	circumstances within three years after the effective date, of group relief, reconstruction relief, acquisition relief or charities relief.		and 9; Schedule 8, paragraph 2
collective enfranchisement	The right exercisable by an RTE company (under the Leasehold Reform, Housing and Urban Development Act 1993) under Part 1 of the Landlord and Tenant Act 1987 or Chapter 1 of Part 1 of the Leasehold Reform, Housing and Urban Development Act 1993.	5.110	section 74
company	• Generally, any body corporate or un-incorporated association, but not a partnership. • For group relief purposes, a company means a body corporate.	5.46	section 100, Schedule 7, paragraph 1(2)(a)
completion	In Scotland, means: (a) in relation to a lease, when it is executed by the parties (that is to say, by signing) or constituted by any means; (b) in relation to any other transaction, the settlement of the transaction.	2.26	section 121
connected persons	Very generally, an individual's spouse, relatives and spouse's relatives; companies under common control; partners and their spouses; trustees of a settlement and their settlors.	4.68	ICTA 1988, section 839
contingent consideration	Consideration that is to be paid or provided, or cease to be paid or provided, only if some uncertain future event occurs. SDLT is initially payable based on a reasonable estimate subject to application to the Revenue for deferral of payment.	4.28	section 51(3)

Term	Definition	Relevant paragraph of this book	Relevant statutory provision (FA 2003 unless stated otherwise)
contract	Includes any agreement, including an agreement for lease.	2.26	section 44(10)
conveyance	Includes any instrument, including the grant of a lease.	2.26	section 44(10)
crofting community right to buy	A right exercisable by a crofting community body under Part 3 of the Land Reform (Scotland) Act 2003.	5.111	section 75
effective date	• Generally, the date of completion. • For a contract which is to be completed by a conveyance or lease grant, the date of substantial performance. • Special rules apply on the chargeability and notifiability of a conveyance or lease grant which completes a contract or sequence of contracts. • On the acquisition of an option or right of pre-emption, the effective date is the date when the option or right is acquired (as opposed to when it becomes exercisable).	2.26	sections 119, 44(4) and 46(3)
exchanges	Exchanges of land interests are treated as two distinct land transactions. Certain transfers of residential property to housebuilders in exchange for a new dwelling are exempt.	3.26, 4.52, 5.35	section 47, Schedule 4, paragraphs 5 and 6, section 58
exempt interest	Licences to use or occupy land; security interests; in England and Wales and Northern Ireland, tenancies at will, franchises, advowsons and manors.	2.10	section 48(2) to (5)
exempt land transaction	A land transaction that is exempt from charge. Transactions which are exempt under Schedule 3 are not notifiable	chapter 5	section 49 and Schedule 3; see also the

Term	Definition	Relevant paragraph of this book	Relevant statutory provision (FA 2003 unless stated otherwise)
	transactions. Other exempt transactions may be notifiable transactions.		Table of exemptions and reliefs at Appendix 2.
implementation date	Expected to be 1 December 2003.	9.5	To be appointed by Treasury Order under Schedule 19, paragraph 2(2)
just and reasonable	The basis upon which consideration which is attributable to two or more transactions or other matters is to be apportioned.	4.40	Schedule 4, paragraph 4
land	Includes (a) buildings and structures and (b) land covered by water.		section 121
land transaction	Any acquisition of a chargeable interest.	2.5	section 43(1)
land transaction return	The return which is required to be delivered to the Revenue, in the form prescribed by regulations, for every notifiable transaction within thirty days after the effective date of the transaction.	8.4	section 76(1)
licence	Generally, a personal right to occupy another person's land which does not amount to a lease.	2.11	section 48(2)(b)
linked transactions	Transactions which form part of a single scheme, arrangement or series of transactions between the same vendor and purchaser or persons connected with either of them.	4.92	section 108

Term	Definition	Relevant paragraph of this book	Relevant statutory provision (FA 2003 unless stated otherwise)
major interest in land	A freehold or leasehold estate either at law or in equity. In Scotland, the interest of an owner (of the *dominium utile*, until Scottish feudal reform) or of a tenant over land.	4.53, 8.8	section 117
market value	Generally, the price which assets might reasonably be expected to fetch on a sale in the open market. There are special rules for the market value of quoted shares, units in unit trust schemes and unquoted shares and securities.	4.73	section 118; TCGA 1992, sections 272–274
net present value	The formula used to calculate the value of rents paid over the term of a lease.	6.13	Schedule 5, paragraph 3
notifiable transaction	• Generally, acquisitions of major interests (freeholds and leaseholds) are notifiable unless exempt from charge under Schedule 3 (so they remain notifiable even if another exemption or relief applies). • But grants of leases for at least seven years are notifiable if there is chargeable consideration. • Grants of leases under seven years are notifiable if SDLT is payable on them or would be payable but for a relief. • Acquisitions other than of a major interest are notifiable if SDLT is payable on them or would be payable but for a relief.	8.6	section 77
option	An agreement entered into between two or more parties binding one or more of them to enter into a land transaction, or to discharge the obligations under the agreement in some other way, if called upon to do so pursuant to the terms of the agreement	3.15	section 46(1)(a) and section 46(2)

Term	Definition	Relevant paragraph of this book	Relevant statutory provision (FA 2003 unless stated otherwise)
partition	Partition or division of a chargeable interest to which persons are jointly entitled.	3.28, 4.56	Schedule 4, paragraph 6
party to a transaction	One of the tests for identifying a purchaser.	2.24	section 43(5)
penalties (for failure to deliver return)	• Flat-rate penalty of £100 if return delivered within three months of filing date and £200 otherwise • Additional tax-related penalty not exceeding the amount of tax chargeable if return not delivered within twelve months of the filing date. • Additional daily penalty up to £60 a day under certain circumstances and under the direction of the Commissioners.	8.20	Schedule 10, paragraphs 3–5
percentage rate of tax	Determines the amount of tax chargeable, based on the chargeable consideration for the transaction. The percentage rate is determined by the amount of the relevant consideration. See the Table of rates at page xxii above.	4.78, 6.30	section 55(2), Schedule 5, paragraph 2
postponed consideration	In determining the chargeable consideration, no discount is given for postponement of the right to receive it or any part of it.	4.27	Schedule 4, paragraph 3
provision of services	Where services (other than the carrying out of building works) are provided as all or part of the consideration, the value is the amount that would have to be paid in the open market to obtain those services.	3.67, 4.13	Schedule 4, paragraph 11
purchaser	• The transferee of an existing interest in land. • The person entitled to a created interest.	2.22	section 43(4) and (5)

Term	Definition	Relevant paragraph of this book	Relevant statutory provision (FA 2003 unless stated otherwise)
	• The person whose interest in land benefits from a surrender or variation. • A person is only a purchaser if he has given consideration for, or is a party to, the transaction.		
rate of tax	The relevant percentage rate of tax.	4.78, 6.30	section 55(7) schedule 5, paragraph 2
relevant consideration	The chargeable consideration for the transaction, used to determine the relevant rate of tax. If the transaction is one of a number of linked transactions, the relevant consideration is the total of the chargeable considerations for all those transactions.	4.92	section 55
reliefs	Reduce or remove the liability to tax, subject in certain cases to clawback if circumstances change within three years. See the table of reliefs in Appendix 2.	5.23	section 57–75
residential property	Generally, property which is used or suitable for use as a dwelling or is being constructed or adapted for such use. Six or more dwellings subject to a single sale or lease are treated as non-residential.	4.85	section 116
Revenue certificate	A certificate by the Revenue that a land transaction return has been delivered in respect of the transaction.	8.49	section 79(3)(a)
reverse premium	A payment by the landlord to the tenant on the grant of a lease, by the tenant to the landlord on the surrender of the lease, or by the assignor to the assignee on the assignment of a lease.	4.64	Schedule 4, paragraph 15

Term	Definition	Relevant paragraph of this book	Relevant statutory provision (FA 2003 unless stated otherwise)
right to buy	A sale or lease of a dwelling at a discount by a relevant public sector body, or in pursuance of a preserved right to buy on disposal to a private sector landlord. Contingent consideration under the right-to-buy transaction is ignored in calculating the SDLT payable.	5.17	Schedule 9
Royal Assent	10 July 2003	9.5	
SDLT transaction	A transaction that is chargeable or notifiable or for which a certificate is required for land registration purposes. Generally, a land transaction whose effective date is on or after the implementation date, unless it is pursuant to a contract entered into on or before 10 July 2003 which is not subsequently varied or assigned. Special rules apply to options and to existing resting on contract transactions.	9.6	Schedule 19
security interest	An interest or right (other than a rentcharge or, in Scotland, a feu duty or similar payment) held for the purpose of securing the payment of money or the performance of any other obligation. These are excluded from the scope of SDLT.	2.18	section 48(3) and (4)
self-certificate	A certificate by the purchaser that no land transaction return is required in respect of the transaction.	8.51	section 79(3) (b) schedule 11
substantial performance (in relation to a contract)	The date when the purchaser takes possession of the land, or becomes entitled to receive rents and profits, or	2.30	section 44(5) to (7)

Term	Definition	Relevant paragraph of this book	Relevant statutory provision (FA 2003 unless stated otherwise)
	when a substantial amount (expected to be taken as 90 per cent) of the consideration is paid or provided or the first rent payment under a lease is made.		
transfer of rights	An assignment (assignation in Scotland), sub-sale or other transaction as a result of which a person other than the original purchaser becomes entitled to call for a conveyance to him.	3.2	section 45(1)
unascertainable consideration	Consideration payable in the future but based on events prior to the effective date, the amount of which has not yet been calculated. SDLT is initially payable based on a reasonable estimate.	4.28	section 51
uncertain consideration	Consideration whose amount or value depends on uncertain future events. SDLT is initially payable based on a reasonable estimate subject to application to the Revenue for deferral of payment.	4.28	section 51(3)

Abbreviations

BSA	Building Societies Act 1986
C&E	HM Customs & Excise
CA	Court of Appeal
Ch	Chancery Division
FA	Finance Act
ICTA	Income and Corporation Taxes Act 1988
IRC	Inland Revenue Commissioners
LLP	limited liability partnership
PACE	Police and Criminal Evidence Act 1984
P&CR	*Property and Compensation Reports*
PFI	Private Finance Initiative
QB	Queen's Bench
Revenue	Inland Revenue
RIAT	Risk Identification Assessment Team
Sch.	Schedule
SDLT	stamp duty land tax
SP	Statement of Practice
SPV	special purpose vehicle
STC	*Simon's Tax Cases*
TC	*Official Tax Cases*
TCGA	Taxation of Chargeable Gains Act 1992
TLTA	Trusts of Land and Appointment of Trustees Act 1996
VAT	value added tax
VATA	Value Added Tax Act 1994

1

Introduction and overview

A new tax on land transactions

1.1 Stamp duty land tax (SDLT) is charged on transactions the subject-matter of which is land situated in the United Kingdom. Tax is charged as a percentage of the purchase price. Unlike its predecessor, stamp duty, SDLT is a directly enforceable tax which is payable by the purchaser. The SDLT legislation is contained in the Finance Act 2003 (FA 2003). The general rule is that SDLT applies to land transactions entered into after 1 December 2003,[1] although this is subject to detailed transitional provisions which are discussed in Chapter 9 below.

1.2 Tax is chargeable on transactions involving residential property where the consideration exceeds £60,000 and on those involving commercial or mixed-use property where the consideration exceeds £150,000. The initial rate is 1 per cent and this increases to a maximum rate of 4 per cent where the chargeable consideration exceeds £500,000. For example, on a straightforward house purchase for £750,000 tax of £30,000 will be payable by the purchaser.[2]

1.3 As the name suggests, SDLT replaces stamp duty on land transactions. Like its predecessor, SDLT is charged primarily on sales of land as a percentage of the purchase price and must be paid before the transaction can be registered with the Land Registry (or the Scottish or Northern Irish equivalents). The increase in the nil-rate band for commercial property to £150,000 is the only change in the rate of tax introduced by SDLT. Nevertheless, despite these similarities SDLT is not a modernisation of stamp duty on land transactions but rather a new tax in its own right.

1.4 SDLT differs fundamentally from stamp duty in two ways. First, the charge to tax is founded on an entirely new set of concepts. Stamp duty[3] was charged on documents which gave effect to a 'conveyance or transfer on sale'. SDLT is charged on the 'acquisition' of a 'chargeable interest' in land whether or not there is any document giving effect to the transaction. The charge to tax

---

[1] The government has announced that 1 December 2003 will be the appointed day for the new regime to commence and has steadfastly refused to delay implementation. However, this needs to be confirmed by an official order made by the Treasury.

[2] The rates of tax are set out in the Table of rates of tax at p. xxii above.

[3] *Ad valorem* stamp duty, as opposed to the £5 fixed duty which was payable on transfers otherwise than on sale.

is discussed in outline at paragraph 1.16 below and in detail in Chapter 2. Secondly, SDLT is a directly enforceable tax accompanied by an extremely onerous compliance regime. The 'purchaser'[4] is liable to pay the tax whether or not he plans to register the land transaction. A self-assessment return must be made to the Inland Revenue (the 'Revenue') within thirty days of the transaction accompanied by a payment of any tax or the taxpayer becomes liable to a penalty. The compliance regime is discussed in outline at paragraph 1.27 below and in detail in Chapter 8.

1.5   Accordingly, SDLT is a new tax founded on fresh concepts and enforced through a rigorous new compliance regime based on self-assessment. The inclusion of the term 'stamp duty' in the name of the new tax indicates its origins and the sort of transactions on which it is to apply. However, the term 'stamp duty' is not only strictly incorrect, because SDLT contains no requirement to stamp any documents, but also misleading insofar as it suggests that the basis of the new tax remains essentially the same as that of stamp duty.

The importance of SDLT

1.6   Stamp duty on land and buildings currently raises in excess of £4 billion of revenue.[5] While nowadays new taxes are introduced under the guise of making the tax system fairer, the purpose of every tax is to raise additional revenue for the state. SDLT is no different: it has been introduced to raise more money than stamp duty on equivalent land transactions. This has huge practical importance because it underlies every provision of the new tax. The substantive provisions of SDLT are designed to close down what the Revenue saw as stamp duty loopholes that were being exploited by tax planners and thereby increase revenue. The new procedural provisions and especially the self-assessment regime are designed to ensure that the new tax is not only directly enforceable but also collected with maximum efficiency.

1.7   The rise in importance of stamp duty, caused by the recent increases in rates, has been a tax phenomenon in the last few years. In 1990, stamp duties as a whole, including stamp duties on shares and other assets, raised only £1.7 billion.[6] This was less than capital gains tax, which in 1990 raised £1.9 billion, and little more than inheritance tax, which then raised £1.3 billion. By 2002, stamp

---

[4] A term of art for SDLT purposes the meaning of which is discussed at para. 2.22 below.

[5] When the consultation exercise which led to the introduction of SDLT was announced in April 2002, the government stated that stamp duty on land transactions currently raised around £4 billion. It is believed that the figure is now closer to £5 billion.

[6] The source for all the figures in this paragraph except for the amount of stamp duty raised on land transactions is the Revenue's table showing 'Annual Receipts of Inland Revenue'. The table gives no figure for stamp duty raised on land transactions, only a figure for stamp duties as a whole including stamp duty and stamp duty reserve tax levied on shares. It is thought that stamp duty on land transactions currently raises around £5 billion. See para. 1.2 and note 5 above.

duties as a whole were raising some £7.5 billion of which around £4 billion was raised on sales of land and buildings, and it is thought that the figure is now around £5 billion. In contrast, capital gains tax raised only £1.7 billion in 2002 and inheritance tax a mere £1.4 billion. Accordingly, stamp duty on sales of land currently raises more than inheritance tax and capital gains tax combined. The introduction of SDLT is designed to generate yet more revenue.

The inadequacy of stamp duty

1.8   The purpose of introducing SDLT is to raise more money from land transactions in a similar way to stamp duty without increasing the rate of tax. In order to understand how SDLT is to achieve this, it is necessary to understand the limitations[7] of stamp duty. The biggest problem faced by the Revenue in trying to enforce stamp duty was that it was not directly enforceable. Although documents were not admissible in evidence or at the Land Registry unless properly stamped,[8] the Revenue could not directly assess any person for the duty. Even if a document had been submitted for stamping, the taxpayer was not required to pay the correct amount of duty but could withdraw the document if the Revenue wanted additional duty.

1.9   The stamp duty legislation was last consolidated in the Stamp Act 1891 and the legislation is scattered throughout subsequent Finance Acts.[9] The increases in rates brought stamp duty to the fore and created a surge in tax planning work. Unsurprisingly, the legislation proved to be hopelessly outdated and inadequate for such an important source of revenue. Not only was the legislation difficult to follow, but it was often possible for taxpayers to reduce the stamp duty charge, or even avoid having to pay it at all, through the use of careful planning.

1.10   Some planning techniques were blocked by piecemeal anti-avoidance legislation. One example was the provisions enacted in the Finance Act 2000[10] which prevented taxpayers transferring land into a connected company so that the shares in that company could then be sold with stamp duty payable at 0.5 per cent on the shares rather than at 4 per cent on the land. That such simple planning was effective into the twenty-first century says everything about how far behind the times stamp duty has been lagging. It was generally agreed that stamp duty was long overdue for fundamental reform.

1.11   In April 2002, the government announced a consultation exercise to reform stamp duty on land and buildings. The three aims were stated to be fairness, modernisation and simplification. This consultation exercise was abruptly

---

[7] Of course, the Revenue viewed stamp duty's limitations as shortcomings and, conversely, taxpayers saw them as advantages.

[8] S. 14 of the Stamp Act 1891.

[9] Although there was a partial consolidation of stamp duty in Sch. 13 FA 1999.

[10] Ss. 119 and 120 FA 2000.

terminated in January 2003 leaving those who participated in the consultation in no doubt that, so far as the Revenue was concerned, clamping down on perceived avoidance was the dominant motive for change. In the Revenue's view, fairness requires the prevention of what they perceive to be tax avoidance because it is unfair for well-advised taxpayers to avoid paying tax through good planning, as this puts an unfair share of the tax burden onto everyone else. It is against this background that the SDLT regime has been enacted in the Finance Act 2003.

The SDLT regime

1.12   The SDLT regime is a comprehensive new code contained in the Finance Act 2003. The legislation is written, or so it is claimed, in plain English. Unfortunately, while the wording of the legislation may be readily understandable, finding the statutory provisions which apply to any particular land transaction is a more difficult exercise because the relevant provisions are scattered throughout the part of the Finance Act 2003 which deals with SDLT and the Schedules to it.

1.13   The SDLT code is an entirely new tax with a new charging mechanism. In theory, there should be no need to refer back to stamp duty. Unfortunately, in practice this is unrealistic because even though the SDLT charge is fundamentally different the new legislation is based upon and often copied from the old stamp duty provisions. Accordingly, what a particular SDLT provision is trying to achieve often cannot be properly understood without referring back to the old stamp duty position. In particular, large parts of the new SDLT regime, including almost all of the main changes from stamp duty, are designed to stop the sort of planning that was being used for stamp duty.

1.14   However, in practice the most important change introduced by the SDLT regime is not substantive but procedural. The introduction of the new self-assessment regime means that SDLT is enforceable and the taxpayer must file a return and pay within thirty days or incur a penalty. Whereas before it was possible to take a more relaxed attitude to stamp duty, it is now absolutely imperative that SDLT is properly complied with.

1.15   The remainder of this chapter contains an overview of the substantive and procedural provisions of the SDLT regime. The aim is to provide a summary of the tax and the major changes in comparison with stamp duty. Each area of the SDLT regime is then discussed separately in more detail in the chapters which follow.

Overview of the charge to SDLT and other substantive provisions

The basis of the charge to SDLT

1.16   SDLT is charged on 'land transactions'. A land transaction means the 'acquisition' of a 'chargeable interest' in land situated in the UK. A chargeable interest is defined widely to include any estate or interest in or right over land; it includes any equitable interest in land but expressly not a licence or a lender's charge. Unlike stamp duty, SDLT is chargeable irrespective of whether there is any instrument effecting the transaction. It is similarly irrelevant whether or not the parties are present in the UK at any time. The charge to SDLT is discussed in detail in Chapter 2 below.

Tax is charged as a percentage of the chargeable consideration

1.17 Tax is charged on a percentage of the 'chargeable consideration' given for the transaction. The principle is the same as for stamp duty. However, the meaning of 'chargeable consideration' is defined very widely and includes consideration in money's worth. No discount is made if the consideration is only payable on a contingency, although an adjustment can be made if the consideration subsequently turns out not to be payable. An assumption of debt by the purchaser expressly counts as chargeable consideration as it did under stamp duty. The rule that a transfer of land to a connected company is deemed to take place at market value is also retained in order to prevent avoidance through land being transferred into a special purpose company which could then be sold on to a purchaser with stamp duty payable at only 0.5 per cent on the share sale. The rules for identifying and valuing the chargeable consideration are explained in detail in Chapter 4 below.

Rates of tax

1.18 The rates of tax are as set out at the start of this book.[11] The rates follow the old stamp duty rates and increase in stages as the chargeable consideration increases. There is a new distinction between residential and non-residential property, although as yet the only difference is the increased nil-rate band for non-residential property of £150,000. Surprisingly, for a supposedly modern tax, there is no tapering of the rate increases. Instead, the rate is simply increased when the consideration reaches a particular figure, a technique aptly described as the slab effect. The real reason why there is no tapering is that the government would need to increase the rates in order to achieve the same yield. If transactions are 'linked' within the meaning of section 108 FA 2003, then the chargeable consideration is aggregated for the purposes of determining the rate of tax. Section 108 is a re-enactment of the old stamp duty 'series of transactions' rule,[12] although once again the wording of the legislation is more widely drafted. The rules for calculating the tax liability are discussed in Chapter 4 below.

Leases

1.19 The new rules for taxing the rent payable on a lease are one of the most important changes brought about by SDLT. The old stamp duty rule that leases

---

[11] See p. xxii above.   [12] Contained in para. 6(1) of Sch. 13 FA 1999.

are charged on a percentage of the average annual rent has been scrapped and replaced with the rule that leases should be charged according to the value of the future rental stream at the time of grant, referred to as the 'net present value'. The net present value of a lease will be calculated using a statutory formula. The charge to SDLT on leases is discussed in Chapter 6 below.

Special rules for particular transactions

1.20   The Finance Act 2003 contains a number of special provisions dealing with how the charge to SDLT is to apply to certain types of transaction. The most important rule is that a contract for the sale of freehold land is now chargeable under section 44 FA 2003 on the earlier of completion (settlement in Scotland) or 'substantial performance'. This is to prevent parties from resting on contract in order to avoid paying tax. Substantial performance occurs as soon as either party obtains what he bargained for: when the purchaser either takes possession of the land or becomes entitled to receive the rents and profits or the vendor receives the purchase price (other than a deposit). The new rule for determining when tax becomes payable on the sale of freehold land and the concept of substantial performance are discussed at paragraph 2.26 below.

1.21   The new rules on sub-sales contained in section 45 FA 2003 follow on from section 44. The general rule is now that both the original sale and the sub-sale will be chargeable to tax unless the original sale is not substantially performed. Relief is given to the extent that completion of the sub-sale contract is deemed not to complete the original sale. The new rule for sub-sales under section 45 is discussed further in Chapter 3 at paragraph 3.2 onwards.

1.22   Options are the subject of a special rule designed to ensure that the grant of an option is always chargeable to SDLT. Exchanges are treated as two separate sales of the properties being exchanged; it is no longer possible to structure an exchange as a single sale of the more valuable property. The transfer of an interest in possession in a trust where the underlying assets include land is also within the charge to SDLT. The tax treatment of options is discussed further in Chapter 3 at paragraph 3.15 onwards.

Exemptions and reliefs

1.23   The exemptions and reliefs for SDLT are based on those which applied to stamp duty. Disadvantaged areas relief is retained and will continue to be very important in practice. This relief exempts some of the most valuable commercial property in the country because the criteria to identify a disadvantaged area are based on residential deprivation. Group relief, reconstruction and acquisition reliefs apply in a similar way as for stamp duty. However, the conditions for their application have been tightened up and each is now subject to a three-year clawback in order to prevent them being exploited by tax planners.

1.24   There is no longer a fixed £5 duty for transactions otherwise than on sale, and transactions which are not made for chargeable consideration are now exempt from SDLT under Schedule 3 FA 2003. The reliefs introduced by SDLT are mostly targeted reliefs aimed at very specialised types of transaction. For example, the new relief in section 58 FA 2003 for purchases made in part-exchange by housebuilders compensates for the abolition of resting on contract and the much more limited sub-sale relief. The exemptions and reliefs from SDLT are the subject of Chapter 5 below.

Commencement and transitional provisions

1.25 The general rule is that from 1 December 2003, the date that will be appointed as the 'effective date' for the implementation of the new regime, all land transactions will be subject to SDLT. Stamp duty is abolished on land transactions but continues to be chargeable on shares and securities. Stamp duty reserve tax continues to be chargeable on agreements to transfer chargeable securities. However, there is an exception from SDLT for transfers of land into and out of a partnership by a partner or former partner and transfers of interests in partnerships. This is a temporary exception until new SDLT provisions are ready to be brought into force. These are expected to form part of the Finance Act 2004.

1.26 There is also a complicated set of transitional provisions to deal with transactions which somehow straddle 1 December 2003. In summary, where the contract for the land transaction is made after 1 December 2003 the transaction will always be subject to SDLT. Conversely, where the contract was made before 11 July 2003, the day after the FA 2003 received Royal Assent, the land transaction will not normally be subject to SDLT even if it is completed after 1 December 2003. If the contract was made after 10 July 2003 then it will be an SDLT transaction unless it is completed before 1 December 2003, even if it was substantially performed before 1 December 2003. The transitional provisions and in particular the special rules for sub-sale are discussed in more detail in Chapter 9.

Overview of the SDLT compliance regime

1.27 The fundamental limitation in the old stamp duty regime was that duty was not directly enforceable. Conversely, the most important change introduced by SDLT is to make tax not only directly enforceable on the purchaser but also the subject of an onerous self-assessment regime. The purchaser must now make a return and pay any tax within thirty days of a 'notifiable transaction'. The return must be in a prescribed form and sent to a central unit in Netherton. A transaction may be notifiable even though there is no tax to pay and a taxpayer who fails to make a return will be liable to a penalty.

1.28 There is a very complicated set of rules to decide whether a transaction is notifiable.[13] Transactions which would be chargeable but for any of the reliefs, for example group relief, will normally be notifiable. Where there is no

---

[13] Discussed in detail at Chapter 8.

chargeable consideration then the transaction will not be notifiable. However, where the transaction is not notifiable, the taxpayer must still self-certify that the provisions of SDLT have been complied with before a transaction can be registered with the Land Registry (or the Scottish or Northern Irish equivalents). Where a return has been made a certificate will be issued by the Revenue.

1.29   Once the return has been made, the Revenue has nine months in which to raise an enquiry into the return. The old stamp duty adjudication procedure has been abolished and there is now no procedure for requiring the Revenue to give rulings either before or after a transaction. However, the Revenue may agree to give a pre-transaction ruling in a particular case,[14] and in any event they have only nine months in which to raise an enquiry. If an enquiry is made the Revenue may issue a further assessment. Should the taxpayer wish to appeal against a Revenue assessment then the appeal will now be heard by the General or Special Commissioners rather than the High Court or the Court of Session.

1.30   The new regime also contains the usual provisions for the Revenue to charge interest where tax is paid late and penalties where returns are not made in time or the compliance provisions are not otherwise satisfied. The Revenue also has wide-ranging information-gathering powers modelled on those for direct taxes contained in the Taxes Management Act 1970. Taxpayers are under a duty to keep the records relating to a land transactions for at least six years. The time limit for making assessments is extended to up to twenty-one years where tax has not been paid owing to negligence or fraud on the part of the taxpayer.

Summary of the substantive changes introduced by SDLT

1.31   The main substantive changes introduced by SDLT in comparison to stamp duty include the following:

1. The mandatory nature of the charge.
2. The different nature of the charge: SDLT is a charge on land transactions however they take effect, whereas stamp duty was a charge on instruments.
3. The abolition of the rule that contracts for the sale of freehold land are only chargeable on conveyance and its replacement with the rule that contracts are chargeable on the earlier of completion or 'substantial performance'.
4. The restriction of sub-sale relief to situations where the original contract of sale is not substantially performed.
5. The introduction of a new formula for leases at a rent designed to charge the value of the rental stream at the time of grant.
6. The tightening up of the anti-avoidance rules in order to prevent the exploitation of reliefs including the extension of the group relief claw-back to three years and the introduction of similar provisions for the reconstruction and acquisition and charities reliefs.

[14] Following Code of Practice 10.

7. The introduction of new reliefs targeted at specific transactions.
8. The abolition of the £5 fixed duty.
9. The increase in the nil-rate band to £150,000 for commercial and mixed-use property.
10. The new rules for valuing contingent and deferred consideration.
11. The abolition of the ability to structure an exchange as a single sale of the more valuable land.
12. The replacement of the stamp duty 'series of transactions' rule with the wider concept of 'linked transactions'.

Summary of procedural changes introduced by SDLT

1.32   The importance of the new procedural regime cannot be overstated. It is discussed in detail in Chapter 8. The procedural changes introduced by SDLT in comparison with stamp duty include the following:

1. Tax is now directly enforceable against the purchaser.[15]
2. The purchaser must file a return on the new form within thirty days of a notifiable transaction including a self-assessment of any tax due, and pay that tax. A return may have to be made even though no tax is payable.
3. The introduction of the new procedure following a return and, in particular, the nine-month window during which the Revenue can open an enquiry.
4. The duty on the taxpayer to keep records for at least six years.
5. The abolition of the adjudication procedure and the lack of any formal clearance procedure under SDLT.
6. The raft of new information-gathering powers exercisable by the Revenue.
7. The rule that the Land Registry (and the Scottish and Northern Irish equivalents) cannot register land transactions without either a certificate of compliance from the Revenue or a self-certificate from the taxpayer that SDLT has been complied with.
8. Appeals are now to the General or Special Commissioners rather than the High Court or the Court of Session.

---

[15] This is both a procedural and a substantive change.

2

The charge to SDLT

Introduction

2.1 The purpose of this chapter is to discuss the core concepts in the charge to tax. SDLT is a tax on 'land transactions'. A land transaction involves the 'acquisition' of a 'chargeable interest' by a 'purchaser'. The purchaser is the person who is liable to pay the tax. Accordingly, this chapter is concerned with the following questions.

- What is a chargeable interest?
- What constitutes an acquisition of a chargeable interest?
- Who is the purchaser?
- When does a land transaction take effect for SDLT purposes and, in particular, what is the tax trigger on a sale of land which requires a separate conveyance?

A tax on land transactions

2.2 SDLT is a tax on land transactions. Unlike its predecessor, stamp duty, which was charged on documents effecting certain transfers, the charge to SDLT is triggered by the transaction itself. Accordingly, the first issue to consider is now whether or not there is a land transaction rather than whether a particular document needs stamping. As a land transaction tax, SDLT applies to all chargeable land transactions, however they take effect. Section 42(2) FA 2003 expressly provides that tax is chargeable whether or not there is any instrument effecting the transaction. Land transactions effected orally which were not chargeable to stamp duty are now within the charge to SDLT.

2.3 It is understandable policy that a land transaction tax should be levied on, for example, a lease irrespective of whether it is created in writing. However, section 43(2) FA 2003 expressly includes within the charge to tax transfers which arise by operation of law, by court order or other authority and by statute.[1] This makes a whole variety of events, including the transfer of title by adverse possession,

---

[1] Although note that a land transaction is exempt from charge if no chargeable consideration is given for it under para. 1 of Sch. 3 FA 2003. A transfer to a connected company is deemed to take place at market value under s. 53 FA 2003 and so is not exempt under para. 1 of Sch. 3.

the acquisition of an easement or servitude by prescription and the creation of constructive trusts, potentially chargeable to SDLT. Tax will only be payable where consideration in excess of the nil-rate band is given, so in practice this should make no difference. Nevertheless, the charge is very broad and the risk that SDLT may be levied in unforeseen circumstances needs to be guarded against.

2.4   An example of where a transfer arising by operation of law may produce difficulties is the case of a merger under foreign law. Under the law of some foreign jurisdictions, for example Delaware, it is possible to effect a true merger, the effect of which is that two entities become one. This is impossible under English law, where a merger is effected through one company acquiring the business of the other. In the past the Revenue has, on occasions, agreed that no stamp duty was payable on the basis that a foreign merger took effect by operation of law, but that analysis will not now prevent SDLT from being chargeable. Whether or not there will be a charge to SDLT will depend on whether the transfer involves an acquisition of a chargeable interest for consideration. If the merger involves an issue of replacement shares by the new entity then it would seem that there is consideration on which SDLT is chargeable but there may still be no acquisition of a chargeable interest.

A land transaction means the acquisition of a chargeable interest

2.5   The concept of a land transaction as defined in section 43(1) FA 2003 requires the acquisition of a chargeable interest. Both 'acquisition' and 'chargeable interest' are key terms of art for SDLT. The meaning of 'acquisition' is discussed at paragraph 2.20 onwards. Whether the concepts used in the charge to SDLT are to be interpreted in a narrower legal sense or in a broader commercial sense is discussed further at paragraph 7.19 below.

Chargeable interest

2.6   Chargeable interest is defined, again in very wide terms, in section 48(1). It includes, under section 48(1)(a), 'an estate, interest, right or power in or over land in the United Kingdom', and, under section 48(1)(b), 'the benefit of an obligation, restriction or condition affecting the value of any such estate, interest, right or power'.

2.7   The meaning of section 48(1)(a) is reasonably straightforward and, naturally, it includes all sales of land and grants of leases. No distinction is drawn between legal and equitable interests, so the acquisition of an equitable interest is within the charge to SDLT. The definition also covers the acquisition of rights over land, such as the granting of an easement or servitude. The inclusion of powers brings in a power of appointment exercisable under a trust.[2] Although it would

---

[2]   In Standing Committee, the Chief Secretary to the Treasury, Mr Paul Boateng, stated that: 'In practice, the only powers that are likely to be caught by the SDLT regime are powers of appointment

be very unusual for trustees to buy such a power, the inclusion of powers brings within the charge to tax the situation where a beneficiary, for example with a life interest in the property, pays the trustees for the surrender of their power of appointment so that they can no longer appoint away from him. The application of SDLT to trusts is considered in more detail at paragraph 3.35 onwards.

2.8   The intention behind section 48(1)(b) is apparently to bring into charge restrictive covenants and similar obligations that bind another's land only where they affect the value of that land.[3] Unfortunately, that is not what the statute says. Instead it is drafted inclusively so that *any* obligation which affects the value of rights over land falls within it. The important limitation inherent in section 48(1)(b) is that the obligation must affect the value of (proprietary) rights over land. In other words, only rights which affect the value of the land are included, and these will usually themselves be proprietary rights. However, rights which affect the value of proprietary rights are not always themselves proprietary.

2.9   For example, if an option-holder agrees to a restriction on the exercise of his option with the vendor then the rights under that contract are personal rights even though the option itself is proprietary. Nevertheless, the variation of the option is within section 48(1)(b). By way of contrast, if A contracts with B, a builder, for B to build an extension to A's house, that contract is not within section 48(1)(b) because the benefit of it is personal to both parties and does not run with A's land so as to affect its value. Similarly, the benefit of a maintenance contract, even if it is assignable, does not affect the value of an interest in land.[4]

Exempt interests

2.10   Certain rights are expressly exempted from the definition of a chargeable interest. The two most important are licences and security interests. The others are tenancies at will, advowsons,[5] franchises[6] and manors.[7] Section 48(5) gives the Treasury power to make regulations to make other interests exempt. The power is most likely to be used to exempt other rare species of interest that most lawyers will probably never encounter in practice.

---

exercised by trustees of land. If such powers were not caught, there will be opportunities for the avoidance of SDLT – a fact that is patently obvious.'

[3] Finance Bill 2003, Notes on Clause 48 para. 8.

[4] It might be argued to the contrary that the benefit of an assignable building or maintenance contract does affect the value of land in the same way as planning permission. Such an argument would be misconceived because there is no difficulty in finding a builder provided that you are prepared to pay; so even if the contract is at a low price the value is contained in the contract rather than the land.

[5] Perpetual rights of presentation to an ecclesiastical living.

[6] A grant from the Crown to hold markets or levy tolls.

[7] Lordships of the manor being equitable interests in land and registrable at the Land Registry.

Licences

2.11   Licences to use or occupy land and tenancies at will are expressly exempted from the definition of chargeable interest by section 48(2)(b). Accordingly, there is no need to consider the difficult question of when, if ever, a licence might have fallen within the wording of section 48(1). The essence of a licence is the permission to enter onto another's land without being a trespasser. Conversely, every permission to enter onto another's land involves the grant of a licence. The exclusion of licences is because they are merely personal rights rather than proprietary rights which bind the land. Although licences concern land, unlike the variation of an option, the grant of a licence does not affect the value of the grantor's proprietary rights because he remains able to dispose of the land free from the burden of any licence and the licensee's only remedy will be against the grantor in person. Similarly, although tenancies at will are interests in land, the chief characteristic of a tenancy at will is that it is terminable at any time without prior notice and therefore it does not affect the value of the landlord's reversion.

2.12   The term licence is not defined in the Act and therefore bears its general law meaning. Accordingly, the *Street* v. *Mountford*[8] line of authorities on the lease/licence distinction will now be used to determine whether or not transactions are taxable. The classic definition of a lease is that it involves exclusive possession for a term at a rent. Although there are many different types of lease, all leases are interests in land. In contrast, the essence of a licence is permission to enter another's land so as not to be a trespasser. A licence is a merely personal right. In Scotland, the concept of a licence is less developed than it is in English law, but if an interest is not in law a lease because it does not exhibit the essential elements of a lease in Scots law (an agreement between parties in relation to specified land for a rent and for a specified or ascertainable period) with no consequent right to quiet enjoyment then it may be regarded as a licence.

2.13   In practice, distinguishing a lease from a contractual licence under English law can be a difficult exercise. A lease is a species of contract but so is a contractual licence. Although rent is indicative of a lease, a lease can exist without the payment of rent either because no payment is made or because payment is made in the form of a premium.[9] Regular ongoing payments can equally be made for a contractual licence. Similarly, although a lease must have a certain term, this requirement has been interpreted liberally, so that, for example, periodic tenancies do not fall foul of the rule.[10] Accordingly, the presence or absence of both a fixed term and rent are not determinative of the question whether something is a lease or a licence.

[8] [1985] AC 809.
[9] See *Ashburn Anstalt* v. *Arnold* [1989] Ch 1; [1988] 2 WLR 706; [1988] 2 All ER 147, CA.
[10] *Prudential Assurance Co. Ltd* v. *London Residuary Body* [1992] AC 386.

2.14   Accordingly, in practice exclusive possession[11] is the most important factor in distinguishing leases from licences. In *Street* v. *Mountford*,[12] Lord Templeman, giving the judgment of the House of Lords, went even further and suggested that exclusive possession was conclusive[13] other than in exceptional cases. However, an alternative view[14] is that, where either analysis is possible, then the intention of the parties should be decisive because, while they cannot create one thing and call it something else, in a situation where they could structure their relations in either of two ways they should be able to choose the one which they consider best.[15]

2.15   In practice, care will need to be taken in ensuring that what the parties believe to be a contractual licence is not in substance a lease on which SDLT must be paid. For those purchasers who are prepared to make do with the lesser rights conferred by a licence or a tenancy at will, this may be a method of saving SDLT. This is discussed in more detail at paragraph 7.25 below.

2.16   Finally, it is worth remembering that the issue of whether a 'licence to occupy land' exists arises for VAT in interpreting the exemption from VAT for land contained in Group 1 of Schedule 9 VATA 1994. However, in VAT the test works differently: the issue is typically whether there is either a licence to occupy land, which qualifies for exemption from VAT in the same way as a lease, or a licence insufficient to amount to a licence to occupy and thus taxable. This area of law is worth knowing about because it is a fruitful source of principles which may be used to support the conclusion that something is a licence rather than a lease.

2.17   If something is not a licence to occupy for VAT purposes, then it would be inconsistent to treat it as a lease for SDLT purposes. However, this is extremely unlikely to happen as the type of rights which have been held not to be licences to occupy land, such as the right to operate as a hairdresser from a particular chair in a salon, do not involve exclusive possession. A more interesting question is whether something which for VAT purposes is a licence to occupy land, for example the right to operate two shops at Heathrow airport,[16] could be a lease for SDLT purposes. The answer is that it could because the VAT authorities are concerned with a different question and cannot be decisive of the lease/ licence distinction for SDLT purposes. Nevertheless, the VAT case law must be something which can be taken into account.

---

[11]   Note that exclusive possession does not require exclusive occupation. A person entitled to the rents may have exclusive possession.

[12]   [1985] AC 809.   [13]   See especially at p. 823D–E and at pp. 826G–827B.

[14]   Although this is not accepted by, for example, the learned editor of *Megarry and Wade's The Law of Real Property* (6th edn, Sweet & Maxwell, London, 2000).

[15]   Cf. *IDC* v. *Clark* (1992) 65 P&CR 179, where it was decided that the parties could create a licence of a right to use a fire escape rather than an easement even though the conditions for an easement were present.

[16]   *British Airports Authority* v. *C&E Commissioners* [1977] STC 36, CA.

Security interests

2.18   The other major exemption from the definition of chargeable interest in section 48 is that for security interests under section 48(2)(a). These are defined[17] as 'an interest or right (other than a rent charge) held for the purpose of securing the payment of money or the performance of any other obligation'.[18] Accordingly, SDLT will not be charged when lenders or creditors take charges over property. Obtaining a mortgage or a remortgage on a property will not trigger a charge to SDLT. Nor does it matter if the loan is used to finance something other than the property purchase such as funds for a business.

2.19   Only straightforward mortgages and charges are made exempt under section 48(2). Other more complex lending arrangements remain within the charge to SDLT even though the economic effect may be no different. There is a relief for alternative finance arrangements made by individuals, including Islamic mortgages, contained in sections 72 and 73. This is discussed further at paragraph 5.101 onwards. However, there is no such relief for companies. Accordingly, sale-and-leaseback arrangements and securitisations will be within the charge to SDLT. It may be that, in the future, limited reliefs will be enacted but the Revenue is very cautious about introducing a relief for securitisations lest it open the floodgates for avoidance through selling securitised interests in land. This is an example of the tax system lagging behind the latest commercial practice. Possible future developments in the field of corporate finance transactions are discussed further at paragraph 9.41.

Acquisition of a chargeable interest

2.20   A land transaction involves the acquisition of a chargeable interest. Under section 43(2), it does not matter how that acquisition takes effect. The concept of acquisition as defined in section 43(3) includes not only transfers and creations of chargeable interests, as might be expected, but also surrenders, releases and variations of them. The charge to SDLT is therefore very wide indeed. Accordingly, the surrender of a lease or the release of a restrictive covenant (or, in Scotland, the discharge of a burden) are both within the charge to SDLT notwithstanding that as a matter of general law no interest is acquired as a result of either transaction. Somewhat inconsistently, the surrender or assignment of a lease for a reverse premium is then specifically exempted from SDLT, as discussed at paragraph 4.64 below.

2.21   The inclusion of surrenders, releases and variations widens the scope of the tax charge in comparison to stamp duty. For example, it will cover payments made to commute rent payable under a lease. This idea was sometimes used for

---

[17] Under s. 48(3)(a).

[18] In Scotland, the reference to a rentcharge is to be read as a reference to a feu duty or a payment mentioned in s. 56(1) of the Abolition of Feudal Tenure etc. (Scotland) Act 2000.

stamp duty planning purposes – such planning is no longer effective. Despite the wide definition, there is some residual uncertainty concerning the scope of the term 'acquisition'. There may perhaps be rare events, possibly arising under foreign law,[19] which do not fit within either the normal meaning of acquisition or the enlarged meaning under section 43(3); see further paragraph 2.4 above.

Identifying the taxpayer: who is the purchaser?

2.22   Who is the purchaser is an important question in practice because that person is obliged to comply with the reporting requirements and to pay any tax. To be a purchaser a person must both acquire a chargeable interest under the rules contained in section 43(3) and either give consideration for or be a party to the transaction under section 43(5). On a straightforward transfer or creation of a chargeable interest, the purchaser is the person who becomes entitled to the interest, as would be expected. So, for example, on the grant of an easement or servitude, the purchaser is the person who becomes entitled to the right. Where a chargeable interest is varied, surrendered or released, then the purchaser is the person whose interest is benefited or enlarged as a result.[20] Accordingly, on the release of a restrictive covenant (or a burden in Scotland), the purchaser is the person whose land is freed from the burden of the covenant or obligation.

2.23   In order to be a purchaser, a person not only must acquire a chargeable interest under the rules discussed earlier in this chapter but also must either give consideration for or be a party to the transaction under section 43(5). The intention behind section 43(5) is to prevent those who receive a benefit from transactions to which they were not a party and for which they have given no consideration from becoming liable to SDLT. For example, if Mrs Smith buys a property to provide a home for her aged mother, the mother is not a purchaser because she has provided no consideration for the transaction and is not a party to it. The purchaser is Mrs Smith because she has acquired the property herself. It does not matter if Mrs Smith directs the vendor to convey the property directly to the mother because Mrs Smith has nevertheless acquired rights over the land.

2.24   Who is a party to a land transaction is not made clear by the Act. Where there is a contract for the land transaction, then the parties who enter into that contract and acquire rights under it must be parties to the land transaction. However, it is not necessary for a person to be a party to a contract in order to be a party to a land transaction. Most simply, the recipient of a gift is a party to the land transaction when he receives the interest because the act of receipt completes the gift. The legislation is unclear as to whether a third party beneficiary under a contract is a party to the land transaction. For example, A contracts with B for B to transfer Blackacre to C. C is not a party to the contract and in the normal case

[19] Although arguably that is not enough because what matters is the characterisation of the event under English law. In other words, a conflict of laws issue would arise.

[20] S. 43(3)(b)(c) FA 2003.

he has no right to enforce it. The contract between A and B will be substantially performed when the purchase price has been paid,[21] yet C will have received nothing and has no right to receive anything. It does not seem right that C should be required to pay tax in this situation. Arguably, the position should be different if C is given the right to enforce the contract under the Contracts (Rights of Third Parties) Act 1999[22] and C proceeds to exercise that right. The land transaction is the acquisition of the chargeable interest and a person who enforces his rights in order to effect the land transaction is a party to it. If C does not acquire rights and cannot be required to pay tax then A will remain liable (because A has acquired the right to compel B to transfer Blackacre to C).

2.25   Section 43(5) restricts the definition of purchaser rather than expanding it. Accordingly, merely giving consideration for or being a party to a land transaction is not alone sufficient to make someone a purchaser because that person does not acquire any chargeable interest. For example, providing the finance for a purchase of land does not make a person liable to SDLT unless he becomes entitled to land rights other than an exempt security interest. There was a concern that, where a land transaction also increased the value of the vendor's interest in land, then the vendor would become a purchaser notwithstanding that he paid no consideration. This concern was raised in Standing Committee by reference to an example[23] of a situation where a lessee pays a landlord to permit him to grant a sub-lease. The sub-lease increases the value of the landlord's interest because the sub-lessee is a more desirable tenant than the existing one. The Chief Secretary to the Treasury confirmed that, in this example, the landlord was not liable for SDLT on the grant of the sub-lease because on these facts two separate land transactions would have occurred. The landlord would not be chargeable on the grant of the sub-lease and would not be a joint purchaser under section 103 FA 2003.[24]

When a land transaction takes effect for SDLT

General rule

2.26   Liability to tax and reporting obligations arise following the 'effective date' of the transaction. Under section 119 FA 2003, the general rule is that the effective date is that of completion. However, this is subject to the rule that, where a contract is to be completed by a conveyance and is 'substantially performed' before it is formally completed, then a charge to SDLT will arise at the time of substantial performance. This is a radical change from the old stamp duty provision and is brought about by section 44 FA 2003. Before discussing section 44, it is worth emphasising that it is the exception. The effective date of transactions where

---

[21] The concept of substantial performance is discussed at para. 2.27 onwards below.
[22] This Act does not apply in Scotland.   [23] Provided by the Law Society.
[24] Tax will still be chargeable on the consideration given by the tenant for the landlord's permission and on the grant of the sub-lease.

there is no preceeding contract is simply that of completion (or, in Scotland, settlement) under the general rule contained in section 119 FA 2003.[25]

Background: treatment of contract requiring separate conveyance under stamp duty

2.27   It is no coincidence that the section dealing with contract and conveyance is located at the very start of the statutory provisions of the SDLT regime. In order properly to understand the importance of section 44 FA 2003 and how it is to apply, it is necessary to refer back to the old stamp duty position. Stamp duty followed the traditional distinction between contract and conveyance, and stamp duty on the sale of a legal estate in land only became chargeable upon completion (although section 115 FA 2002 introduced an exception where the purchase price exceeded £10 million). Accordingly, where a separate conveyance was required to effect the transfer provided for by a contract, then no duty was payable until then and the contract was not stampable. Although following the contract and the payment of the purchase money the purchaser became beneficially entitled to the property, the contract was not stampable as the sale of an equitable interest because that was not the transfer provided for in the contract but instead one which arose by operation of law.[26]

2.28   This rule was frequently exploited in tax planning by the parties deliberately choosing not to complete transactions but instead to 'rest on contract'. If the parties chose not to complete a contract for the sale of land in order to avoid stamp duty, then the courts regarded that as legitimate tax planning. In *IRC* v. *Ingram*,[27] Vinelott J stated[28] that '[the] fact that parties to . . . a sale agreement do not intend that it will be completed by a conveyance is not a reason for describing it as a sham'. Resting on contract was only possible where the purchaser was prepared to make do without the legal title. Accordingly, it was only available in practice when the parties trusted one another and the purchaser did not require a mortgage. Nevertheless, it was hugely important to stamp duty planning, both as a structure in its own right and as part of more sophisticated arrangements. Similar structures were employed in Scotland subject to variations to reflect the fact that Scots law does not recognise equitable interests, and a purchaser obtains a mere personal right against the seller under a purchase contract and not an equitable interest enforceable against third parties.

Contract requiring separate conveyance

2.29   The purpose of section 44 is to prevent parties avoiding postponing tax by resting on contract. Section 44 applies in situations where a conveyance is required in order to complete the sale of land. If the transaction is completed

---

[25] Note that the effective date of an option within s. 46(1) FA 2003 is expressly the date of grant under s. 119(2) and s. 46(3) FA 2003.

[26] See especially *IRC* v. *Angus* (1889) 23 QBD 579.

[27] [1985] STC 835.   [28] *Ibid.*, p. 843e.

without previously having been substantially performed, then the effective date is the date of completion, as under the old stamp duty rules.[29] However, under section 44(4), where the contract is substantially performed before completion, then the effective date is when the contract is substantially performed. Where substantial performance precedes completion, then the contract is deemed to be the transaction which it provides for under section 44(4), so that there is both a deemed acquisition of the land agreed to be transferred and a deemed payment of the purchase price. The intention is that, where there is both a contract and a completion by conveyance, then SDLT will be charged on the earlier of those two events. SDLT will only be charged once on the same consideration. Nevertheless, where the contract is substantially performed before it is completed, then both events are notifiable transactions with each requiring a land transaction return to be submitted by virtue of section 44(8)(a). However, under section 44(8)(b), tax is only chargeable on completion to the extent that it is greater than the tax chargeable under the contract. The intention of section 44(8)(b) is that additional tax should be payable on completion to the extent that additional consideration is given. However, this will rarely be the case because section 44(4) deems the contract to be the transaction it provides for, with the result that tax is chargeable on the entire consideration payable under the contract. Accordingly, section 44(8) applies only where the purchaser gives additional consideration not provided for by the contract.

Substantial performance

Introduction

2.30   The new concept at the heart of section 44 is substantial performance. As a corollary to triggering the tax charge on a sale of freehold land under section 44 FA 2003, substantial performance also effectively determines whether or not sub-sale relief is available under section 45 FA 2003 because sub-sale relief is only now available if the original contract is not substantially performed (the treatment of sub-sales is discussed further in Chapter 3 at paragraph 3.2 onwards). A contract is substantially performed under section 44(5) when either 'the purchaser takes possession of the whole or substantially the whole of the chargeable subject-matter of the contract' or 'a substantial amount of the consideration is paid or provided'. The principle behind these provisions is that, once either party has received in substance and economic reality the benefit of what he bargained for, then SDLT will become payable. It does not matter that the formality of transferring the legal title has not yet happened or that a small amount of the purchase price remains outstanding.

2.31   Once again, section 44 has been drafted widely. The charge to SDLT is triggered once either party has received substantially what that party bargained for.

---

[29] S. 44(3).

Accordingly, in order to avoid the charge, neither party must receive substantially what he bargained for. If the sale is called off before the purchase price is paid or the purchaser has gone into occupation, then there will have been no substantial performance. However, the ability to 'rest on contract' is only available to this limited extent under SDLT. Deferring substantial performance for as long as possible may help mitigate the tax charge (see further paragraph 7.44 below).

Purchaser takes possession of the whole or substantially the whole
of the subject-matter of the contract

2.32   A contract is substantially performed under section 44(5)(a) when the purchaser takes possession of the whole, or substantially the whole, of the land which is the subject-matter of that contract. Under section 44(6)(a), a purchaser takes possession if he receives or becomes entitled to receive rents or profits. It is immaterial whether the purchaser takes possession under the contract or under a lease or licence of a temporary character. The subject-matter of the contract as defined by section 43(6) includes not only the chargeable interest but also any interest or right pertaining to it that is acquired with it. Accordingly, when the purchaser takes possession of a property or the purchaser of an investment property begins receiving rent, then the contract will have been substantially performed and a charge to SDLT may arise.

2.33   However, in some cases the question of whether the purchaser has taken possession of substantially the whole of the property is much more difficult. Section 44(6) provides some clarity by confirming that a purchaser takes possession if he receives or becomes entitled to receive rents and that it makes no difference if he takes possession under a temporary lease or licence rather than under the contract itself. Nevertheless, uncertainty remains on the question of when exactly a purchaser takes possession of the whole or substantially the whole of the subject-matter of the contract and this has been left to the courts to resolve. If the contract is for the sale of two or more properties, then each sale is a separate land transaction and must be analysed separately. However, there remains doubt as to how section 44(5)(a) will apply in relation to the particular property. An important point to note is that taking possession of the property for the purposes of fitting out the premises will normally trigger a charge to SDLT. This uncertainty is particularly unfortunate because substantial performance triggers the requirement to make a land transaction return.[30] If the Revenue believes that a return is submitted late the taxpayer may have to pay interest and penalties.

A substantial amount of the consideration is paid or provided

2.34   Substantial performance occurs under section 44(5)(b) when a substantial amount of the consideration is paid or provided. A distinction is drawn between

---

[30] Under s. 76(1) FA 2003. Substantial performance provides the trigger when it is the effective date of the land transaction.

rent and other consideration in section 44(7). If the consideration is not rent, then the contract is substantially performed when the whole or substantially the whole of it is paid. If the only consideration is rent, then the first payment amounts to substantial performance. If the consideration is a mixture of both rent and other consideration, then substantial performance takes place on the earlier of either a payment of rent or the payment of substantially the whole of the other consideration.

2.35   How much consideration is substantially the whole is again left to the courts to decide. The Revenue has its own view as to what amounts to substantially the whole of the consideration, which is that it is 90 per cent of the total. However, that figure has not been enacted in order to prevent it being deliberately circumvented by tax planners. The thinking is that, by not specifying a particular figure, the Revenue and ultimately the courts will be able to do justice in a particular case. The Chief Secretary's speech in Standing Committee gives a good insight into the Revenue's thinking on this matter.

> That is clearly an area in which we have to ask whether enshrining any particular proportion in the wording of the statute would benefit anyone other than those seeking to exploit some sort of advantage. It could enable an unscrupulous minority to plan around that wording with a view to reducing the revenue take. We do not want that to happen. We shall, however, issue guidance in due course. Part of the reason for subsection (4) is to prevent payment of a deposit from triggering a charge. That is clearly unacceptable in relation to house purchases. The guidance will indicate that 'a substantial amount of the consideration' is equal to or greater than 90 per cent. That was the approach taken for the Finance Act 2002, and it will inform the guidance to be issued in due course . . . It would not help anyone but the unscrupulous minority . . . were we to go further than that.
>
> Allowing someone into possession for fitting-out purposes will often trigger the first payment of rent. In those circumstances, subsection (6)(b) will of course apply. In other circumstances, however, the person will continue to occupy or trade from those premises once the fitting out works are completed, in which case subsection (4) will apply. Again, the treatment of such cases will be covered by guidance to be published by the Revenue. There is nothing unusual or sinister about that: it is the traditional way in which we have proceeded in order to avoid the mischief that I mentioned.

2.36   While this thinking is understandable, a counter argument is that it would have been better to enact a particular figure in order to provide certainty. It is desirable to have maximum certainty in a provision which triggers both a charge to tax and reporting requirements.

Events following substantial performance

2.37   Where the contract is completed following substantial performance, then both transactions are notifiable, but credit is given on completion for the tax that became chargeable on the contract under section 44(8), as discussed at paragraph 2.29 above. Where a transaction is substantially performed before it is completed this will trigger the obligation to make a return. The requirement to make a land transaction return under section 76 FA 2003 is discussed in paragraph 8.4 onwards below. If completion takes place before the land transaction return is made, in other words within thirty days of substantial performance, then it should be possible to make only one return.

2.38   If the contract is rescinded, annulled or otherwise not carried into effect following substantial performance, then the overpaid tax is refundable under section 44(9). Accordingly, in the case of a conditional contract, SDLT is chargeable once the contract is substantially performed, although it becomes repayable if the condition is subsequently unfulfilled. For example, if a sub-lease is granted subject to the landlord's consent and the sub-lessee takes possession, then the contract is substantially performed when the sub-lessee takes possession of the property notwithstanding that the condition is never fulfilled. When the condition is not satisfied, then the tax can be reclaimed.

3

The application of the charge to SDLT to specific transactions other than ordinary sales

Introduction

3.1   Chapter 2 focused on the core concepts upon which the charge to SDLT is founded, and considered how tax is charged on a straightforward sale of land. This chapter follows on from that, and is concerned with certain types of transaction where the charge to SDLT is governed by specific provisions within the Finance Act 2003.

Sub-sales and successive transactions

Introduction

3.2   Section 45 FA 2003 deals with sub-sales and assignments of rights under a contract of sale. The situation envisaged is where, after a contract for sale has been entered into but before completion, the original purchaser agrees to sell on to a third party sub-purchaser and directs the original vendor to convey the property directly to that sub-purchaser. The same result can be achieved by the original purchaser assigning his rights to a third party purchaser. Under the old stamp duty regime, tax was only charged on the consideration given by the sub-purchaser.[1] However, under SDLT, both transfers are now chargeable unless the original contract is not substantially performed or completed other than as part of completion of the sub-sale. Section 45 provides relief to this limited extent.

3.3   In order properly to understand section 45, it is necessary to refer back to the old position under stamp duty. Stamp duty was only chargeable on completion unless the consideration payable under the contract exceeded £10 million.[2] Accordingly, where it was contemplated that the immediate purchaser of land intended to sell on to a sub-purchaser, often the parties would choose not to complete the first sale but instead to rest on contract. The legal title would then

---

[1] See s. 58(4) of the Stamp Act 1891. Although the rule was subject to exceptions, the most important of which was that a contract of sale where the consideration exceeded £10 million was itself stampable under s. 115 FA 2002.

[2] See s. 115 FA 2002. Although note that a limited sub-sale relief was available where s. 115 applied under Part 2 schedule 36 FA 2000 so that where there was a sub-sale stamp duty in was only chargeable to the extent that the chargeable consideration for the sub-sale exceeded the chargeable consideration on the original sale chargeable under s. 115.

be transferred from the original vendor to the sub-purchaser on completion of the second sale.

3.4   The technique of combining resting on contract with a sub-sale was often used by land developers. Typically, the developer would purchase a site from the original vendor. Although the development agreement would provide for the sale of the land to the developer, that sale would remain uncompleted. Once the developer had built the development, for example ten houses, each house would be sold to the ultimate purchaser by the developer and the developer would direct the original vendor to make a conveyance to the ultimate purchaser. This is one type of planning which sections 44 and 45 are designed to stop. Planning involving sub-sales always involved the parties resting on contract. The ability to rest on contract has been abolished by section 44 and replaced by the doctrine of substantial performance. Accordingly, planning involving sub-sales where a contract is substantially performed would be ineffective anyway without section 45, owing to section 44.

3.5   The government has confirmed that it is considering targeted replacements for sub-sale relief. The relief for part-exchanges of residential property between individuals and housebuilders in section 58, discussed at paragraph 5.35 below, is an example of such a relief. Other reliefs are likely to be similarly targeted at narrow areas.

The operation of section 45

3.6   Section 45 applies in the situation 'where a contract for a land transaction (the "original contract") is entered into . . . which . . . is to be completed by a conveyance, and . . . there is an assignment, sub-sale or other transaction . . . as a result of which a person other than the original purchaser [(the "ultimate purchaser")][3] becomes entitled to call for a conveyance to him'.[4] For convenience, the term 'sub-sale' will be used to refer to any situation to which section 45 applies, in particular to the situation where the original purchaser assigns his rights to a third party. The sub-sale can relate to the whole of the subject-matter of the original contract or only to part.

3.7   Section 45 is a curious piece of drafting. The most important words in section 45 are the final words of section 45(3) which provide that 'the substantial performance or completion of the original contract at the same time as, and in connection with, the substantial performance of the [sub-sale] shall be disregarded'. In other words, completion of the sub-sale is deemed not to complete the original contract, as would otherwise have been the case, by section 45(3) but if prior to completion of the sub-sale the original contract is substantially performed then SDLT is chargeable in respect of the original contract and no

---

[3] The term 'ultimate purchaser' is adopted for convenience; it is not a term of art introduced by the legislation.

[4] S. 45(1).

sub-sale relief is available. The result of section 45(3) is that sub-sale relief is available to this limited extent.

3.8 Surprisingly, then, the first issue to consider in determining the tax treatment of a sub-sale situation governed by section 45 is whether the original contract is substantially performed under section 44 otherwise than as a consequence of the completion of the sub-sale itself. If the original contract is substantially performed apart from the sub-sale, then tax becomes chargeable on the original contract in the normal way. The question of when a contract is substantially performed is discussed above at paragraph 2.30 onwards.

3.9 The tax treatment of the sub-sale is dealt with by section 45(2) and (3). These provisions also operate oddly because they first deem the sub-sale not to be a land transaction and then deem a fictional transaction to have taken place. The sub-sale agreement is, counter-intuitively, deemed not to be regarded as a land transaction entered into by the purchaser by section 45(2). Section 45(3) is again the important provision; its final words have already been discussed above. The first part of section 45(3) provides for a deemed contract under which the ultimate purchaser is the purchaser and the consideration is so much of the consideration under the original contract as is to be paid directly by the ultimate purchaser to the original vendor together with the consideration given for the sub-sale. The consideration given by the ultimate purchaser to the original vendor includes consideration provided indirectly by the ultimate purchaser or a person connected with him.

3.10 The effect of section 45 is best explained by an example.[5] A agrees to sell Whiteacre to B for £100,000. B pays A a deposit of £10,000. B then assigns his rights under the original contract to C for £20,000. C completes the original contract in place of B and A conveys Whiteacre directly to C. C pays the £90,000 balance due under the original contract to A.

3.11 C will pay SDLT on a total £110,000 of chargeable consideration by virtue of section 45(3). This is the aggregate of the £90,000 which he pays indirectly under the original contract and the £20,000 given for the transfer of rights. It is the total of what he pays for the land.

3.12 B's position depends upon whether his contract with A is substantially performed apart from the completion of the sub-sale. If it is substantially performed, for example by B taking possession[6] of the property, then SDLT is chargeable on the full amount of the consideration under the original contract of £100,000. However, if the original contract is not substantially performed or completed other than as part of the completion of the sub-sale, the original contract is not chargeable owing to the operation of section 45(3).

---

[5] This is based on the example given by the Revenue in the Notes to the Finance Bill and subsequently discussed and amended during Standing Committee.

[6] This prevents the sub-sale structure being used by a developer if he takes possession himself.

3.13   If the contract between A and B is not substantially performed, then it will not be chargeable to SDLT at all. This means that, where there is a sub-sale and the original contract is not chargeable to SDLT owing to section 45(3), then no SDLT is chargeable on the deposit paid under the original contract. The deposit is not chargeable under the original contract because the payment of the outstanding purchase money and the transfer of the legal title to the ultimate purchaser are deemed not to complete the original contract. Nor is it chargeable under section 45 because it is not given by the sub-purchaser or a person connected[7] with him. In practice, this should make no difference because where unconnected parties enter into a sub-sale agreement the price paid by the ultimate purchaser will incorporate any deposit paid by the original purchaser. In the above example, the price charged by B for the assignment of his rights consisted of the value of the deposit B had paid to A together with B's profit.

3.14   Where there are successive sub-sales then section 45(3) applies in relation to each of them by virtue of section 45(4). Completion or substantial performance of a subsequent sub-sale is not treated as completing an earlier sub-sale.

Options and rights of pre-emption

Introduction

3.15   Options and rights of pre-emption are dealt with expressly by section 46. A right of pre-emption typically involves the situation where the purchaser is given the right of first refusal to buy a property but the sale price has not been agreed. For convenience, the term 'option' will be used throughout the following discussion to refer to both options and rights of pre-emption.

3.16   Structures involving options have recently been popular in stamp duty planning, and section 46 has been enacted with the intention of preventing such avoidance. Bizarrely, however, section 46 only applies to options not otherwise chargeable to SDLT. Accordingly, most options will be chargeable under the general charge to tax because an option is a right over land (though not in Scotland, where the option-holder acquires a purely personal right against the grantor of the option and does not acquire any equitable interest in the land itself).[8] The main type of option to which section 46 applies is a 'put option', where the vendor buys an option to sell land to the purchaser. A put option is a personal right against the purchaser rather than a right over land and so would not otherwise be chargeable to tax.[9] It is not very satisfactory that there are

---

[7] Again defined by reference to s. 839 ICTA 1988 under s. 45(6). For a discussion of s. 839, see para. 4.7 below.

[8] There is some doubt as to whether a Scottish option falls within the general definition of a chargeable interest under s. 48. However, there is no doubt that Scottish options are now chargeable owing to s. 46.

[9] Although a put option effectively sets a minimum price for the sale of the land, the better view is that this does not affect the value of the land because the right is a personal one exercisable only

now two charging regimes for options. A simpler alternative would have been to tax all options under section 46. Nevertheless, the grant of an option over UK land is now undoubtedly not only chargeable to tax but also a notifiable[10] transaction. Accordingly, planning based around the idea of using options and not reporting the grant to the Revenue is now not only ineffective but will also have potentially very serious penal consequences.

Further background to the SDLT treatment of options

3.17 In order to better understand section 46, it is necessary to refer back to some of the history behind its enactment. Options were a popular planning device in the old stamp duty regime. The idea was that, instead of a straight sale, land was sold in two stages consisting of the grant and exercise of an option. Typically, the option was granted for a substantial consideration and the document providing for the grant was not submitted for stamping. On exercise, the conveyance was stamped only on the price paid for the conveyance itself.

3.18 As the Revenue pointed out in issue 3 of the *Stamp Taxes Bulletin*,[11] these structures were not necessarily effective. It was long ago settled, in *George Wimpey* v. *IRC*,[12] that the grant of an option to purchase land was a sale of property and therefore stampable in its own right. Moreover, the exercise of the option formed part of a series of transactions so that it was not possible to certify that the lower rates of tax could apply to the consideration given on exercise.[13] The Revenue also took the view that, in order to satisfy the requirement under section 5 of the Stamp Act 1891 to set forth all the facts and circumstances affecting the liability of an instrument to duty when submitting it for stamping, the option agreement itself had to be submitted for stamping. Finally, if the exercise was pre-ordained, then probably so also was the initial grant, so it was not possible even to certify that the lower rates applied to the consideration for the grant.

3.19 Nevertheless, whether or not the Revenue's view of section 5 of the Stamp Act 1891 was correct, it is believed that not all taxpayers submitted the option agreements for stamping alongside the final conveyance of the freehold, and the Revenue's view was that many option agreements were not being stamped in practice. Accordingly, the purpose of section 46 is to put beyond all doubt that all option agreements are now taxable irrespective of whether the option agreement falls within the general definition of a chargeable interest in section 48(1).

Options chargeable otherwise than under section 46

3.20 Section 46 is a strange section. At first glance it appears to be the section in the Act which sets out the tax treatment of options. However, by virtue of section 46(4), it does not apply 'to so much of an option or right of pre-emption

against the grantor of the option. Accordingly, the grant of a put option is outside the definition of chargeable interest in s. 48(1).
[10] See para. 8.6 onwards below.   [11] 3 June 2002.
[12] [1975] 2 All ER 45; [1975] 1 WLR 995.   [13] Under paras. 4 and 6 of Sch. 13 FA 1999.

as constitutes or forms part of a land transaction apart from section 46'. The acquisition of most options will be a land transaction in its own right under the general charging rules and therefore section 46 will not apply to them. Accordingly, when considering the tax treatment of an option, the first issue is not whether and how section 46 applies but whether the transaction is a land transaction under the general charging rules discussed in Chapter 2. Most options and rights of pre-emption are within the general charge, and it will therefore be quite rare for section 46 to actually apply.

3.21   For example, A pays £100,000 for an option to acquire Blackacre from B for £450,000. Six months later, A exercises his option and buys Blackacre for £450,000. Both the grant of the option and the subsequent exercise are land transactions in their own right. When the option is granted, A acquires a right over land. The purchase of the freehold is another acquisition of a chargeable interest. Each transaction is chargeable separately under the general charge to SDLT. Accordingly, there is no need to refer to section 46.

3.22   An important issue is whether the rules on 'linked transactions' in section 108 FA 2003 apply to options so that the consideration is aggregated for the purposes of determining the rate of tax under section 55. The rules governing linked transactions are discussed in more detail from paragraph 4.92 onwards below. The exercise of an option will undoubtedly be linked to the original grant because they form a series of transactions. This follows from the old stamp duty treatment as confirmed by the Revenue in issue 3 of the *Stamp Taxes Bulletin*.[14] Accordingly, the consideration payable for the grant of the option (£100,000) is aggregated with the consideration payable on exercise (£450,000) for the purpose of determining the rate of tax payable on exercise under section 55(4)(b). Accordingly, tax is chargeable on the £450,000 payable on exercise at the 4 per cent rate rather than the 3 per cent rate which would have otherwise applied had the transactions not been linked. Tax of £18,000 is therefore payable on exercise.

3.23   The more difficult issue is whether the original grant of the option will itself be linked to the subsequent exercise so that all the consideration which may become payable under the option agreement is aggregated for the purposes of determining the rate of tax that is to apply to the initial grant. The SDLT charge on grant depends on whether or not the grant is linked to the subsequent exercise under section 108. If the grant is linked, then the £450,000 payable on exercise is aggregated with the £100,000 for the purposes of determining the rate of tax applicable to the grant. It does not matter that the £450,000 is contingent on the option being exercised because of section 51 FA 2003.[15] Accordingly, if the transactions are linked, the charge to SDLT on the grant will be £4,000 (£100,000 at 4 per cent) whereas if not it will be only £1,000, assuming that the land is residential. The better view is that, provided the option is a genuine

---

[14] 3 June 2002.   [15] See para. 4.28 below.

commercial option rather than one acquired for tax planning purposes, the grant of an option will not be linked with the subsequent exercise. Support for this view is found in section 46(1), which states that the grant and exercise of an option 'may be "linked transactions"' and conversely may not be. However, if there was an arrangement that the option would be exercised at the time of grant, in other words the option was bought for tax planning purposes only and its exercise was pre-ordained, then the grant will be linked with the subsequent exercise. This accords with the Revenue's view of the position under stamp duty that the grant of an option was only linked with the subsequent exercise (as opposed to the other way round) if its exercise was pre-ordained.[16] The linked transactions rules are discussed further at paragraph 4.92 onwards: see especially paragraph 4.109.

Options and rights of pre-emption chargeable under section 46

3.24   Only where the grant of the option or right of pre-emption is not otherwise chargeable is it necessary to consider section 46. Section 46 applies to options which bind the grantor to enter into a land transaction and rights of pre-emption which restrict the grantor from entering into a land transaction. Such transactions are deemed to be land transactions separate from any subsequent exercise of the right. Section 46(3) confirms that the effective date is the date of the acquisition of the option rather than the date of exercise.

3.25   Under section 46(2), binding the grantor to enter into a land transaction includes an option 'requiring the grantor either to enter into a land transaction or to discharge his obligations in some other way'. This refers to an option which gives him the choice to perform in either of those ways rather than an option to do either of those two things. Otherwise, an option to sell shares, for example, would fall within section 46. The definition of option means that section 46 applies to 'put options' where the purchaser of the option is the vendor of the land, as discussed at paragraph 3.16 above. This is because the option binds the grantor to purchase the land and therefore the purchaser of the option does not acquire any rights over land on its grant. The purchase of the land is a land transaction and therefore section 46 applies to it. This type of option, commonly known as a 'put option', is common in share dealings but more unusual in land dealings. Section 46 has been enacted to prevent any tax planning using put options and to put beyond doubt that Scottish options are chargeable to SDLT.

Exchanges and partitions

3.26   The general rule is that an exchange of a major interest[17] in land is treated under section 47 FA 2003 as two separate transactions each of which is chargeable

---

[16] See again the *Stamp Taxes Bulletin*, issue 3, 3 June 2002.
[17] A major interest in land means a lease or freehold: see s. 117 FA 2003. The meaning of 'major interest' is discussed further at para. 4.54 below.

to SDLT on the market value of the interest acquired. An exchange can no longer be structured as a single sale of the more valuable property. Once again, this section has been designed to counter perceived avoidance by taxpayers taking advantage of the single-sale route. Section 47 applies when a purchaser enters into a land transaction in consideration of his entering into another land transaction as vendor. Exchanges are always governed by section 47 even if other consideration is also given. Each of the transactions may be entered into alone or jointly and there is no requirement that the parties be identical. For example, if A, B and C enter into a tripartite contract under which A agrees to sell Blackacre to B, B agrees to transfer Whiteacre to C and C to transfer Greenacre to A, then all three will be chargeable under section 47.

3.27   Where section 47 applies, the exchange is treated as two separate land transactions each of which is chargeable to SDLT. Accordingly, it is no longer possible to structure an exchange as the sale of the more valuable property for a consideration consisting of property and cash. The charge to SDLT is triggered by the fact that land is being transferred for a consideration. In a simple exchange what matters is that there are two pieces of land being transferred rather than there being only one bargain.

3.28   The wording of section 47 also covers partitions, because a partition involves the acquisition of a chargeable interest in exchange for the giving up of another. A partition includes the situation where co-owners of a piece of land divide it into two separate portions and take one each. However, tax should not be chargeable on a simple partition where property is divided according to the parties' existing entitlements because of the rule contained in paragraph 6 of Schedule 4. This particularly obscure rule is discussed further at paragraph 4.56 onwards below. The tax treatment of a partition is of particular importance on the dissolution of a partnership. At present, the dissolution of a partnership is outside SDLT and remains within the stamp duty regime. However, when the new SDLT regime for partnerships is introduced, this is one area which will need to be covered. For the SDLT treatment of partnerships, see paragraph 3.44 below.

3.29   The definition of an exchange also covers the surrender and regrant of a lease, including one which takes effect by operation of law. The relief for the surrender and regrant of a lease under paragraph 14 of Schedule 4, discussed at paragraph 4.65 below, only applies where the new lease is on the same terms as the old one. Accordingly, if a tenant surrenders his lease to the landlord in exchange for a new lease of a longer duration, both the value of the surrendered lease and the value of the new lease are chargeable to SDLT. The Chief Secretary to the Treasury was pressed on this point during Standing Committee. He accepted that there would be a charge in situations not covered by paragraph 14 of Schedule 4. However, he thought that a tax charge on the surrender and regrant of a lease was something that could be fairly easily avoided and should not normally arise in practice. The Chief Secretary made the following statement:

> At the instigation of the Law Society of Scotland, the Hon. Member for Hertford and Stortford pointed out how the change will affect surrenders and regrants that arise from operation of law. We touched on that earlier. Surrender and regrant of a lease can occur by operation of law when the duration of that lease or its area is amended. It is assumed that the existing lease is replaced with a new lease on the same terms save for the amended duration or area. That could lead to a fresh liability to pay stamp duty land tax on the new lease. There is nothing new about that, because it was also a potential problem in relation to stamp duty. In the modernised regime, we want to improve the situation by including paragraph 14 of Schedule 4, which we will discuss later. The tax will still be payable based on the net present value of the rents due under the regranted lease. In fact, a surrender and regrant by operation of law can be fairly easily avoided and it is not something that should normally arise; for example, an extension of a let area could be documented by way of a supplementary lease of the additional area. We do not therefore see any pressing need for a further change to stamp duty as a result of modernisation.
>
> Further representations have been received from a variety of sources that want more reform that would go beyond that that is available in relation to the stamp duty regime. We will happily consider any representations during the consultation on lease duty. I hope that on that basis the Hon. Gentleman will, for the time being, feel that the point made by the Law Society of Scotland has been dealt with.

3.30   Accordingly, the surrender and regrant of a lease is an area where care needs to be taken in practice. This is discussed further at paragraphs 4.65, 6.37 and 7.42 below.

Calculating the chargeable consideration

3.31   Special rules apply for calculating the chargeable consideration on an exchange. These are contained in paragraphs 5 and 6 of Schedule 4 and are discussed in more detail at paragraph 4.52 onwards below. The general rule is that, where a piece of freehold land is exchanged wholly or partly in consideration for another freehold, then in both cases the chargeable consideration will be the market value of the land acquired.

3.32   For example, D agrees to sell Blackacre (market value £200,000) to E in exchange for Whiteacre (market value £100,000) and an additional £100,000. This is treated as two separate land transactions. D will pay SDLT on the value of Whiteacre, although not on the £100,000 of cash received. E pays SDLT on the value of Blackacre. Accordingly, the value of everything received by each party is chargeable.[18] The Chief Secretary to the Treasury confirmed in

---

[18] This is a reversal of the general rule that SDLT is payable on the consideration given by each purchaser.

Standing Committee that a simple exchange of properties will not be covered by the linked transactions rules.

3.33   Paragraph 6 of Schedule 4 contains a special rule for calculating the chargeable consideration on a partition. It provides: 'In the case of a land transaction giving effect to a partition or division of a chargeable interest to which persons are jointly entitled, the interest held by the purchaser immediately before the partition or division does not count as chargeable consideration.' What this is intended to achieve is unclear because the chargeable consideration on an exchange under paragraph 5(4) of Schedule 4 is what is acquired rather than what is given up. The better view, and what paragraph 6 appears to be intended to achieve, is that, where paragraph 6 applies, paragraph 5 no longer applies because the giving up of the original interest is ignored and therefore not treated as consideration for a sale so that there is no exchange within the definition of paragraph 5(1). The meaning of paragraph 6 of Schedule 4 is discussed further at paragraph 4.56 below.

3.34   Finally, section 58 contains a relief for exchanges where the purchaser is a housebuilding company. The policy is to incentivise and reward housebuilders and their customers through making part-exchange an attractive method of acquiring recently built properties. This relief is considered in more detail at paragraph 5.35 below.

Transactions involving interests under trusts

Introduction

3.35   On a straightforward purchase of land by trustees SDLT is chargeable in the normal way. Who is responsible for paying tax depends, under Schedule 16, upon whether or not the beneficiaries of the trust are absolutely entitled. If the beneficiaries are absolutely entitled then they must pay the tax; if not, it is the responsibility of the trustees. The question of who is responsible to pay SDLT following a purchase by a trust is discussed further at paragraph 8.90 above.

3.36   A particular issue which arises is whether and under what circumstances the acquisition of a beneficial interest under a trust might produce a charge to SDLT. Clearly, an interest under a bare trust of land is a chargeable interest. An interest in possession under a trust whose assets include land is also a chargeable interest and the sale of such an interest will be chargeable to tax. It is useful to distinguish three situations.

Bare trusts

3.37   The first situation is where the trustees hold the property on a bare trust of land, the paradigm case being where land is held on trust for co-owners. Under English law, each co-owner has an equitable interest in the land under the trust of land by virtue of the Trusts of Land and Appointment of Trustees Act 1996 (TLTA 1996). These interests are undoubtedly chargeable interests in the land owing to the abolition of the doctrine of conversion for trusts of land in the TLTA 1996. Accordingly, there will be a straightforward charge to SDLT if the interest is sold. As to the position regarding trusts under Scots law or non-UK laws, see paragraph 3.40 below.

Beneficial Interest in Underlying Trust Property

3.38   The second situation is where the beneficiary has an interest in the underlying trust property, in which case he has a chargeable interest. Typically, a beneficiary will have an interest in the underlying land when he has either the right to live in it or the right to receive income from the property as it arises. When the beneficiary has an interest in possession in the trust property, he will have a chargeable interest in it to the extent that the trust property consists of land.[19] Accordingly, a life interest under a trust is a chargeable interest to the extent that its value is attributable to underlying assets of UK land.[20]

3.39   For example, A and B are two brothers who each inherit life interests in a trust set up by their grandparents. The trust owns a £1 million house in the UK and a £500,000 share portfolio. A agrees to acquire B's interest under the trust for the value of B's share on the straightforward assumption that it is worth half the value of the assets, which is £750,000. Two-thirds of the purchase price is attributable to the land and so A must pay SDLT on £500,000. Moreover, in the situation where beneficiaries under two trusts swap beneficial interests, SDLT will be chargeable on the value of the land element in each interest as an exchange under the rules contained in section 47.[21] Accordingly, if beneficiaries swap life interests under two separate trusts, the tax charge will be a maximum 4 per cent of the UK land owned by each trust.

3.40   Paragraph 2 of Schedule 16 extends the definition of chargeable interest to include the situation where 'property is held in trust under the law of Scotland, or of a country or territory outside the United Kingdom, on such terms that, if the trust had effect under the law of England and Wales, a beneficiary would be regarded as having an interest in the trust property'. Under paragraph 2, the beneficiary is treated as having an interest in the property notwithstanding that the law of the trust does not treat him as having such an interest. The intention of paragraph 2 is to include beneficial interests under trusts and their equivalents that do not treat the beneficiary as having an interest in the land.

---

[19] Under English law, an interest in possession means that the beneficiary has the ability to claim something now, usually the right to the property and the entitlement to any income which it produces. See e.g. *Gartside* v. *IRC* [1968] AC 553 especially at p. 607 *per* Lord Reid. It does not matter that the trustees might be able to terminate that entitlement prospectively. The relevance of an interest in possession is that it gives the beneficiary certain rights over the trust property and the beneficiary is treated as having rights in that property.

[20] This may not be true of an interest under a will trust created before 1997 to which the doctrine of conversion does not apply under s. 3 TLTA 1996.

[21] Discussed at para. 3.26 above.

However, in practice, this is likely to throw up some difficulties because it involves construing a Scottish or foreign document through English eyes.[22]

3.41   In Scots law, the interest of a beneficiary under a trust (other than perhaps a bare trust) is fundamentally a personal interest, and the beneficiary has no property interest in the underlying assets of the trust. However, for most tax purposes, the Scottish situation is assimilated with England and the tax treatment is the same notwithstanding the technical legal differences. However, paragraph 2 must be viewed as unsatisfactory from the point of view of a Scottish lawyer who has no training in English law and may be unaware of the circumstances under which a beneficiary under a trust might under English law be regarded as having an equitable interest. Ultimately, how the terms of the trust are to be looked at is for the courts to decide. The Revenue's view will be that, where someone has the present right to enjoy the benefit of land, then that is a chargeable interest.

Discretionary trusts

3.42   The third situation is where a beneficiary's only interest is as the potential object of a discretionary power exercisable by the trustees. A discretionary interest is not a chargeable interest for SDLT purposes. This was confirmed by the Chief Secretary to the Treasury in Standing Committee, who stated that:

> I have been asked how SDLT will apply to trusts. The Chartered Institute of Taxation asked for confirmation that [what is now section 48(1)] will not cover the interests of a discretionary beneficiary, other than as provided for under paragraph 2 of Schedule 16. I shall give a detailed answer to avoid any doubt, and I shall choose my words particularly carefully. Paragraph 2 of Schedule 16 does not cover discretionary interest, but equitable interest. A person who has a discretionary interest in a trust does not have an equitable or any other interest in assets under English law. If someone is named as a beneficiary of a trust when the trustees have a discretion over the disposition of assets, that person does not acquire an interest in land so there is no land transaction. That will mean, for example, that the purchase of a reversionary interest and an interest in possession trust when the asset is land is a land transaction. That seems obvious and necessary to stop avoidance mechanisms.

3.43   However, there is still a charge to SDLT if a discretionary beneficiary pays trustees to exercise their discretion to give him land because that is the acquisition of a chargeable interest. If there was any doubt that the general charge applies, paragraph 7 of Schedule 16 provides expressly that, where a chargeable interest is acquired by a person through the exercise of a power of appointment or a discretion then any consideration given for that person becoming an object of the trustees' discretion is chargeable consideration for the transfer. In other words, paragraph 7 of Schedule 16 prevents the parties contending that any

---

[22] In other words, there is a Conflict of Laws issue.

consideration was provided for the person becoming a discretionary beneficiary rather than a subsequent exercise of the power.[23] The Chief Secretary to the Treasury made the following statement in Standing Committee:

> None of what I have described affects discretionary interest [*sic*]. Paragraph 7 of Schedule 16 applies to the exercise of a discretion, and the explanatory notes set out how that paragraph works. In essence, if a person pays trustees to exercise their discretion to give him land, the acquisition of the interest in land is a land transaction under the general rules. That is obviously necessary, otherwise one would again have an avoidance mechanism. The payment to the trustee is consideration for that land transaction. It closes down what would otherwise be a straightforward way in which to avoid the tax. The purchaser could argue that the payment was for something other than for acquiring land. Paragraph 7 of the Schedule applies in the same way to a payment to exercise a power of appointment. The mischief that it is designed to avoid is the same mischief: the use of something artificial, the power of appointment or the payment of a consideration to make a trustee exercise his discretion in a particular way. However, the provision does not cover all the possibilities in respect of trusts. It is possible to avoid a charge to SDLT using trusts and powers in another way, so it is necessary to be vigilant in that regard to stop abuse.

Transactions involving partnerships

Introduction

3.44   The purchase of property by a partnership from a third party is chargeable to SDLT in the normal way under Part 2 of Schedule 15 FA 2003. The partners are made jointly and severally liable to pay the tax under paragraph 7 of Schedule 15. The compliance responsibility of partnerships for SDLT is discussed further at paragraph 8.89 below. The meaning of a partnership for SDLT purposes, as defined in paragraph 1 of Schedule 15, includes partnerships under the Partnership Act 1890, limited partnerships under the Limited Partnerships Act 1907 and limited liability partnerships under the Limited Liability Partnerships Act 2000 or the Limited Liability Partnerships Act (Northern Ireland) 2002 and an entity of similar character established in a foreign jurisdiction. The general definition of a partnership is that contained in section 1(1) of the Partnership Act 1890, which provides: 'Partnership is the relation which subsists between persons carrying on a business in common with a view to profit.' Under SDLT, land held by a partnership is treated as being owned by or on behalf of all the partners under paragraph 2 of Schedule 15 so that the partnership is transparent for tax purposes.[24] This accordingly disapplies for SDLT purposes the usual position in Scots law (though not in English law) that a partnership does

---

[23] Merely paying to become a discretionary object does not itself create a land transaction.

[24] Sch. 15, para. 2.

have legal personality separate from its partners, but it is consistent with the approach of other taxes which treat Scottish partnerships as tax transparent – in particular capital gains tax which treats the capital gains of a partnership (whether English or Scottish) as those of its partners.

Partnership transactions outside SDLT

3.45   SDLT does not apply to transactions involving the acquisition of an interest in a partnership, by virtue of paragraph 11 of Schedule 15. Nor does SDLT apply where land is transferred into or out of a partnership by a partner or former partner in exchange for a corresponding variation in that partner's partnership share, by virtue of paragraphs 10 and 12 of Schedule 15. This includes the formation or termination of a partnership. An SDLT regime for transactions involving acquisitions and disposals of partnership interests and transfers of land into and out of a partnership by the partners is currently being prepared. See paragraph 9.40 below. In the meantime, stamp duty continues to apply to these transactions. Ironically, the reason that the stamp duty rules remain in place is that this is a very difficult area of the law. This has made modernising it a difficult task, especially when the Revenue is wary of opening up new opportunities for tax planning. Accordingly, for the moment the old rules, defective as they are, remain in force.

3.46   A detailed discussion of the stamp duty rules on partnership transactions is outside the scope of this book, which is concerned with SDLT. What follows is a summary of the major points. There is no special regime in the stamp duty legislation for partnerships and very little that directly governs transfers of partnership interests and transfers of property into and out of a partnership. Accordingly, it is a matter of applying the general charging principles. However, applying those general principles is often not easy. In practice, the starting point has been to refer to the *Stamp Office Manual*.[25] Although whether the Revenue's analysis is entirely correct is doubtful, it at least makes a sensible attempt to apply the law fairly. In relation to Scots law, the *Stamp Office Manual* makes it clear that the approach it takes does not apply to Scotland, no doubt due to the rule that a Scottish partnership, though not a body corporate, has legal personality separate from its partners. In practice, however, the Stamp Office appears to apply the same rules in the same way as between English and Scottish partnerships.

Contribution of assets to partnerships

3.47   The Revenue's view is that a contribution of assets to a partnership in return for an increased partnership share is not a conveyance on sale because no consideration is given by a third party purchaser.[26] The partnership share is received by the partner in consequence of the transfer rather than as consideration for it. Accordingly, both the formation of a partnership and the transfer of assets into

---

[25] Available via the Revenue website, www.inlandrevenue.gov.uk.
[26] *Stamp Office Manual*, para. 4.444.

a partnership by an existing partner are chargeable with £5 duty. However, if a new partner pays cash to the existing partners in exchange for a partnership share, then that will be a sale.[27] Conversely, if the property is transferred subject to a liability, then the other partners will be assuming a liability of the transferor and giving consideration under section 57 of the Stamp Act 1891 so that *ad valorem* stamp duty is chargeable on the transfer.

3.48   The rule that a contribution of assets into a partnership is not a conveyance on sale is thought not to apply to limited liability partnerships (LLPs). This is because an LLP is a body corporate and has a legal personality distinct from its partners and therefore the premise upon which the treatment in the *Stamp Office Manual* is based does not apply. The transfer would then be treated as an exchange of land for property (the interest in the LLP) and chargeable as an exchange under section 241 FA 1994. However, this point has never been tested before the courts. In practice, it is rarely a problem because the conversion of an existing partnership into an LLP is exempt from stamp duty under section 12 of the Limited Liability Partnerships Act 2000.[28]

Distributions of partnership assets to partners

3.49   A distribution to a partner in accordance with his partnership share under the partnership agreement is not treated as a conveyance on sale.[29] Instead, it is a partition or distribution *in specie*. The same applies if the partnership is dissolved in accordance with the partnership agreement. These distributions are chargeable to £5 fixed duty only (even in Scotland, even though a Scottish partnership has legal personality separate from its partners).

3.50   However, if the distribution to the partner is made otherwise than in accordance with the partner's strict entitlement under the partnership agreement then the transfer is a conveyance on sale. If the outgoing partner has to make a payment to the other partners for equality or any other reason, then *ad valorem* stamp duty is chargeable under the partition or division provisions of Schedule 13 FA 1999 if the payment exceeds £100.[30] Conversely, if the outgoing partner requires the discharge of his partnership debts and an indemnity against any future ones in addition to the full value of his partnership interest then this is again chargeable as a conveyance on sale.[31]

Transactions with an overseas element and the territorial scope of SDLT

3.51   SDLT is chargeable on the acquisition of chargeable interests in UK land under section 48(1) FA 2003. Section 42(2) FA 2003 specifically states that it does not matter whether or not the instrument effecting the transaction is executed inside or outside the UK or indeed whether there is any instrument at all. Accordingly,

---

[27] *Ibid.*, para. 4.445.   [28] Provided that the conditions of the relief are met.
[29] *Stamp Office Manual*, paras. 4.446 and 4.447.
[30] Para. 21(1) of Sch. 13 FA 1999.   [31] *Stamp Office Manual*, para. 4.447.

there is nothing to be gained from executing the documents overseas. Nor does it matter if any of the parties are non-resident. In short, whenever and wherever UK land is sold, SDLT is potentially chargeable. The definition of the United Kingdom is not extended to include the continental shelf.

3.52   For example, if UK land is sold between two US companies in the US and all the documentation is signed in New York, then SDLT remains payable. Conversely, if the transaction does not concern UK land, then it is outside the scope of SDLT even if the documentation is executed in the UK.

SDLT and the Private Finance Initiative

The stamp duty treatment of PFI transactions

3.53   The Private Finance Initiative (PFI) transactions will raise particular SDLT issues. The application of stamp duty to typical PFI transactions gave rise to some problems. As a result a Contract Group for PFI was established[32] to work with HM Treasury and the Revenue to identify and resolve the tax issues obstructing the operation of PFI. As a result of the discussions of the Contract Group with the Revenue, there was published in *Tax Bulletin* 43 (October 1999) an article setting out the Stamp Office's practice in relation to certain 'typical' PFI transactions.

3.54   The article sets out the Stamp Office's view of the correct stamp duty treatment of the documents likely to be encountered in a typical PFI scheme. It is stressed that the correct treatment depends upon the exact facts, but the article does contain useful guidance where there is a 'traditional' structure of a sale or a lease followed by a leaseback with a master project agreement and perhaps a transfer of surplus land. Clarification is given, in particular, on the following specific issues.

3.55   As regards the initial sale, if the sale or lease is expressed to be in consideration of the leaseback, the stamp duty 'exchange' provisions of section 241 FA 1994 apply to charge duty based on the full value of the leaseback. If, however, the sale or lease and leaseback are separate transactions and the only consideration for the sale or lease is the operator's undertaking to carry out for example certain building works, the sale or lease attracts only fixed duty of £5.

3.56   If the leaseback is granted to an exempt body, for example an NHS trust, there will be no duty. Otherwise, but only where the lease is granted at a peppercorn rent, there should be fixed duty. The Stamp Office indicated that it will consider whether part of the unitary charge will be properly treated as rent which will usually result in increased duty. In these circumstances, the taxpayer is invited to suggest how much of the unitary charge should be so treated, and the indications are that the Stamp Office will usually accept the suggested amounts.

---

[32] Comprising representatives of Allen & Overy, KPMG, PricewaterhouseCoopers and Berwin Leighton Paisner.

3.57   The project agreement itself will normally have the effect of operating both as an agreement for the lease (if the sale is for the grant of a lease) and also as an agreement for the leaseback, and therefore will be liable to the same duty (or exemptions) as the actual lease and leaseback.

3.58   The usual rule for time of payment of duty on the agreement for lease applies – within thirty days of the execution of the agreement unless it is to be presented with the lease granted. The Stamp Office confirms that, if the leases are not subsequently granted, if for example there is a dispute, it will take this into account as a factor in potentially mitigating any penalties (but not interest) on late submission of the agreement and payment of the duty. If the lease is subsequently granted, any duty paid on the agreement will generally be credited against the duty payable on the lease, assuming that the lease is in conformity with the agreement. The article in the *Tax Bulletin* recognises that there may be a major change during the PFI scheme and states that the Stamp Office will apply this rule in a 'common sense way'.

3.59   The article notes that the consideration for the surplus land transfer will usually be an upfront monetary amount, but recognises that there are other options giving rise to different stamp duty consequences:

- Where there is monetary consideration, there will (usually) be duty at the appropriate rate on the amount of the consideration.
- If (unusually) the consideration is expressed to be the grant of the leaseback (or *vice versa*), there would be duty under section 241 FA 1994 on the value of the leaseback (or land transfer).
- If the transfer is described as a contribution to the operator's cost, there will be fixed duty only.
- If the transfer is in satisfaction of amounts of future unitary charge, or in satisfaction of acceptance of a lower level of unitary charge, there will usually be no stamp duty.

3.60   The article is generally a helpful guide to the Stamp Office's views and does not contain anything particularly controversial.

PFI transactions and SDLT

3.61   With the introduction of SDLT, however, a number of the potential issues which were present before the article in the *Tax Bulletin* have re-emerged, with the addition of some new ones. In general, the structure of a typical PFI transaction as set out at the beginning of the article is still the same, but with one major difference. Over the last two years or so, it has become more common for no headlease or leaseback to be granted. Instead, the private sector operator often acts as a contractor to design and construct the building and subsequently to provide maintenance and other services. It does not acquire any proprietary rights in relation to the land itself apart from the minimum licence or right of access necessary to enable it to perform its services. In these circumstances, the following potential concerns arise.

SDLT on an exchange

3.62   In the less frequent situation, where a lease or leaseback is granted in exchange, section 47 is applicable as discussed at paragraph 3.29 above, with the result that there is a double charge. If, following consultation, relief is not provided here, then thought should be given to structuring the transaction to fall outside section 47.

SDLT on the headlease

3.63   Where a lease is granted, the effect of paragraph 10 of Schedule 4 FA 2003 is to charge SDLT on the 'value of the works', which is the amount which would have to be paid in the open market for the carrying out of the works.

3.64   Paragraph 10(2) contains an exemption, but three cumulative conditions have to be met. First, the works must be carried out after the 'effective date of the transaction'. Clearly, this circumstance would apply in cases where the lease is granted up front before any works are carried out, but not otherwise. Secondly, the works must be carried out on land acquired or to be acquired under the transaction by the operator. This condition would normally be satisfied. Thirdly, it must not be a condition of the transaction that the works are carried out by the vendor (i.e. the public authority in question) or a person connected with it. Normally, this requirement is met.

3.65   In the case therefore where the lease is granted at the outset of the project and before works have commenced, it seems to be the case that the exemption should apply. There will, however, be projects where a lease is to be granted but only upon completion of the works. Such projects would not fall within the exemption provided by paragraph 10(2).

Transitional provisions

3.66   As is made clear in Chapter 9, a lease should not attract SDLT under the new provisions if the 'effective date' of the land transaction falls before the implementation date. Where it is possible to arrange for the lease to be granted before such implementation date, SDLT should not apply. This will, however, not always be possible and as a result the transaction would be within the scope of SDLT unless the project agreement has been signed before Royal Assent (11 July 2003) and so long as there is no variation of the agreement after that date. It seems from paragraph 3 of Schedule 19, however, that any variation of the project agreement (which will normally cover the entire project) could disapply the exemption. On a complex PFI transaction, it is very likely that there would be such variations.

Provision of services

3.67 PFI contracts typically involve the provision of services by the operator to the purchaser over a period. In return, the purchaser makes periodic payments. It does not seem correct to say that the consideration for the grant of the headlease is the provision of services (other than building works). That is the way project agreements are usually drafted. It is to be hoped that the Revenue will accept this analysis.

Chargeable interests

3.68 Section 48 describes 'chargeable interests' as including a right or power over land in the UK, but specifically excludes licences to use or occupy land. Normally, the operator is granted a licence or right of access in relation to the project site to enable it to carry out the initial building works and, following completion of those works, to provide ongoing services. Although the point is yet to be clarified, it is thought unlikely that the acquisition of these types of right is intended to constitute a 'chargeable interest' which might be the subject of a charge.

Surplus land

3.69 Guidance was published in the stamp duty context in the *Tax Bulletin* about the treatment of surplus land. Clearly, that guidance does not apply for SDLT purposes, and therefore clarification will be needed as to the position there. The SDLT position in relation to the above questions has not yet been resolved but the government has indicated that it will discuss issues arising with the PFI Contract Group in the context of the ongoing consultation on complex commercial transactions. See further paragraph 9.42 below.

4

Calculating the liability to SDLT

Introduction

4.1 This chapter is concerned with how the SDLT on a chargeable land transaction is calculated. In practice, it is often better to consider first whether a transaction is exempted or relieved from charge before seeking to calculate what the charge might be. However, because several of the reliefs take effect by ignoring the chargeable consideration rather than simply exempting the transaction, it is necessary to consider first how the charge to SDLT operates in order to explain properly the mechanics of those reliefs.

4.2 SDLT is charged as a percentage of the chargeable consideration for a land transaction. Calculating the tax charge is a two-stage process. First, it is necessary to identify and value the chargeable consideration using the rules contained in sections 50–54 and Schedule 4 FA 2003. The basic rule is that the chargeable consideration is the price paid by the purchaser. Inevitably, this is subject to a number of modifications and exceptions, the most important of which is that transfers of land to a connected company are deemed to take place at not less than market value.

4.3 The second stage is to find and apply the appropriate rate of tax to the chargeable consideration to calculate the tax payable. The rates of tax are set out in section 55.[1] A distinction is drawn between residential and non-residential property. However, at present, the only difference in rates is that a sale of residential property for over £60,000 and not more than £150,000 is chargeable to tax at 1 per cent whereas a sale of non-residential property at that price is exempt.

4.4 Where the consideration consists of rent, then the special regime for leases contained in Schedule 5 applies. This is the subject of Chapter 6 below.

Identifying the chargeable consideration

4.5 The general rule is that the chargeable consideration is everything given by the purchaser. In a straightforward sale this means the purchase price. However, the chargeable consideration is defined by paragraph 1 of Schedule 4 to mean 'any consideration in money or money's worth given ... directly or indirectly,

---

[1] The rates are also set out at p. xxii above.

by the purchaser or a person connected with him'. This definition is intended to be as broad as possible so as to bring everything given in return for the land transaction within the charge to SDLT.

4.6   The definition of consideration for SDLT is wider than for either stamp duty or stamp duty reserve tax. Although *ad valorem* stamp duty was chargeable on 'the consideration for the sale',[2] a sale requires a price in money paid or promised.[3] Accordingly, the basic rule for stamp duty was that only money was taken into account. However, the rule was extended to include consideration in the form of an assumption of debt,[4] a transfer of shares or securities,[5] and any other property given in exchange under section 241 FA 1994. The charge to stamp duty reserve tax is made on 'consideration in money or money's worth'.[6] The aim of paragraph 1 of Schedule 4 FA 2003 is to extend the definition of what counts as consideration even further. However, in one respect the SDLT definition of consideration is narrower because it does not include consideration given by an unconnected third party.

4.7   As discussed at paragraph 2.22 onwards above, not everyone who provides consideration for a transaction is a purchaser because the purchaser must acquire a chargeable interest. Consideration provided by an unconnected third party is not chargeable consideration, although in practice it will be very rare for such a person to provide consideration. Nevertheless, in a more complex scenario the first issue is, strictly, to identify the purchaser or purchasers. A purchaser is anyone who both acquires rights over land and is either a party to the transaction or provides consideration for it. If a person other than a purchaser provides consideration, then the next issue is whether that person is connected with the purchaser. Whether parties are connected is determined by applying the test in section 839 of the Income and Corporation Taxes Act 1988 (ICTA 1988). In summary,[7] section 839 provides that individuals are connected with their spouses, their relatives and their spouses' relatives. A relative means a sibling, ancestor or lineal descendant. Companies are connected with one another if they are under common control. Persons acting together to control a company are connected with both one another and that company. Partners are connected with each other and their spouses except in relation to disposals and acquisitions of partnership assets under *bona fide* commercial arrangements. Trustees of a settlement are connected with the settlors and certain companies in which the trustees are interested but not, perhaps surprisingly, the beneficiaries of the trust.

---

[2] Under para. 2 of Sch. 13 FA 1999.
[3] *Littlewoods Mail Order Stores Ltd* v. *IRC* [1963] AC 135, especially at p. 152.
[4] S. 57 of the Stamp Act 1891.   [5] S. 55 of the Stamp Act 1891.   [6] S. 87(1) FA 1986.
[7] What follows is a summary of s. 839 ICTA 1988. As an anti-avoidance provision, it is very widely drafted, and detailed reference should be made to the wording of s. 839 in any case where it may apply.

4.8   For example, B agrees to buy a house from C for £200,000. £100,000 of the purchase price is paid directly to C by D. D is not a purchaser because he is not party to the transaction and acquires no rights in the land. Whether or not the money given by D forms part of the consideration depends on whether or not B and D are connected. If D is B's father, then they are connected and the £100,000 is part of the chargeable consideration. However, if D is B's uncle, then they are not connected because D is not an ancestor and therefore not a relative. Accordingly, the parties are unconnected and D's contribution to the sale is not chargeable to SDLT provided that D has given the money himself and it has not been given indirectly by B's father or someone else connected to B.

4.9   As mentioned in paragraph 4.6 above, this change actually relaxes the old stamp duty rule. Stamp duty was charged on the consideration for a sale irrespective of who provided it, whereas SDLT only charges consideration provided by purchasers and connected parties. Finally, section 50(2) and (3) FA 2003 expressly gives the Treasury the power to amend the legislation for the purposes of determining both what counts as chargeable consideration and the value of that consideration. This is in addition to the general power to vary the legislation contained in section 109 FA 2003.

4.10   Although the situation where an unconnected third party is prepared to make a gift in order to fund the purchase of land will rarely arise in practice, there will be occasions when it does. One example would be where a rich benefactor wishes to make a gift of money to an organisation which is not a charity to assist them in the purchase of a property. If the donor makes a gift to the organisation which buys the property, then SDLT is chargeable in the normal way. However, if the donor contributes to the purchase price of the building, then no SDLT is payable on his share. Arguably, this rule is unfair to those taxpayers not lucky enough to have rich benefactors to help them buy property. The intention behind paragraph 1 of Schedule 4 was certainly not to relax the rule as to what counts as consideration and the law may well be changed to remove this anomaly.

Valuing the chargeable consideration

4.11   Having identified the chargeable consideration the next step is to value it. The legislation contains a series of rules for doing so.

Non-monetary consideration

4.12   The general rule is that non-monetary consideration is charged on its market value at the effective date of the transaction under paragraph 7 of Schedule 4. However, this is subject to anything in the Act providing otherwise and in particular to the rules which apply to the assumption of debt contained in paragraph 8 of Schedule 4.

Provision of services

4.13   Where the purchaser provides consideration to the vendor in the form of services, other than those to which paragraph 10 applies, then the open market value of obtaining those services is chargeable consideration by virtue of paragraph 11. The Revenue intends to issue guidance on the sorts of services to which paragraph 11 will apply and how they will be valued.

Debt as consideration

4.14   Where the purchaser agrees either to pay off a debt of the purchaser or to release him from a liability, then the value of that debt or liability is chargeable consideration under paragraph 8 of Schedule 4. This is subject to the limitation that the chargeable consideration brought into account cannot exceed the market value of the land. As consideration includes everything given by the purchaser in money's worth, it is questionable whether paragraph 8 is needed at all. For example, if A releases B from a debt which B owes to A in exchange for B transferring Greenacre to A, B has certainly received money's worth. The inclusion of an express provision confirming that the assumption of debt is consideration is a hangover from stamp duty. Unfortunately, there remains some uncertainty as to the circumstances under which transferring land subject to a debt will be chargeable to SDLT under paragraph 8 of Schedule 4.

Background

4.15   In order to understand paragraph 8 of Schedule 4 properly it is necessary to refer back to the old stamp duty position. As has already been mentioned, stamp duty was charged on sales of land. Four elements are necessary for a sale to exist as a matter of general law: parties competent to make a contract; mutual assent; property transferred from a seller to a buyer; and a price in money paid or promised.[8] Under the general law, if A agrees to transfer land to B in exchange for B agreeing to pay off A's debts to C, then there is no sale because there is no price in money paid or promised.

4.16   Such transactions were brought within the charge to stamp duty by section 57 of the Stamp Act 1891. Section 57 provided that, where property was conveyed in consideration of a debt due to the purchaser or subject to the payment of any money, then that debt or money was consideration for the transfer. However, uncertainties remained as to the precise scope of section 57. The Revenue sought to clarify the position by publishing Statement of Practice 6/90. SP 6/90 stated that section 57 applied only to sales and not to gifts. Accordingly, it applied in cases where the transferee agreed to assume a liability of the transferor, whether expressly or impliedly.

4.17   However, SP 6/90 was itself unclear on the position where property is gifted subject to a mortgage. The problem is that, although section 57 does not expressly

---

[8]   See *Littlewoods Mail Order Stores Ltd* v. *IRC* [1963] AC 135 at 152.

deem there to be a sale where the transferee agrees to assume a liability to pay a debt of the transferee, that is its effect. Nevertheless, SP 6/90 implied otherwise by suggesting in paragraph 3 that section 57 does not apply where a mortgaged property held in the name of one spouse is transferred into the joint names of both. However, in paragraph 6, SP 6/90 then restates the orthodox position that section 57 only applies where the transferee does not assume liability for the mortgage. In other words, where property was transferred between, for example, spouses and the transferee agreed to assume liability for the mortgage then section 57 applied and SP 6/90 does not help. However, it was possible to take a broader reading of SP 6/90 and some uncertainty remained.

Treatment of debt under paragraph 8 of Schedule 4

4.18   Paragraph 8 applies in two situations. First, where the chargeable consideration consists wholly or partly in the satisfaction or release of a debt either due to the purchaser or owed by the vendor, and, secondly, where the chargeable consideration consists wholly or partly of the assumption of an existing debt by the purchaser.

4.19   Where the purchaser takes the property wholly or partly in satisfaction of either a debt due to him or a debt owed by the vendor, then the transfer falls within paragraph 8(1)(a). It is not necessary that the debt should have been owed by the vendor to the purchaser. Instead, it suffices that the debt was owed either by the purchaser or to the vendor. Accordingly, if land is given by a person in satisfaction of a debt owed by, for example, his son, then the amount of the debt satisfied is treated as chargeable consideration for the transaction. The chargeable consideration is the amount of the debt satisfied rather than the value of the property.

4.20   The assumption of an existing debt by the purchaser is taken account of under paragraph 8(1)(b). An existing debt means a debt created before the effective date of the transaction and otherwise than in connection with it.[9] This is intended to exclude any mortgage taken out by the purchaser in order to acquire the property.

4.21   However, the assignment of a property subject to an existing mortgage is not exempted. Accordingly, where land is transferred subject to a mortgage and the transferee agrees to take over the mortgage payments, then SDLT is chargeable. This rule can cause difficulties when families and their private companies wish to transfer assets between themselves, perhaps to obtain benefits in relation to other taxes. In the past, this difficulty could be overcome by resting on contract. However, while SDLT has removed the ability to rest on contract, the charge when land is transferred subject to a liability, which was formerly imposed by section 57 of the Stamp Act 1891, is retained. Obviously, one course now is

[9] See para. 8(3)(b).

to pay the mortgage off so that the property is transferred free from it. If the transfer is a gift other than into a connected company, then no SDLT would then be payable.

4.22   An example of where paragraph 8 can apply is where there is a transfer of a property subject to a mortgage between co-owners or former co-owners. Suppose that A and B are unmarried co-habitees who own a flat together as tenants in common in equal shares. The flat is worth £300,000 and is subject to a £200,000 mortgage which A and B have taken out jointly. A and B split up and it is agreed that A will purchase B's share in the flat for £50,000. If A agrees to assume liability for B's share of the mortgage, then the value of the liability assumed is chargeable consideration under paragraph 8(1)(b). The value of the liability assumed is £100,000, being B's share of the outstanding debt as between A and B. It might be possible to argue that A has assumed no liability because A was jointly and severally liable to the bank for the mortgage anyway. However, if the bank releases B from liability for the mortgage, then the value of the debt released is chargeable under paragraph 8(1)(a) and the Revenue might argue that if A assumes no liability B is released from liability for the whole value of the mortgage rather than just his own half share. However, the better view is that, in this example A will in practice be chargeable to SDLT on consideration of £150,000, being the £50,000 cash together with the £100,000 debt assumed.

4.23   Paragraph 8 will only not apply if the transferee does not assume liability for the mortgage and the transferor is not released from any liability. This might be the case, for example, where a wife transfers a half share in property to her husband and continues paying the mortgage herself. However, if the husband assumes liability for half the mortgage, then paragraph 8 still applies. It is still possible that the Revenue may issue a new statement of practice to mitigate the full rigours of paragraph 8, but this cannot be relied upon. Paragraph 8 is an important provision to watch out for in practice because its effect is that SDLT may be chargeable on a transaction which would not normally be thought of as a sale.

4.24   Paragraph 8(1)(b) also creates two new uncertainties of its own. The first is whether or not an agreement by the assignee of a lease to take over the payment of rent is within paragraph 8(1)(b). Under stamp duty, an agreement by the assignee of a lease to pay rent did not count as chargeable consideration. The liability to pay rent was inherent in the nature of the lease. This was decided in *Swayne* v. *IRC*[10] on the basis that section 57 applied to 'a liability to pay money arising in some way other than as incident to and inseparably connected with the property conveyed'.[11]

4.25   Paragraph 8 is worded differently to section 57, so whether *Swayne* remains good law is now uncertain. The better view is that paragraph 8 should be

---

[10] [1899] 1 QB 341, confirmed [1900] 1 QB 372.   [11] *Per* Bruce J at 341.

construed in the same way so that a debt means a debt separate from the property rather than inherent in it. The Revenue has made no mention of changing the law in this area so that is likely to be accepted as the correct interpretation. However, there is no guarantee that the Revenue or the courts will construe paragraph 8 so restrictively.

4.26   The second area of uncertainty is whether paragraph 8(1)(b) applies to consideration given by a party connected with a purchaser. Paragraph 8(1)(b) applies to 'the assumption of existing debt by the purchaser'. Unlike in paragraph 1(1) of Schedule 4, no mention is made of connected parties. However, if a debt assumed by a connected party is not within paragraph 8(1)(b) then it might be argued by the Revenue that it is within the general charge under paragraph 1(1) of Schedule 4 as money's worth.

Deferred consideration

4.27   Where part of the consideration is postponed, then paragraph 3 of Schedule 4 provides that no discount is made for the delay in the right to receive it. If payment is dependent upon a contingency, then section 51 FA 2003 applies (see the next paragraph below).

Contingent, uncertain or unascertainable consideration

4.28   Section 51 FA 2003 deals with contingent, uncertain or unascertainable consideration. In practice, these are quite different things; the link is that, in all cases, it is hard to value the consideration at the date when the transaction takes place. As with deferred consideration, the general rule is that these types of consideration are chargeable immediately. However, if the consideration ultimately turns out not to be payable, then a repayment of tax may be made under section 80 FA 2003.

4.29   Where part of the consideration is contingent, then SDLT is charged immediately on the maximum possible consideration. Contingent is defined as being dependent upon the occurrence of some future event. Section 51(1) is deliberately structured so that whichever way round the contingency is structured the maximum duty will be payable. If it becomes clear that less consideration is payable as the contingency has not been satisfied or, alternatively, because it has occurred, then the SDLT overpaid can be reclaimed under section 80(4).

4.30   If the consideration is uncertain or unascertained, then the amount to be taken into account is based on a 'reasonable estimate'. What is a reasonable estimate is not defined in the Act. However, in Standing Committee, the Chief Secretary to the Treasury gave the following guidance:

> The Hon. Member for Hertford and Stortford asked what is meant by 'reasonable estimate'. As is the case with self-assessment generally, it will be up to the taxpayer to supply the most appropriate estimate. The

evidence that is appropriate to support the estimate will depend on the facts of the case. For a good reason, and to the great benefit of lawyers, the law always shies clear of defining 'reasonable'. In reality, a commercial tenant will usually have a good idea of the amount that they expect to pay over the term of the lease. There are business forecasts and management accounts, for example. The Revenue does not intend to challenge *bona fide* estimates, as long as they are reasonable, based on the facts available at the time. Issues that enable taxpayers to make a judgment will be laid out in guidance.

4.31   Uncertain consideration does not bear its ordinary meaning but is defined to mean 'that its amount or value depends upon uncertain future events'. An example of uncertain consideration given by the Revenue is where it depends upon profits in accounts which have not yet been finalised. For example, A agrees to sell Blackacre to BCo and BCo agrees to pay A half its profits from the development which it plans to build on the land. The value of the consideration is therefore unknown at the time of sale because it is dependent upon how much BCo receives for the development. The consideration will, therefore, have to be determined by best guess at the time of sale.

4.32   Consideration is unascertained when it is ascertainable but has not yet been determined. For example, consideration is unascertained when A agrees to sell land to B in consideration of B paying A half of B's profits for the financial year just ended. That figure is currently unknown because B's accounts have not been drawn up. Accordingly, it is ascertainable but not yet ascertained.

4.33   Again, where uncertain or unascertained consideration becomes known, an adjustment can be made under section 80. If the actual consideration is higher than the original estimate so that more SDLT is payable then the taxpayer must, under section 80(2), make an additional return and pay the extra tax. If less SDLT tax turns out to be payable, then it is up to the taxpayer to reclaim the overpayment.

4.34   However, where section 51 would otherwise apply, the purchaser may apply, under section 90, to defer payment of all tax where the consideration is contingent or uncertain. At least part of the consideration must be potentially payable more than six months after the effective date of the transaction. Section 90 provides for the Revenue to make regulations about the making of such applications. At the time of writing, no regulations have yet been made.

4.35   The SDLT provisions dealing with deferred consideration broadly mirror the capital gains tax treatment of deferred consideration. Under sections 48 and 49 TCGA 1992, no discount is made from the sale proceeds for either deferred consideration or liabilities assumed by the vendor. However, as with SDLT, if the consideration becomes irrecoverable or the liability arises, then an adjustment is made. Where the consideration is payable by instalments over a period exceeding eighteen months, then the taxpayer can apply to pay the tax in instalments under section 280 TCGA 1992. Where tax is deferred under section 280, it is payable at 50 per cent of the consideration received until the tax is paid off rather than by tax simply being paid on each instalment as it becomes due. Regulations made under section 90 FA 2003 may well be in similar terms.

Consideration includes VAT

4.36   The chargeable consideration includes any VAT chargeable on the transaction by virtue of paragraph 2 of Schedule 4. However, VAT is not included if the election to charge VAT[12] is made after the effective date. Accordingly, in the case of a lease, if VAT becomes payable on the rent only after the effective date for SDLT, then the VAT does not form part of the chargeable consideration if the election is made after that date. For SDLT purposes, it is therefore more attractive if the vendor makes the election to charge VAT only after the effective date. However, for VAT or other reasons the vendor may not wish to do so.

4.37   There may be other circumstances in which it is possible to avoid paying SDLT on the VAT element of the purchase price by ensuring that the effective date for SDLT falls before the option to charge VAT is exercised. However, such circumstances are likely to be very rare in practice because the time of supply for VAT on a sale of freehold land will be triggered on the earlier of the making of a payment by the purchaser or the land being made available to him.[13] Accordingly, the time of supply for VAT is unlikely to be after the effective date for SDLT.

4.38   The Chief Secretary to the Treasury in Standing Committee stated that VAT is only chargeable to SDLT on a transaction if it is actually charged. This is a consequence of the rule that SDLT is only chargeable on the consideration given for the transaction. However, if the vendor has the right to charge VAT under the contract but mistakenly fails to do so, then that should be taken into account for SDLT because the purchaser remains liable and so has given consideration.

Foreign currency

4.39   Consideration paid in foreign currency is valued according to the London closing exchange rate on the effective date of the transaction under paragraph 9 of Schedule 4. However, if the parties have used a different rate in their own contract, then that rate applies instead. If the effective date is not the date on which payment is made then the purchaser may be taxed on a higher or lower sum than it actually pays.

Apportionment

4.40   Where the purchaser pays one consideration for two land transactions or partly for one land transaction and partly for something else, then it is to be apportioned

---

[12] Under Sch. 10 VATA 1994.   [13] See especially s. 6 VATA 1994.

on a just and reasonable basis under paragraph 4 of Schedule 4. The starting point is the market value of the various assets and accordingly there will be a spectrum of values that is acceptable. If the figure given by the parties is not justifiable on the basis of market value, then it will not be a reasonable apportionment.

4.41   Paragraph 4(3) specifically stops the parties from artificially apportioning consideration to different assets by providing that consideration given for what is, in substance, one bargain is attributable to all the elements of that bargain even though the parties may have purported to expressly apportion the consideration or even structured the bargain as several separate transactions. This prevents, for example, attributing artificially large amounts of the purchase price to chattels on the sale of a house.

The carrying out of building works

Introduction

4.42   Paragraph 10 of Schedule 4 is designed to deal with the situation where as part of the consideration for the land transaction the purchaser agrees to construct or improve a building on the land. Unless the conditions set out in paragraph 10(2) are met, the value of the works is taken into account as chargeable consideration. It appears somewhat odd that work which the purchaser undertakes on his own land should be consideration for the sale. However, paragraph 10 is aimed at the situation where a purchaser acquires land and under the same agreement agrees to construct a new building on the land to do some other work which is of benefit to the vendor.

4.43   An example of the sort of arrangement to which paragraph 10 is intended to apply is the grant of a building lease, where there is an agreement for a lease a term of which is that the lessee must erect a building on the land. Another example is where the purchaser buys land from a public authority and there is an agreement under section 106 of the Town and Country Planning Act 1990 (or section 75 of the Town and Country Planning (Scotland) Act 1997 or Article 40 of the Planning (Northern Ireland) Order 1991) that the purchaser will construct a building on the land. Where paragraph 10 applies, the value of the building is not taken into account as part of the purchase price.

Operation of the relief under paragraph 10

4.44   Paragraph 10 is actually a relieving provision because where the three conditions in paragraph 10(2) are met then the value of the building works, which would otherwise be chargeable to SDLT as money's worth under paragraph 1 of Schedule 4, is not chargeable to tax. Where part of the consideration for a land transaction involving the acquisition of a major interest in land consists of the carrying out of works of construction, improvement or repair of a building (or other works to enhance the value of land), those works are taken into account as chargeable consideration by virtue of paragraph 10(1) unless the three conditions contained in paragraph 10(2) are met. These are, first, that the works are carried out after the effective date of the transaction.[14] Secondly, and very importantly, that it is not a condition of the transaction that the works are carried out by the vendor or a person connected with him.[15] The third condition is 'that the works are carried out on land acquired or to be acquired under the transaction or on other land held by the purchaser or a person connected with him'.[16] It would be unusual for the vendor to want the purchaser to build a building on other land but if so then relief is not available.

4.45   If any of these conditions is not met, then the value of the works is taken into account as chargeable consideration. The three conditions are in substance the test for the relief to apply, so in order to understand the operation of paragraph 10 it is necessary to understand them. The most important requirement is contained in paragraph 10(2)(c): 'that it is not a condition of the agreement that the works are carried out by the vendor or a person connected with him'. The effect of this is that paragraph 10 does not apply in the situation where the purchaser buys land from a developer and the sale agreement also provides that the developer will construct a building on the land at the purchaser's expense. However, this does not mean that tax is always chargeable when in a sale-and-build situation for the reasons given at paragraph 4.47 below. Paragraph 10(2)(c) only provides that no relief is available under paragraph 10 in a sale-and-build situation. The other conditions of paragraph 10(2) are less important but restrict the operation of the relief to a building-lease-type scenario.

4.46   If the three conditions in paragraph 10(2) are not met, then the value of the works is taken into account as chargeable consideration under paragraph 10(1)(b). The value of the works is the amount that would have to be paid in the open market for the carrying out of the works, by virtue of paragraph 10(3)(b).

Sale-and-build situations

4.47   The charging aspect of paragraph 10 of Schedule 4 raises concern as to the tax treatment of sale-and-build situations. The situation envisaged is where a purchaser buys a plot of land from a developer and at the same time the developer agrees to construct a building on the land at the purchaser's expense. In summary, the stamp duty position was that, provided the sale and building contracts were kept separate, duty was not chargeable on the building contract, and this should remain the same for SDLT. However, the law in this area is not straightforward.

4.48   The treatment of sale-and-build contracts for stamp duty was determined in *Prudential Assurance Co. v. IRC*.[17] In *Prudential*, the purchaser entered into two simultaneous agreements with a developer under a sale-and-build arrangement.

---

[14] Para. 10(2)(a).   [15] Para. 10(2)(c).   [16] Para. 10(2)(b).   [17] [1992] STC 863.

The first was a sale of the land. The second was an agreement for the developer to complete a development upon that land. The Revenue sought to charge stamp duty on the total consideration payable by the purchaser on the basis that there was an agreement for a sale of land with completed buildings thereon. Sir Donald Nicholls V-C rejected the Revenue's arguments on the basis that the contracts were legally independent and capable of independent performance.

4.49   In the wake of the *Prudential* decision, the Revenue issued Statement of Practice 8/93 which set out their interpretation of the law. The Revenue's view was that a single sale-and-build transaction could be effected by entering into two separate contracts. Where the contracts were genuinely independent, then stamp duty was only payable on the consideration given for the land transaction and not the consideration for the building contract. Unfortunately, the only guidance as to whether or not the contracts were 'genuinely independent' was that contracts were not independent if default on one rendered the other unenforceable. Difficulty arises in determining whether contracts are legally separate where the developer is unwilling to sell the land without the purchaser entering into the building contract.

4.50   The effect of paragraph 10 upon *Prudential* and SP 8/93 is now unclear. It is understood that the Revenue intended paragraph 10 to reproduce the old law. However, it is Parliament's intention rather than the Revenue's which ultimately counts. The issue here is whether a building contract entered into as part of a sale-and-build agreement is 'consideration' for the land transaction within the meaning of paragraph 10(1). The better view is that paragraph 10(1) is to be understood as being in accordance with *Prudential* and SP 8/93. Accordingly, where the contract for the sale of land is legally separate and enforceable by itself, it cannot be said that the building contract is consideration for it and paragraph 10 does not apply. If the building contract is entered into separately, then by definition it is not consideration for the sale of the land because it is not given in return. In practice, it is important that the land should not be sold at an undervalue and the price for the building contract inflated so that the Revenue cannot argue that the building contract is entered into at an unfavourable price and thereby represents consideration for the sale of the land.

4.51   Moreover, even in a situation where it is a condition of the agreement that the vendor constructs a building on the land, then it may be arguable that paragraph 10 still does not apply because the consideration for each agreement is the money the purchaser agrees to pay under each agreement and not the making of the other agreement. The difficulty in this situation is that the Revenue may argue that the true bargain is for a sale of land with a completed building thereon, following *Prudential*. Accordingly, great care needs to be taken when structuring the contracts in a sale-and-build situation in order to ensure the taxpayer both obtains the benefit of *Prudential* and is outside paragraph 10 of

Schedule 4. Not only must the contracts be legally separate but also the building contract must not be consideration for the land transaction.

Exchanges

4.52 Where land is exchanged, this is treated as two separate sales, as discussed at paragraph 3.26 below. The consideration for each sale is the market value of the land acquired under paragraph 5(3) of Schedule 4. If the interest acquired is a lease at a rent, then the rent is also included in the consideration together with the market value of the new lease under paragraph 5(3). Apart from leases, additional consideration is not taken into account. An example of how the charge to tax applies on an exchange is given at paragraph 3.32 below.

4.53 If the subject-matter of the exchange does not consist of major interests in land, then the market value of the interests being exchanged is not taken into account, by virtue of paragraph 5(4) of Schedule 10. In such a case, only any additional consideration, usually the money, is chargeable to SDLT. Paragraph 5(4) has practical importance in situations such as where developers constructing neighbouring tower blocks exchange easements of light.

4.54 A major interest in land is an important concept for SDLT. It is defined in section 117 FA 2003 to mean 'an estate fee simple absolute' or 'a term of years absolute' subsisting in either law or equity; in other words, any freehold interest or lease whether legal or equitable. For example, the interest of a co-owner under a trust of land qualifies as a major interest in land. In Scotland, a major interest in land means the interest of an owner of land or the tenant's right over or interest in a property subject to a lease. Until the appointed day for the purposes of the Abolition of Feudal Tenure etc. (Scotland) Act 2000, the reference in section 117(3)(a) to the interest of the owner is to be read in relation to feudal property as a reference to the estate or interest of the proprietor of the *dominium utile*. In Northern Ireland, a major interest means any freehold estate or any leasehold estate, whether subsisting at law or equity.

4.55 Confusingly, the term major interest in land is also used in VAT, but with a slightly different definition. In VAT, a major interest means a freehold or a lease for a term exceeding twenty-one years, under section 96(1) VATA 1994. Accordingly, a lease for a term of twenty-one years or less is a major interest in land for SDLT but not for VAT.

Partitions

4.56 Where land is partitioned or an interest in land is divided, paragraph 6 of Schedule 4 provides that 'the share of the interest held by the purchaser before the partition or division does not count as chargeable consideration'. Otherwise, the general rules for exchanges contained in paragraph 5 of Schedule 4 apply.

4.57   The meaning of paragraph 6 is particularly unclear. The chargeable consideration on an exchange, under paragraph 5 of Schedule 4, is the value of the interest acquired. Accordingly, by disregarding the interest disposed of, paragraph 6 does not achieve anything. The best interpretation of paragraph 6 is that, because the interest being disposed of is ignored in determining the chargeable consideration, the words in paragraph 5(1) do not apply to a partition because the acquisition is not made 'in consideration' of any disposal. Alternatively, paragraph 6 might simply mean that, when calculating the chargeable consideration on a partition, the value of the parties' existing interests is subtracted from the value of what they acquire. This interpretation would be more sensible but unfortunately that is not what the legislation says.

4.58   For example, A, B and C together own Blackacre as tenants in common in equal shares. Suppose Blackacre is uniform land of sixty acres and on a partition each party receives twenty acres. The intention of paragraph 6 is clearly that, in this situation, none of the co-owners is chargeable. However, suppose A receives thirty acres and B and C fifteen acres each. If no other consideration is given by A, then it does make a difference how paragraph 6 is interpreted. If the correct interpretation is that the interest given up is ignored so that paragraph 5 does not apply, then A will not be chargeable to SDLT. This makes sense because B and C have made a gift to A in this example. However, if paragraph 6 means that the value of the existing interest is subtracted from what is acquired, then A would be chargeable on the value of the additional ten acres which he received over and above the value of his existing interest.

Transactions entered into by reason of employment

4.59   Paragraph 12 introduces a new charge to SDLT in the situation where an employee is given living accommodation which is provided to him by his employer and is chargeable to income tax. Where the employee is chargeable to income tax under Chapter 5, Part 3, of the Income Tax (Earnings and Pensions) Act 2003, then the amount chargeable to income tax as a benefit is added to the chargeable consideration.

4.60   However, paragraph 12 will not apply where the employee occupies by virtue of a licence rather than a lease, because giving the employee a licence is not a land transaction. Accordingly, it may be possible to plan around the charge to SDLT, although not the charge to income tax.

Exempt consideration

4.61   The consideration given for certain transactions is expressly excluded from the definition of chargeable consideration under Schedule 4, thereby making the transactions themselves effectively exempt from SDLT. Why these transactions could not simply have been made exempt is not immediately apparent. However, it does have compliance consequences. A transaction where the consideration is not chargeable under Schedule 4 is a transaction for no chargeable consideration within paragraph 1 of Schedule 3 and, accordingly, should never be a notifiable transaction requiring the purchaser to file a return. This is discussed further at paragraph 8.4 onwards below.

Lease obligations

4.62   Certain obligations assumed by the tenant on the grant of a lease are exempted from being chargeable consideration by virtue of paragraph 13 of Schedule 4. The exemption covers covenants of repair and undertakings to insure the property entered into by the tenant. Also expressly excluded is the value of any undertaking by the tenant to reimburse the landlord's costs of management. Accordingly, the obligation to pay service charges is excluded. Finally, there is a general exclusion for any other obligation undertaken by the tenant that would not affect the rent that a tenant would be prepared to pay in the open market. The obligation to pay rent or a premium is not excluded.

4.63   Paragraph 13(3) provides that the assumption or release of the obligations listed in paragraph 13(1) does not count as chargeable consideration on the assignment of the lease. The effect of paragraph 13 is partially to replicate the stamp duty position and in particular the effect of *IRC* v. *Swayne*,[18] as discussed at paragraph 4.24 above. On its terms, paragraph 13 is much less generous and it could be read as saying that the assumption of the liability to pay rent by the new tenant on the assignment of a lease will count as chargeable consideration under SDLT. However, the better view is that this is not correct and that paragraph 13 does not affect the principle of *IRC* v. *Swayne* because it only states what does not count as chargeable consideration rather than what does. The obligation to pay rent is inherent in the lease and therefore its assumption by the new tenant is not consideration at all.

Reverse premiums

4.64   Reverse premiums are exempted from SDLT under paragraph 15. Reverse premium is given an expanded meaning to include three types of payment. The first is the standard reverse premium where a tenant pays a landlord to terminate his lease. The second is an inducement paid by the landlord to the tenant on the grant of a new lease. The third is a payment from the assignor to the assignee on the assignment of a lease. In contrast, an inducement to surrender a lease paid by the landlord remains chargeable to SDLT. In other words, surrenders of leases are chargeable where the landlord pays the tenant to give up the lease but not if the tenant pays a reverse premium.

---

[18]   [1899] 1 QB 341, confirmed [1900] 1 QB 372.

Surrender and regrant of lease on identical terms

4.65   There is an exemption in paragraph 14 of Schedule 4 on the grant of a new lease where it is granted on the surrender of an existing one. Where paragraph 4 applies then neither the grant of the new lease nor the surrender counts as chargeable consideration. Unfortunately, the exemption is drafted in very restrictive terms. For the exemption to apply, the new lease must be of the 'same or substantially the same premises' and on the 'same or substantially the same terms'. The duration of the new lease must be for the same or substantially the same term as the old one. Accordingly, the exemption will not apply if the new lease is for a longer or shorter term than the old one. The use of the term 'substantially the same' allows there to be minor differences without the exemption ceasing to apply. This is a stringent relief and careful thought needs to be given to the stamp duty consequences on the surrender of a lease when the tenant is going to take a new one. It may be better to vary the terms of the old lease before surrender. The possibility of a charge arising on the surrender and regrant of a lease is discussed further at paragraph 3.29. How an unnecessary tax charge might be avoided on the surrender and regrant of a lease where paragraph 14 of Schedule 14 does not apply is considered at paragraph 7.41 below.

Indemnities

4.66   Finally, paragraph 16 of Schedule 4 exempts indemnities given by the purchaser to the vendor in respect of liabilities of the vendor to a third party in relation to the land. Neither the agreement itself nor any payment made under it counts as consideration. Other indemnities owed by the purchaser to the vendor are not exempt.

Consideration paid in the form of an annuity

4.67   Section 52 FA 2003 provides that, where the consideration consists of an annuity payable for a definite period exceeding twelve years, an indefinite period or for life, then the consideration taken into account is limited to twelve years' annual payments. There is no provision for adjustment under section 80 if the consideration actually paid turns out to be different. Section 52 is aimed primarily at equity release schemes where the taxpayer sells his house to a life insurance company in exchange for the right to live in it until his death and an annuity. Although a similar economic effect could be achieved by mortgaging the property, which would be exempt from SDLT, an equity release is something different. An annuity is not restricted to a narrow meaning but is defined as any consideration other than rent that falls to be provided periodically.

Transfers to connected companies deemed to take place at market value

Introduction

4.68   Where land is transferred to a connected company, then, subject to exceptions, section 53 deems that transfer to take place at market value. The reason for this is that sales of shares in companies are only chargeable to stamp duty at 0.5 per cent.[19] Accordingly, an old method of saving stamp duty was to transfer the property intended to be sold into a company set up for the purpose ('Newco'). No stamp duty was payable on that transfer because it was either a gift or a sale for a nominal consideration. The shares in Newco could then be sold on to the purchaser with stamp duty payable at 0.5 per cent. This arrangement was stopped by section 119 FA 2000. Section 53 FA 2003 is intended to achieve the same result for SDLT.

The rule in section 53

4.69   Section 53 applies where land is transferred to a company and either the transferor is connected to the company or at least some of the consideration consists of the issue or transfer of shares in a company with which the vendor is connected. Whether the parties are connected is determined in accordance with section 839 ICTA 1988, which is discussed further at paragraph 4.7 above. The inclusion of situations where the consideration consists of the issue or transfer of shares in a company with which the vendor is connected under section 53(1)(b) appears to be targeted at bringing in other non-arm's length transactions where the vendor and the company are unconnected. In other words, it is designed to prevent the anti-avoidance provision being circumvented by ensuring that the vendor and the company are unconnected.

4.70   Although section 53 is an anti-avoidance provision, its application is mandatory. An important area where it applies is on the incorporation of a business or on a transfer of assets to a company for no consideration. In both of these situations capital gains tax holdover relief is available under sections 162 and 165 TCGA 1992. However, no relief from SDLT is available. Under the old stamp duty regime, one solution was to rest on contract, but this is no longer possible because of section 44 FA 2003. The application of section 53 in this way is quite deliberate. The government were pressed on it in Standing Committee and responded that, because of the nil-rate band threshold for commercial property, only businesses owning property worth over £150,000 need worry about this. Unfortunately, this is little comfort to everyone else.

4.71   The only comfort is that, if the land is transferred to a company, then, on the law as it stands at present, it will be possible to take advantage of the 0.5 per cent rate of stamp duty on shares by selling the company rather than

---

[19] Para. 3 of Sch. 13 FA 1999.

the land when the land comes to be sold. However, it is possible that legislation will be introduced aimed at preventing the avoidance of SDLT by buying and selling special purpose land-owning companies[20] as originally proposed by the government in Budget 2002. Moreover, even if the law does not change, it is not always possible, in practice, to sell the company rather than the land, for example because the company is continuing to trade. There are also specific disadvantages for direct tax which though important are outside the scope of this book.

4.72   Where section 53 applies, the chargeable consideration is 'not less than the market value of the subject-matter of the transaction'. Accordingly, section 53 only operates to increase the amount of tax chargeable up to the market value of the property. If the purchaser pays an amount equal to or in excess of the market value, then tax is charged on the actual consideration given.

4.73   Market value is determined in accordance with the definition in section 272 TCGA 1992[21] which provides that it is the price which the land might reasonably be expected to fetch on a sale in the open market. While market value is a familiar concept, no indication is given as to whether account is to be taken of mortgages and charges. In capital gains tax, the issue never arises because assets are treated as being free of any security interests at the time of disposal under section 26(3) TCGA 1992. SDLT has no provision equivalent to section 26(3) TCGA 1992. Accordingly, for SDLT purposes, the value of a mortgage or other debt secured on the property does operate to reduce its value. The very essence of market value is what people will pay for something, and nobody will pay the full value of an unencumbered freehold for one which is subject to a charge in favour of a third party.

4.74   For example, Mr A transfers the freehold of his shop to BCo upon incorporation of the business. The shop is worth £500,000 but has a mortgage secured on it of £300,000. The market value of the freehold is therefore £200,000. BCo receives the property subject to the mortgage and agrees to assume liability for the mortgage so that it is chargeable under paragraph 8 of Schedule 4. SDLT is charged only on the value of the mortgage (£300,000) because the amount of chargeable consideration under the normal rules is greater than the market value of the freehold (£200,000). It is unclear whether the Revenue would accept this as being the correct analysis.

Exceptions to the deemed market value rules

4.75   Section 54 FA 2003 provides for an exception to section 53 in three cases. In these cases, the only chargeable consideration will be that actually paid. The first case is an exception for professional corporate trustees, and applies where

---

[20] Often referred to as special purpose vehicles or SPVs.   [21] See s. 118 FA 2003.

the purchaser holds the land as trustee in the course of a trust management business.[22] The second case is where the purchaser company holds the land on trust and the vendor is connected with the company only by reason of section 839(3) ICTA 1988.[23] Section 839(3) provides that settlors and persons connected with settlors are connected with trusts. In other words, case two exempts transfers to companies where the company holds the property on trust but the settlor and persons connected with him do not control that company. The third case exempts the situation where the transferor is another company and the transaction is a distribution of the assets of that company whether or not on winding up.[24] Case three does not apply if the vendor has claimed group relief in a transaction that has taken place during the three years prior to the transaction.

4.76   The exemptions in section 54 have been restrictively drafted in an attempt to prevent avoidance. These exemptions to the deemed market value rule were formerly found in section 120 FA 2000. However, not all the stamp duty exemptions have been incorporated into SDLT. In particular, the exceptions for trusts have been drafted much more narrowly to prevent properties being routed through trusts in order to avoid the connected companies rule. Where property is already held on trust and the legal title is transferred to the beneficial owner, then section 53 will apply, but there will be no charge to SDLT because the legal title has only nominal value.

Calculating the amount of tax chargeable

Introduction

4.77   The amount of tax payable is calculated under section 55 FA 2003, except to the extent that it consists of rent in which case section 55 does not apply and tax is calculated according to the rules in section 56 FA 2003 and Schedule 5 (see Chapter 6 below). Tax is charged on a percentage of the chargeable consideration. There are two sets of rates. Which applies depends upon whether or not the property is 'residential'. However, in practice, the only difference is that the nil-rate band ends and the 1 per cent charge begins at over £60,000 for residential property but over £150,000 for non-residential or mixed property. If the transaction is one of a number of 'linked transactions' under section 108 FA 2003, then the consideration for all those linked transactions is aggregated for the purposes of determining the rate under section 55(4)(b). Accordingly, the rate at which tax is levied on the chargeable consideration may be greater than would have been charged on a stand-alone transaction.

Rates of charge

4.78   The percentage rate at which tax is levied depends upon whether or not the land consists entirely of residential property.

[22] S. 54(2).   [23] S. 54(3).   [24] S. 54(4).

4.79   If the land consists entirely of residential property, the rates in Table 4.1 apply under section 55(2)(a).

Table 4.1 Rates of SDLT on land transactions (other than leases) for residential property	
Relevant consideration	*Percentage*
Not more than £60,000	0 per cent
More than £60,000 but not more than £250,000	1 per cent
More than £250,000 but not more than £500,000	3 per cent
More than £500,000	4 per cent

4.80   If the land includes any land which is not residential property then Table 4.2 applies.

Table 4.2 Rates of SDLT on land transactions (other than leases) for non-residential or mixed-use property	
Relevant consideration	*Percentage*
Not more than £150,000	0 per cent
More than £150,000 but not more than £250,000	1 per cent
More than £250,000 but not more than £500,000	3 per cent
More than £500,000	4 per cent

4.81   Except for increasing the nil-rate band for property which is not exclusively residential to £150,000, SDLT merely replicates the old stamp duty rates of charge. As with stamp duty, there is no tapering of the rates. So, if A buys a home for £249,000 he pays £2,490 SDLT at 1 per cent. However, if he pays £251,000 for it he will pay £7,530 SDLT at 3 per cent. Accordingly, by paying an additional £2,000 for the property his house purchase has worked out an additional £6,030 more expensive.

4.82   The tax rates simply rising when they hit a particular figure in this way is known as the slab effect. This is an apt expression for what is a crude system of rates. The Revenue is under pressure to reform the rates and replace them with a modern tapered rate. In the Standing Committee debates, the Chief Secretary to the Treasury indicated that this would be looked at in due course. Such a crude rate system does not sit well with a modern tax, and reform is likely to be sooner rather than later. The downside is that, when the reforms are implemented, the rates of tax will almost certainly be increased to compensate for the loss of revenue that would otherwise occur.

Is the land entirely residential property?

4.83   SDLT introduces a new distinction in rates between residential and commercial property. More precisely, the test under section 55(2) is whether or not the relevant land consists entirely of residential property. At present, this distinction is of little practical importance as regards the rates because the only difference is that 'residential' property is chargeable at 1 per cent rather than nil over £60,000 and up to £150,000. Nevertheless, it merits discussion because in time the rates for residential and non-residential property are likely to diverge further.

4.84   Whether property is residential or non-residential is also a key distinction in disadvantaged areas relief. However, confusingly, mixed-use property is treated differently in these two contexts. In determining the rate of tax under section 55, the property must be entirely residential or the non-residential rate will apply.[25] Accordingly, a property with a shop downstairs and a flat above is taxed at the non-residential rate under section 55. This is surprisingly generous because it might have been made necessary for the property to be entirely commercial for the increased nil-rate band to apply. Disadvantaged areas relief apportions the consideration between residential and non-residential use.

The meaning of residential property

4.85   The distinction drawn by the Act is between residential and non-residential property. There is no separate concept of commercial property, only property that is non-residential. Residential property is defined in section 116 FA 2003 to mean a building that is used as or suitable for use as a dwelling. A building that is being constructed or adapted for use as a dwelling qualifies as residential property under section 116(1)(a). The garden or grounds of a dwelling are included by virtue of section 116(1)(b). There is no restriction on the area that can count as the garden or grounds, unlike in capital gains tax private residence relief or the SDLT relief for housebuilders contained in section 58 FA 2003. Section 116(1)(c) confirms that interests in and rights over the building or garden are also residential property.

4.86   The concept of residential property as defined in section 116 includes a building suitable for use as a dwelling. Accordingly, if it is only a plot of land that is being sold and there is no building in the process of being constructed, then the land is non-residential. In the same way, an existing building that is to be demolished and converted into houses is not residential. Accordingly, if A buys a plot of land on which he intends to build a house, then he might be surprised to learn that it is non-residential property. However, at present, the only difference in rates is the increased nil-rate band for non-residential property. In the above example Mr A will be pleased to learn that, if he has paid £100,000 for his plot of land, there will be no SDLT to pay rather than the £1,000 he would have had to pay if it were residential property.

4.87   The test under section 116 looks at the character of the building rather than the use to which it is being put by the purchaser. Accordingly, if a residential investment property is sold for £70,000, then SDLT is chargeable at 1 per cent

---

[25] See s. 55(2)(a) FA 2003.

because the land is entirely residential property. It makes no difference that the property is being both sold and acquired as a commercial investment. However, there is a specific exception under section 116(7) in a case where six or more dwellings are the subject of a single transaction involving the transfer of a major interest in or a lease over them. In such a case, those dwellings are not treated as residential property. For example, if eight residential investment properties are sold at once, the sale will be at the commercial rate. The chargeable consideration will be aggregated to determine the rate of tax because even if the transaction is structured as eight separate sales the sales will almost certainly be linked under section 108. Accordingly, at present, section 116(7) is very unlikely to affect the rate of tax because it would be very rare to buy six properties for under £150,000 nowadays. Section 116(7) is, however, important for disadvantaged areas relief.

4.88   Buildings used for the following purposes are residential property by virtue of section 116(2):

1. residential accommodation for school pupils;
2. residential accommodation for students, other than accommodation falling within category 2 of section 116(3);
3. residential accommodation for members of the armed forces; and
4. an institution that is the sole or main residence of at least 90 per cent of its residents and does not fall within section 116(3).

4.89   Although they may be suitable for use as a dwelling, buildings currently being used for the following purposes are not residential property under section 116(3):

1. a home or other institution providing residential accommodation for children;
2. a hall of residence for students in further or higher education;
3. a home or other institution providing residential accommodation with personal care for persons in need of personal care by reason of old age, disablement, past or present dependence on alcohol or drugs or past or present mental disorder;
4. a hospital or hospice;
5. a prison or similar establishment; and
6. a hotel or inn or similar establishment.

4.90   Where a building is currently not being used, then it will normally be residential where it is suitable for use as a dwelling under the general rule in section 116(1)(a). Section 116(5) provides a tie-breaker test when a building that is not being used is suitable for at least one of the purposes specified in each of section 116(2) and (3). In that case, the building is characterised according to the use for which it is most suitable. If the building is equally suitable for both sets of uses, then it is treated as residential. However, section 116(5) only applies where the building is suitable for one of the uses in section 116(2) and at least one of those in section 116(3). Oddly, section 116(2) does not include an ordinary house or a conversion into flats. Accordingly, the treatment of an empty public house, for example, is not determined under section 116(5) because it is not suitable for any of the uses set out in section 116(2). Whether or not an empty public house is residential property is determined by whether or not it falls within the general definition of residential property under section 116(1). If it is suitable for use as a dwelling or in the process of conversion then it will be residential. However, in other cases it will not, even if it is suitable for conversion.

4.91   From what has been said above, it will be apparent that the distinction between residential and non-residential property is sometimes a difficult area. The Revenue recognises this, and section 116(8) expressly permits the Treasury to amend section 116 when it appears necessary and expedient to do so. Accordingly, in practice much will turn on the Revenue's interpretation of this area. If the rates for commercial and residential property diverge, then more disputes will arise. Finally, the issue of whether property will be used for residential purposes also arises for VAT in connection with whether or not the option to tax under Schedule 10 VATA 1994 applies. The two tests are completely separate.

Linked transactions

4.92   If the land transaction is one of a number of linked transactions within the meaning of section 108 FA 2003, then by virtue of section 55(4)(a) the relevant land is all land comprised in all of those transactions, and under section 55(4)(b) the relevant consideration is the chargeable consideration for all of the transactions. The effect of section 55(4)(a) is that, if any of the land transferred is not residential property, the residential property rate will not apply to any of the transactions because once aggregated none of the transactions will consist entirely of residential property for the purposes of section 55(2)(b). In other words, section 55(4)(a) prevents taxpayers from making separate disposals of residential property if they form part of a large transaction with a non-residential element. Why taxpayers should wish to achieve this when the only difference in rates is in favour of non-residential property is not apparent. This may be a pointer to future policy; in the meantime it is helpful to taxpayers.

4.93   The aggregation of the chargeable consideration for linked transactions by section 55(4)(b) is currently of far more practical importance. The mischief at which this section is aimed is taxpayers artificially splitting up one larger transaction into a number of small transactions in order to take advantage of the reduced rates where the consideration is smaller. Where the transactions are linked, then each transaction is chargeable at the same rate as if the consideration for it was the total consideration for all the linked transactions. For example, A agrees to sell Blackacre, an empty development site, to B for £600,000. In the absence of the linked transactions rules, the parties could split the land up into six lots and sell them separately for £100,000 each. No tax would be payable because each transaction would be within the £150,000 nil-rate band for commercial property. The linked transactions rule operates to aggregate the chargeable consideration for the purposes of determining the rate so that, in this example, each sale will be chargeable at the maximum 4 per cent rate. The amount of consideration chargeable is not affected by the linked transactions rules but only the rate of tax.

4.94   Transactions are linked under section 108 when they 'form part of a single scheme, arrangement or series of transactions between the same vendor and purchaser' or persons connected with them. Whether persons are connected is again defined by reference to section 839 ICTA 1988 (see paragraph 4.7 above). What is a 'single scheme, arrangement or series of transactions' is not defined. The old wording of the equivalent stamp duty provision[26] was 'larger transaction or series of transactions'. Unsurprisingly, the SDLT rule has been drafted in wider terms. In particular, the word 'arrangement' is capable of very broad interpretation and is intended to make the new rule wider. The discussion will first consider the meaning of a single scheme or series of transactions in the light of the stamp duty case law on the meaning of 'larger transaction or series of transactions'. How far the new rule for linked transactions is wider owing to the inclusion of 'arrangement' will then be considered.

Single scheme or series of transactions

4.95   The terms 'single scheme' and 'series of transactions' are clearly a re-enactment of the old stamp duty terms 'larger transaction' and 'series of transactions'. These are two separate concepts. There is a single scheme where the transactions form part of some pre-agreed plan or larger transaction. A series of transactions is present where the transactions are entered into sequentially between identical or related parties. However, it is settled that it is not enough that a series of transactions takes place as a matter of fact; there must also be some integral connection or interdependence between those transactions for them to constitute a series of transactions.

4.96   The sole authority on the meaning of series of transactions is *Attorney-General v. Cohen*.[27] The facts of that case were that the taxpayer bought six dwelling-houses at auction from the same vendor. The majority of the Court of Appeal decided that this was not a series of transactions.

4.97   Greene LJ stated that:[28]

> The statement that a transaction forms part of a series involves a tacit finding as to the meaning of the word 'series' in its context, and, for my part, I am unable to take so easy a path in order to arrive at a solution of the present difficulty. It is, in my judgment, incumbent upon those who assert that a

---

[26] Sch. 13, para. 6(1) FA 1999.   [27] [1937] 1 All ER 27.   [28] At pp. 37G–38A and 38D–39B.

number of transactions constitute a series within the meaning of the section at least to point to some quality in them which, upon some intelligible ground, removes them from the category of separate transactions and unites them under the head of a series . . .

I now turn to a consideration of the crucial words of the section. The word 'series' must be read in its context, which is 'part of a larger transaction or of a series of transactions'. The expression 'part of a series' suggests, to my mind, that by a series is meant something of which it can be said there is some integral relationship between its parts. It does not, I think, convey the idea that all that is required is that the transaction should be one of a number of transactions related to one another in time or space or both. This view is, I think, strengthened by the fact that the expression 'part of a series of transactions' stands in juxtaposition to the expression 'part of a larger transaction'. Many instances can be thought of where it might be doubtful whether a transaction could properly be described as 'part of a larger transaction', but where, by reason of the presence of an integral relationship with other transactions, it could be said to form 'part of a series of transactions'. And here it is of importance to remember that the class of transactions effected by documents covered by the section is a varied one. Thus, it covers the case where in one action (or under one reference) by successive orders of the court (or of commissioners) different parts of a property become vested in a purchaser. Again, a builder developing a building estate might have under one contract an option to purchase different plots at different times, so that each option, when exercised, would create a separate contract. In each of these cases, it would at the least be a matter of doubt whether a particular order or conveyance could be said to form part of a larger transaction, but there would, I think, be in each case such an integral relationship between the transactions as to constitute each indubitably part of a series of transactions. In my opinion, read in its context, the phrase 'part of a series of transactions' is intended to sweep in cases where the relationship between the transactions is an integral, and not a fortuitous one, depending merely on such circumstances as contiguity of place, but is such that it would not, or might not, be sufficient to bring them within the phrase, 'part of a larger transaction'.

4.98   Although the wording may have altered slightly for SDLT, the principle stated by Greene LJ remains valid: for transactions to be linked there must be some integral connection between them. In other words, to be linked, transactions must form part of or follow from the same bargain; one example is the exercise of an option. A difficult question for stamp duty was whether the vendor and the purchaser had to be identical for there to be a series of transactions. The accepted view was that, if the parties were sufficiently related, then there would still be a series. Section 108(1) now provides a definitive answer by stating that the linked transactions rules apply to transactions which take place between the same parties or 'persons connected with them'.

Arrangement

4.99   The new linked transaction provision for SDLT is wider than the equivalent stamp duty provision owing to the insertion of the term 'arrangement'. The idea behind inserting the term 'arrangement' is to give the Revenue maximum flexibility as to when the linked transaction rules should apply. 'Arrangement' is used in various different contexts throughout the tax legislation with slightly different meanings.[29] The key concept behind an arrangement is that it does not require a formal and legally enforceable agreement. Nevertheless, an arrangement does require at least two parties to enter into it. If a person decides to go to lunch tomorrow at one o'clock, that is not an arrangement. Nor is there an arrangement if that person decides he would like to fix up lunch with one of his friends. An arrangement only comes into existence when one of those friends agrees to have lunch with him. If they agree to sort out the details of when and where to meet there may still be an arrangement albeit less definite. The same ideas apply equally in deciding whether there is an arrangement to sell land.

4.100   What is an arrangement is not defined for the purposes of section 108. However, 'arrangement' is defined for the purposes of the SDLT group relief and reconstruction relief clawback provisions in Schedule 7 FA 2003 as 'including any scheme, agreement or understanding, whether or not legally enforceable'.[30] This is a wide definition but one which well illustrates the key features of an arrangement. An arrangement covers situations which fall well short of the requirements for a contract. However, there must be two or more persons for an arrangement to exist. Accordingly, if something is done merely in contemplation that something else might happen in the future and no other party is involved, that is not part of an arrangement.

4.101   Problems exist in determining when an arrangement can be said to exist when another party is in the picture. The definition in Schedule 7 attempts to define arrangement as broadly as possible by including the concept of understanding. Clearly, an understanding falls well short of a contract, but when one exists is extremely uncertain. A practical answer to this question is that the Revenue is likely to argue that an understanding or arrangement is present when a taxpayer is trying to obtain the benefit of group relief or the lower rates in circumstances in which the Revenue believes he is not entitled to it. The Revenue may claim that this is good policy but it is very bad law. In practice, taxpayers will have to self-assess and if the taxpayer forms the view that there is no arrangement

---

[29]   See, for example, s. 410 ICTA 1988 and s. 660G ICTA 1988. Section 410 is concerned with restricting the availability of corporation tax group relief in order to prevent people selling losses. Section 660G is concerned with defining the existence of a settlement in the broadest possible terms.

[30]   Para. 4(8) of Sch. 7 FA 2003.

in circumstances in which the Revenue may disagree then it will be especially important to make this clear on the self-assessment return.

4.102   However, the problem of when an arrangement exists still remains. Whether or not the courts decide that the group relief definition can be referred to in interpreting section 108 probably does not matter because what amounts to an understanding is as equally vacuous and uncertain as what constitutes an arrangement.

4.103   There are at least three Revenue Statements on the meaning of the word 'arrangement' in the context of other statutory provisions. However, these are as notable for what they do not say about the meaning of arrangement as for the guidance given. Statement of Practice 3/98 dealt with the interpretation of the old stamp duty group relief provisions, where the extended SDLT definition found in paragraph 4(8) of Schedule 7 FA 2003 was not present. SP 3/98 stated that:

> In this context, arrangement means the plan or scheme in pursuance of which the things identified in sections 27(3), 151(3) have been or are to be done – *Shop and Store Developments Ltd* v. *IRC* [1967] 1 AC 472, 493, 494. The arrangement need not be based in contract. It is sufficient if the intra-group transaction is made in connection with that plan or scheme. The intra-group transaction may be the first bilateral step by which legal rights and obligations are created in pursuance of the arrangement. If there is an expectation that a disqualifying event will happen in accordance with the arrangement and no likelihood in practice that it will not, relief will be refused.
>
> The words 'in connection with' are very broad. In *Escoigne*,[31] there was a gap of four years between the two steps in issue.

4.104   In other words, for an arrangement to exist there must be both evidence of a plan to do something coupled with no practical likelihood that the plan would not materialise. Accordingly, if the taxpayer could demonstrate that there were matters which could in practice have occurred to prevent the plan materialising no arrangement existed. Notwithstanding SP 3/98 there have been indications in Stamp Office practice recently that the Revenue has wanted to take a broader view of the term 'arrangement' and to equate it with a mere intention or expectation that a particular event will occur. However, the extended definition for group relief does not attempt to try and achieve this, and it is settled that the term arrangement requires a minimum of two parties and that a mere intention by one person to do something is not an arrangement.

4.105   Statement of Practice 3/93 deals with the meaning of arrangement under section 410 ICTA 1988. Paragraphs 6–8 state that:

---

[31]   *Escoigne Properties Ltd* v. *IRC* [1958] AC 549; [1958] 2 WLR 336; [1958] 1 All ER 406, HL.

6. Where a holder of shares or securities in a company is preparing to dispose of them, straightforward negotiations for the disposal will not give rise to the existence of 'arrangements' before the point at which an offer is accepted subject to contract or on a similar conditional basis. Equally, unless there are exceptional features, an offer made to the public at large of shares or a business will not at that stage bring 'arrangements' into existence.

7. If a disposal requires the approval of shareholders, operations leading towards disposal will not give rise to the existence of 'arrangements' before that approval is given or until the directors become aware that it will be given.

8. If following negotiations with potential purchasers a holder of shares or securities concentrates on a particular potential purchaser this will not of itself be regarded as bringing 'arrangements' into existence. But 'arrangements' might exist if there were an understanding between the parties in the character of an option. For example, an offer, whether formally made or not, might be allowed to remain open for an appreciable period so that the potential purchaser was allowed to choose the moment to create a bargain.

4.106   Accordingly, it seems that, just because a particular person is in mind and negotiations may have taken place, that will not yet amount to an arrangement or understanding, and something more is required. The unanswered question is at exactly what point that additional something will be present and the parties reach an understanding. The better view is that there is no arrangement until the parties make a plan to do something. The facts of the particular case will determine this.

4.107   A second issue is whether if the sales of two pieces of land have been negotiated together that will necessarily mean that they constitute a single arrangement. This situation arises where a purchaser agrees to buy two separate properties from the same vendor otherwise than at auction. For example, suppose A agrees to buy two separate farms from B. If the agreement is structured as two separate sales then there is no single scheme. However, the Revenue might argue that there is an arrangement here.

4.108   If two sales have been negotiated together, does that make them necessarily part of a single arrangement? The better view is that it does not, and provided that each sale would have been entered into irrespective of the other then the transactions will not be linked. This follows from the principle laid down in *Prudential Assurance Co.* v. *IRC*,[32] as discussed at paragraph 4.48 above. Conversely, if the transactions would not have been entered into separately, they will be linked transactions. Accordingly, in the above example, if A would buy either of the farms irrespective of the other, then the transactions do not form

[32] [1992] STC 863.

part of a single arrangement and are not linked. However, if the purchases, even though they may have been structured as separate sales, are in fact interdependent, then they will form part of a single arrangement and the consideration must be aggregated. In the above example, this might be the case if the farms were two separate pieces of land only viable as one business.

Linked transactions in practice

4.109   An important area where the linked transactions rules may apply in practice is the tax treatment of options. This is discussed further at paragraph 3.22 above. In summary, the grant of a genuine option, in other words where the purchaser buys it because he may want to exercise it later, will not be linked to any future exercise. This is because the purchaser does not know whether he will wish to exercise the option at some point in the future and accordingly by definition there can be no understanding with the grantor of the option that he will. If the purchaser knows he is going to exercise the option because he has only acquired it for tax planning purposes, then the grant is linked with the future exercise and the consideration must be aggregated for the purposes of determining the rate. The exercise of the option will be linked to the initial grant because it arises from the same contract and therefore forms an interdependent series. Accordingly, the consideration on the exercise of an option must always be aggregated with that paid on grant for the purposes of determining the rate.

4.110   The problem of whether the sale of two properties negotiated at the same time constitutes a single arrangement arises, for example, in the case of a retail takeover where the purchaser buys the property portfolio as part of one transaction. The better view is that these will probably be linked transactions because they are commercially interdependent. However, the contrary is arguable, so it may be that some taxpayers will self-assess on the basis that the transactions are not linked, and wait to see if the Revenue challenges them.

4.111   The equivalent provision in stamp duty caused theoretical difficulties, but often these were not tested in practice because of the unenforceability of stamp duty and the availability of the adjudication procedure. The nature of SDLT will bring the area of linked transactions to the fore, and there are likely to be cases in this area in the near future. The Revenue may also produce guidance on the operation of the linked transactions rules and in particular on when an arrangement will exist.

5

Exemptions and reliefs

Introduction

5.1 This chapter is concerned with transactions which are not chargeable to SDLT owing to the operation of a specific exemption or relief. The provisions of the Finance Act 2003 which deal with exemptions and reliefs are Schedule 3 and sections 57–75, and the discussion will focus on these provisions. However, there are at least six other ways in which transactions involving land may not be chargeable to SDLT.[1]

5.2 First, land situated outside the UK is not within the charge to SDLT at all, as discussed at paragraph 3.51 above. Secondly, licences, security interests and certain less important rights are not chargeable interests under section 48, as discussed at paragraph 2.10 above. Thirdly, no SDLT is payable if the consideration does not exceed the nil-rate band.[2] Fourthly, certain types of consideration, for example reverse premiums, are excluded from being chargeable consideration under paragraphs 10 and 13–16 of Schedule 4.[3] Fifthly, section 107 provides that tax is not required to be paid if it would ultimately be borne by the Crown and that a land transaction is exempt from charge if the purchaser is a Minister of the Crown or a parliamentary body. Sixthly, transactions involving acquisitions and disposals of land into and out of a partnership by the partners and of interests in a partnership are for the moment exempt from SDLT under Part 3 of Schedule 15 and remain chargeable to stamp duty under section 125(8); these are discussed further at paragraph 3.44 onwards above.

5.3 Removing transactions from the charge to tax in so many different ways is confusing, and means that the legislation is difficult to follow. Unfortunately, it is not simply a matter of wading through the various tests to decide if any tax is ultimately payable. Although no tax may actually be payable, the taxpayer may still be required to file a return if the transaction is a notifiable transaction. Whether a transaction is notifiable where no tax is payable depends upon whether the

---

[1] Another example is where a land transaction is neither completed nor substantially performed otherwise than as part of the completion of a sub-sale so that s. 45(3) FA 2003 relieves it from charge.

[2] See Chapter 4 above, especially at para. 4.77 onwards.

[3] See Chapter 4 above, at para. 4.61 onwards.

transaction is a notifiable transaction under section 77 FA 2003. Transactions exempted under Schedule 3 are almost always not notifiable, whereas those relieved from charge under section 57 onwards generally are. For example, a sale of land exempted from charge by the operation of group relief is always a notifiable transaction. The issue of when a land transaction return must be made is discussed at paragraph 8.4 below.

5.4   Owing to these different compliance consequences, the approach of the discussion will be to consider first the reliefs contained in Schedule 3 and then those contained in sections 57–75. In reading what follows, it is important to bear in mind that the reliefs are, unsurprisingly, subject to strict conditions. The discussion will aim to focus in greater detail on those reliefs which are likely to be of more importance in practice and on those areas where the legislation is unclear.

Transactions exempted under Schedule 3

No chargeable consideration

5.5   Transactions for no chargeable consideration are exempt from charge under paragraph 1 of Schedule 3. Most importantly, this means that gifts are exempt from SDLT. All other transfers for no consideration are also exempt from tax.[4] These will include transfers involving trusts such as an appointment of trust assets in favour of a beneficiary or the appointment of a new trustee. A transfer of land to shareholders on a liquidation or to beneficiaries under a will or on an intestacy will similarly be exempt. Acquisitions taking effect by operation of law will, in practice, usually be exempt for the same reason.[5] The reason why transfers taking effect by operation of law are included within the charge under section 43 is no doubt to prevent a general exemption being exploited for tax planning purposes.

5.6   The general exemption for transfers without chargeable consideration is a welcome change from the position under stamp duty where transactions otherwise than on sale were stampable with a fixed duty of £5 unless specifically exempted under the Stamp Duty (Exempt Instruments) Regulations 1987. Both transactions that were formerly exempt and those that were chargeable with fixed duty are now exempt from charge. However, that does not mean that SDLT can be forgotten about because the compliance position needs to be ascertained. A transfer for no chargeable consideration is normally, but not always, not a notifiable transaction under section 77(3).

---

[4] Although not, of course, transfers of land to a connected company, which are deemed to take place at market value under s. 53 FA 2003.

[5] A merger under foreign law may be an exception to this. See further the discussion at para. 2.4 above.

5.7   Finally, transactions where the consideration is not chargeable consideration for SDLT purposes[6] are also within paragraph 1 of Schedule 3. For example, a reverse premium within paragraph 15 of Schedule 4 paid on the surrender of a lease is not chargeable consideration. Accordingly, it falls within paragraph 1 of Schedule 3. This does not affect the amount of tax payable because that is nil in any event. However, it does mean that the surrender of a lease for a reverse premium is not a notifiable transaction under section 77(3). Whether a transaction is notifiable is discussed further at paragraph 8.6 below.

Transactions in connection with divorce

5.8   A transaction between the parties to a marriage is exempt from charge under paragraph 3 of Schedule 3 when it is done pursuant to either a court order in matrimonial proceedings or an agreement between the parties in contemplation of the ending of the marriage or a judicial separation. In short, the effect of paragraph 3 is that, provided the parties intend to get divorced in the normal way, no SDLT will be payable on any resulting property transfers. It does not matter if the agreement is made before any divorce proceedings are issued because the exemption applies to agreements made in contemplation of the dissolution of the marriage.

5.9   The exemption does not extend to unmarried co-habitees. This is an area where the government is under pressure to introduce reforms throughout tax law and some taxpayers are claiming that unmarried co-habitees and same-sex couples deserve equal treatment under the Human Rights Act 1998. On a more practical level, if co-habitees are merely partitioning their existing interests in property, then they should be able to benefit from the rules dealing with partitions which prevent the value of existing interests being taken into account as chargeable consideration.

5.10   However, the situation is more problematic if the property is subject to a mortgage because of the rules on the assumption of debt contained in paragraph 8 of Schedule 4, discussed at paragraph 4.14 onwards above. For example, suppose A and B own a flat together as tenants in common in equal shares. The flat is worth £300,000 and is subject to a £200,000 mortgage. A and B split up and A wants to buy out B's half-share and take over the whole mortgage. A will also pay B £50,000 for his share of the equity. It appears that, in the normal case A must pay SDLT on the chargeable consideration, which comprises the £50,000 paid for B's half-share together with the £100,000 of liability for the mortgage which has been assumed. The issue of whether a charge arises on the assumption of the debt in this situation is discussed further as part of the discussion of paragraph 4 of Schedule 8 at paragraph 4.22 above.

---

[6] Under Sch. 4 FA 2003; see Chapter 4 para. 4.61 onwards above.

Variation of testamentary dispositions

5.11 A variation of the dispositions taking effect on death under section 142 of the Inheritance Tax Act 1984 and section 62 TCGA 1992 is exempt from charge under paragraph 4 of Schedule 3. Post-death variations are ineffective for inheritance tax and capital gains tax when they are effected for consideration other than the variation of another disposition. Paragraph 4 of Schedule 3 prevents that other variation being taken into account as chargeable consideration. When drafting such variations it will no longer be necessary to certify that Category M of the Stamp Duty (Exempt Instruments) Regulations 1987 applies unless the estate also contains other property chargeable to stamp duty.

Public sector housing

5.12 The Finance Act 2003 contains three sets of relieving provisions relating to the public housing sector. For convenience, these are discussed together. The exemption for certain leases granted by registered social landlords is contained in paragraph 2 of Schedule 3. The other reliefs are outside Schedule 3 and are provided for by sections 70 and 71 and Schedule 9 FA 2003.

Registered social landlords

5.13 Leases granted by registered social landlords to individuals pursuant to arrangements between the landlord and a housing authority are exempt under paragraph 2 of Schedule 3. The exemption is only available where the landlord itself has obtained the accommodation for a term of five years or less. A registered social landlord means a body, normally a housing association, registered as such under the Housing Act 1996.[7] The lease must be for an indefinite term or terminable at less than one month's notice. A housing authority is defined in paragraph 2(3) of Schedule 3 to mean certain types of public authority.

Acquisitions by registered social landlord

5.14 There is a separate exemption under section 71 FA 2003 for certain purchases by registered social landlords. A registered social landlord is a body registered as such under the Housing Act 1996.[8] Many registered social landlords are also charities and accordingly charities relief may be available in situations where relief under section 71 is not.

5.15 Acquisitions are exempt under section 71 in three situations. The first is where the registered social landlord is controlled by its tenants. Under section 71(2), a registered social landlord is controlled by its tenants if the majority of its

---

[7] Or the Housing (Scotland) Act 2001 or the Housing (Northern Ireland) Order 1992.

[8] Or the equivalent provisions for Scotland and Northern Ireland: the Housing (Scotland) Act 2001 and the Housing (Northern Ireland) Order 1992: see s. 121.

board members occupy properties owned or managed by it. A board member is a director, trustee or member of the management committee. The second situation is where the vendor is a qualifying body within section 71(3). The list of qualifying bodies includes other registered social landlords and certain other public bodies. The third exempt situation is where the acquisition is funded with a public subsidy. A list of the relevant kinds of payment is given in section 71(4).

Right-to-buy transactions and shared-ownership leases

Introduction

5.16   Schedule 9 introduces special rules for certain transactions involving the purchase of public sector housing. Several distinct situations are dealt with and each has its own rules. The common factor is that these transactions are structured in ways that, in the absence of special provisions, would produce unintended charges to SDLT.

Right-to-buy transactions

5.17   Paragraph 1 of Schedule 9 disapplies the rules on contingent consideration contained in section 51 FA 2003 in the case of a right-to-buy transaction. The value of any consideration payable under a contingency is not taken into account. Moreover, even if the contingency arises and the additional consideration is paid, it is still not chargeable consideration for SDLT purposes. The purpose of paragraph 1 of Schedule 9 is to ensure that, where a council home is sold under the right-to-buy legislation, there is only one charge to SDLT. Even if the property is sold on so that additional consideration becomes payable no further charge to SDLT arises.

5.18   A right-to-buy transaction is defined for the purposes of paragraph 1 as the sale of a dwelling or the grant of a lease either at a discount by a relevant public sector body or in pursuance of the right to buy under the Housing Act 1985 or the Housing (Scotland) Act 1987. Paragraph 1(3) contains a list of relevant public sector bodies which includes government ministers, local councils, housing authorities, social housing bodies and new town and development corporations; in other words, everybody against whom the right to buy might be exercised.[9]

Shared-ownership leases

5.19   Where a lease of public sector housing is granted containing a provision for the lessee to acquire the reversion, then, provided the conditions set out in paragraph 2(2) of Schedule 9 are met, the lessee may elect for a one-off SDLT charge to apply on the grant of the lease. The lease must be granted either

---

[9] Para. 1 of Sch. 9 is based on the stamp duty reliefs contained in s. 107 FA 1981 and s. 110 FA 1984.

by one of the qualifying bodies listed in paragraph 5 of Schedule 9 or under the right to buy contained in the Housing Act 1985. The qualifying bodies are housing associations and similar entities. For paragraph 2 of Schedule 9 to apply, the consideration for the grant of the lease must be partly in the form of rent and partly premium. The lease must contain a statement of the market value of the dwelling. Where the purchaser elects, then the chargeable consideration is that market value. No further tax is payable on the transfer of the reversion to the purchaser, by virtue of paragraph 3 of Schedule 9.

5.20   Paragraph 4 provides for the situation where the lease contains provisions for the freehold to be acquired in steps, known as staircasing. Where the purchaser makes an election, then the chargeable consideration is the minimum rent stated in the lease plus the premium stated to be obtainable on the open market.[10]

Rent-to-mortgage or rent-to-loan

5.21   A 'rent-to-mortgage' transaction means an acquisition of a dwelling arising from the exercise of a right to acquire on rent-to-mortgage terms under Part 5 of the Housing Act 1985. The 'rent-to-mortgage' scheme allows council tenants to buy their own homes by paying part of the right-to-buy price up front with a mortgage to acquire part of the property, and buying out the landlord's share later. A 'rent-to-loan' transaction means the execution of a heritable disposition in favour of a person who is exercising the rights to purchase a house by way of the 'rent-to-loan' scheme under Part 3 of the Housing (Scotland) Act 1987.

5.22   The chargeable consideration in these circumstances is deemed under paragraph 6(3) of Schedule 9 to be the price that would have been payable had the purchaser been exercising the right to buy. This special treatment is needed because otherwise the 1 per cent rate could apply to houses worth less than the £60,000 nil-rate band owing to the way the schemes work.[11]

Other exemptions and reliefs

5.23   The following reliefs are contained in sections 57–75 of the Act. The heading 'Reliefs' is confusing because all the important reliefs simply operate to exempt the transaction from charge. Similarly, section 49(2) FA 2003 provides that some transactions are exempt from charge under Schedule 3 and '[o]ther transactions are exempt from charge under other provisions of this Part'. However, as mentioned above, section 77 draws a distinction between exempt transactions under Schedule 3 and those which would be chargeable but for a relief in determining whether or not a transaction is notifiable. The meaning of relief is not defined. However, given that the heading above section 57 is

---

[10] The reliefs for shared-ownership leases are based on the stamp duty reliefs contained in s. 97 FA 1980 and s. 108 FA 1981.

[11] Para. 6 of Sch. 9 is based on the stamp duty reliefs in ss. 202 and 203 FA 1993.

'Reliefs', the term 'relief' must refer to these provisions. It is not arguable that group relief, for example, is not a relief. However, this is in spite of the wording of section 49 and many of the relieving provisions themselves.

Disadvantaged areas relief

Introduction

5.24   As the name indicates, disadvantaged areas relief is designed to stimulate regeneration of poorer areas within the UK. Disadvantaged areas relief was introduced for stamp duty purposes on 30 November 2001. It is now contained in section 57 and Schedule 6 FA 2003 which are designed to consolidate the stamp duty provisions dealing with it. In summary, all acquisitions of non-residential property are exempt along with purchases of residential property up to £150,000. This is a very important relief in practice.

Identifying a disadvantaged area

5.25   The criteria for identifying disadvantaged areas are based on residential deprivation. Accordingly, some of the most valuable commercial property in the UK, including Canary Wharf,[12] is exempt from SDLT because it is situated in a poor residential area. The aim of the relief is to brings jobs to workers. The list of disadvantaged areas is contained in the Stamp Duty (Disadvantaged Areas) Regulations 2001,[13] which specifically continue to apply for SDLT purposes by virtue of paragraph 2 of Schedule 6. The regulations list 1,997 disadvantaged areas. The areas are defined in England and Northern Ireland by electoral wards, in Wales by electoral districts and in Scotland by postcode.

5.26   A list of the designated areas can be found online at the Revenue's website.[14] Alternatively, advantage may be taken of an online tool published by the Revenue. This requires the user to input the postcode for the relevant land, and gives an indication as to whether the land is situated in a designated area. Note that the postcode test is not conclusive and errors have been known to occur. This stems for the most part from the test using current postcodes instead of electoral wards and postcodes applicable at the relevant date (7 May 1998 for England, 1 April 1998 for Wales, and 21 April 1991 for Scotland and Northern Ireland). Clearly, ward boundaries and postcodes sometimes change (for example, in the case of ward boundaries, this is caused by reorganisations of local government) and, therefore, to get a definitive decision as to whether the relief is applicable for land in England, Wales and Northern Ireland the user faces the onerous task of perusing a map of the relevant ward boundary as at the relevant date applicable for the transaction in question before comparing this to the location

---

[12] Situated in the Blackwall ward in London.
[13] SI 2001 No. 3747.   [14] www.inlandrevenue.gov.uk.

of the property in question. The user should also check the postcode as at the relevant date for the land, since if the postcode straddles the boundary of a ward all properties covered by that one postcode will be considered to fall within the ward and will qualify for the exemption.[15] For land in Scotland, the user should seek out the postcode as at 21 April 1991 for the land in question. Any land which as at the relevant date applicable for each of the four nations did not fall within any of the designated wards or areas but, as at 27 November 2001, had a postcode which was identical to the full postcode of land which at the relevant date did fall within one of those wards or areas will qualify for the relief. Where uncertainty exists, for example where no postcode has been designated for the land, the situation is not helped by the absence of any opportunity for the enquirer to get an advance ruling from the Inland Revenue Stamp Taxes Office.

Non-residential property

5.27   If land situated in a disadvantaged area is non-residential property, then its acquisition is exempt under paragraph 4 of Schedule 6. Whether property is non-residential is determined in accordance with section 116 FA 2003 as discussed at paragraph 4.85 onwards above. Non-residential property is defined by exclusion as property not falling within the definition of residential. Whether property is residential is determined primarily by reference to what the occupier uses it for rather than the intentions of the purchaser. Accordingly, a purchase of a residential investment property is a residential purchase and therefore not automatically exempt. Purchasing a warehouse in order to convert it into flats would be exempt providing the conversion has not yet begun.[16]

Residential property

5.28   Residential property is exempt from charge under paragraph 5 of Schedule 6 provided that the value of the consideration does not exceed £150,000. If the consideration is rent then the relevant rental value as determined for the purposes of paragraph 2(3) of Schedule 5[17] must not exceed £150,000. If the relevant rental value does not exceed £150,000, then the transaction remains exempt.

5.29   Where the consideration for residential property consists of both rent and other consideration, then provided that both the annual rent is less than £600 and the other consideration does not exceed £150,000, no SDLT is chargeable under paragraph 5(4)(a) of Schedule 6. In other words, the annual rent is ignored if it is not more than £600. However, if the annual rent exceeds £600, then the consideration other than rent is treated as falling within the 1 per cent band by virtue of paragraph 5(4)(b) of Schedule 6. This rule is arbitrary.

---

[15] See Stamp Taxes – Customer Newsletter: Disadvantaged Areas Stamp Duty Exemption (December 2001).
[16] See s. 116(1)(a).   [17] See para. 6.13 below.

5.30   For example, A grants a lease to B of land in a disadvantaged area for a rent of £500 per year in exchange for a premium of £120,000. No SDLT is payable because the rent on the lease is not more than £600 per year and the other consideration is not more than £150,000. However, if the rent on the lease had been £650 per year, then the other consideration would have been chargeable at 1 per cent, producing a charge to SDLT of £1,200.

Mixed-use property

5.31   If land is partly residential and partly non-residential, then the consideration is apportioned on a just and reasonable basis under paragraph 6. In consequence, the distinction between residential and non-residential property operates more restrictively for disadvantaged areas relief than it does in distinguishing the different rates of tax under section 55. In determining the rate of tax under section 55, if the property is not used entirely for residential purposes, then it is non-residential; whereas in Schedule 6 the consideration is apportioned according to the different uses. If the consideration attributable to the residential element is not more than £150,000, then the exemption applies unless the consideration consists of or includes rent, in which case the same rules as for an exclusively residential property again apply as described above.

Land situated partly outside a disadvantaged area

5.32   If the land is situated partly inside a disadvantaged area and partly outside, then, under paragraph 7 of Schedule 6, the consideration is again apportioned on a just and reasonable basis. This will be the case, for example, where a development site crosses the boundary of two electoral wards only one of which is a disadvantaged area. Part 3 of Schedule 6 sets out the rules which apply in this situation. After the consideration has been apportioned on a just and reasonable basis under paragraph 7, then the rules apply in the same way as before. Accordingly, in the case of a partly residential property which is partly in an area qualifying for relief, there will be two apportionment calculations to perform.

Overview of disadvantaged areas relief

5.33   The disadvantaged areas rules are fairly straightforward to apply in practice, although they are more complicated if the property is partly residential or straddles the boundary of a disadvantaged area. The new regime brings the charging and exemption provisions together into one Schedule whereas for stamp duty the provisions dealing with residential land are in regulations[18] separate from the main body of provisions in the Finance Act 1992. Finally, the Revenue recently published Statement of Practice 1/2003 which sets out how the relief is to apply for stamp duty. This provides some useful guidance and it is likely to be made applicable to SDLT.

---

[18] Variation of Stamp Duties Regulations 2001 (SI 2001 No. 3746).

Possible future reform of disadvantaged areas relief

5.34   Disadvantaged areas relief has produced some political controversy owing to the fact that high-value commercial property such as Canary Wharf now qualifies for relief. At the end of 2003, it is planned to update the indices upon which the areas are currently designated. The updated indices will take into account for the first time data obtained from the 2001 Census. Further, the continuation of this relief is dependent upon its status as a lawful state aid under European Union law. The next review in the state aid rules will be in 2005. Accordingly, there are likely to be significant changes in the areas which qualify for relief in the next few years. Organisations should bear this in mind when valuing their property holdings.

Sales of residential property to housebuilding company in exchange for new main residence

5.35   Section 58 FA 2003 provides relief where a housebuilding company or a company connected with it acquires an individual's main residence in part-exchange for a new dwelling. This bargain is treated as two separate land transactions under the rules dealing with exchanges in section 47 FA 2003. Section 58 gives relief for the acquisition of the individual's old house by the housebuilder. SDLT remains payable on the market value of the new house upon its acquisition in the normal way. The relief is designed to be a targeted relief following the limitation of sub-sale relief and the abolition of the ability to structure exchanges as a single sale of the more expensive property. It operates by reducing the chargeable consideration to nil.

5.36   The relief applies where a new dwelling is acquired by one or more individuals from a housebuilding company. A new dwelling means a building or part of a building which has been either constructed or adapted for use as a single dwelling and has not previously been occupied. According to the notes accompanying the Finance Bill, it is not intended to cover a situation where a single dwelling has simply been refurbished. Accordingly, a warehouse converted into flats would qualify as a new building. A farmhouse converted into flats or holiday cottages would qualify, but one which was simply renovated would not.

5.37   The individual must give his former residence in exchange and be intending to occupy the new dwelling as his only or main residence. It does not matter if the housebuilder provides additional consideration for the acquisition because the individual is downsizing. Relief is restricted where the garden and grounds of the old house acquired by the housebuilder exceed the permitted area.[19] The permitted area follows the definition for the capital gains tax only or main

---

[19] S. 58(2).

residence exemptions.[20] It is limited to either 0.5 hectares or such larger area as is required for the reasonable enjoyment of the dwelling with regard to its size and character. There is a plethora of case law and Revenue guidance on the meaning of permitted area for the purposes of capital gains tax which it is beyond the scope of this book to discuss.[21]

5.38   Where the housebuilder acquires land in excess of the permitted area, then he is taken to give chargeable consideration equal to the value of the land outside the permitted area. The idea behind restricting the relief to the permitted area is to bring it into line with the capital gains tax relief. This is a strange policy because the reliefs have different functions and are targeted at different taxpayers. The capital gains tax relief is targeted at the former homeowner and relieves gains on private residences. On the other hand, the SDLT relief is designed to help new housebuilders, and what the housebuilder buys will be determined by what his purchaser wishes to part-exchange. The justifications for the restrictions are, first, that, where a developer acquires a property which has excess land, he is likely to develop that land separately and accordingly should pay SDLT, and, secondly, to restrict the relief to part-exchanges of ordinary homes.

5.39   Finally, while this relief helps housebuilders to sell new properties by allowing them to enter into part-exchange deals without having to pay SDLT, the purchaser still has to pay SDLT on his new house. Meanwhile, the housebuilder is left with a house which he has to sell, and SDLT will be payable on that sale by the purchaser in the normal way.

Relocation relief

5.40   Section 59 FA 2003 provides an exemption when an employer or specialist re-location company acquires an individual's main residence where that individual moves home because his place of employment has changed. Like section 58, this relief is designed to compensate for the limitation of sub-sale relief in a tar-geted situation. Once again, strict conditions must be met for the relief to apply. The individual must have occupied the building as his only or main residence at some time during the period ending with the date of acquisition. So, for exam-ple, if the individual has been working somewhere else for a year, then the relief will only be available if the individual can show that he occupied the house at some time during the year and at that time it remained his main residence.

5.41   The acquisition must result in a change of residence caused by a relocation of the individual's employment. The relocation may arise from the employee joining a new organisation or a change of either the employee's role or his place of employment with an existing employer. Under section 59(4), the change

---

[20]   See s. 222 TCGA 1992.
[21]   See the Inland Revenue Capital Gains Tax Manual at paras. 64800–34.

must be wholly or mainly to allow the individual to have his residence within a reasonable daily travelling distance of his new place of employment and his former residence must not be within a reasonable daily travelling distance. This definition is based on the rules in Chapter 7 of Part 2 of the Income Tax (Earnings and Pensions) Act 2003.

5.42   What is a reasonable daily travelling distance is not defined and is therefore uncertain. It is suggested that travelling time as well as distance must be taken into account. The nature of the employee's job must also be relevant. Some employees, such as caretakers for example, will be required to live much closer, although a caretaker is perhaps unlikely to receive a relocation package. As with section 58 the relief is restricted to the dwelling and the permitted area. If the purchaser acquires land in excess of the permitted area, again the value of the excess area represents chargeable consideration. A relocation company is defined narrowly as one whose business includes providing the service of acquiring dwellings in connection with a relocation of employment. Finally, while an employer includes both present and future employers, a small point to watch is that it does not include other group companies.

Group relief, reconstruction relief and acquisition relief

Introduction

5.43   These are probably the most important reliefs of all. The provisions for them are contained in Schedule 7 FA 2003. Part 1 deals with group relief, and Part 2 contains the provisions dealing with the reconstruction and acquisition reliefs. Although all three reliefs are separate, each is subject to strict conditions and a three-year clawback provision in order to prevent the relief being exploited for tax planning purposes. Reconstruction and acquisition reliefs share common anti-avoidance and enforcement provisions. The discussion will follow the structure of the Act by first considering group relief and then the reconstruction and acquisition reliefs together. All three reliefs are based on the old stamp duty provisions.

Group relief

Introduction

5.44   The purpose of group relief is to allow companies under common ownership to restructure by transferring land around the group without triggering SDLT charges. However, if companies could claim group relief on all transfers of land between group companies, it would be possible first to transfer land which the group wanted to sell into a new company specifically created for the purpose and then to sell the shares in that company to a third party with a charge to stamp duty at 0.5 per cent rather than to SDLT at 4 per cent. Group relief has therefore been made subject to both restrictions and a three-year clawback intended to prevent the exemption being exploited for tax planning.

5.45   Accordingly, care needs to be taken to ensure that the anti-avoidance provisions are not triggered either at the time of the initial transfer or within the next three years. The requirements for the existence of a group in the first place are also strict and more onerous than they appear at first glance. Finally, the consequences of an intra-group transfer of land for other taxes and especially the corporation tax charge on capital gains need to be borne in mind. Land can be transferred between group companies without triggering an immediate chargeable gain where the conditions of section 171 TCGA 1992 are met. However, section 171 is also subject to anti-avoidance provisions and in particular the de-grouping charge under section 179 TCGA 1992.

The availability of group relief

5.46   A transfer of land between group companies is exempt from charge under paragraph 1(1) of Schedule 7. The relief applies to what would otherwise be chargeable transactions whether involving a transfer of freehold land or a lease.[22] It does not matter for SDLT whether or not any consideration is given. For group relief purposes, a company means any body corporate.[23] Accordingly, foreign companies qualify for group relief provided that they are sufficiently similar to an English company to fall within the meaning of body corporate. A body corporate is an entity with a legal personality of its own. The Revenue does not treat a Scottish partnership as a body corporate even though it has separate legal personality. Accordingly, a body of trustees or a partnership[24] does not amount to a body corporate. The meaning of body corporate is an area which gives rise to some difficult questions in practice. The Revenue's *Stamp Office Manual*[25] provides a helpful list of foreign entities which do qualify.[26] However, unresolved issues still remain, including the position where the structure includes shares owned by a partnership such as a Dutch *commanditaire vennootschap*. It is suggested that a Delaware limited liability corporation might qualify as a body corporate when it issues shares in accordance with Revenue Interpretation 224.[27]

5.47   Companies are members of the same group if either one is the 75 per cent subsidiary of the other or both are 75 per cent subsidiaries of a third company. Three tests have to be met for one company to be the 75 per cent subsidiary of another. First, the parent must be the beneficial owner of at least 75 per cent of the ordinary share capital of the subsidiary.[28] The ordinary share capital means all the issued share capital by whatever name called except capital which gives the holder the right to a fixed-rate dividend but no other rights to share in the

---

[22] Stamp duty dealt separately with transfers on sale chargeable under Part I Sch. 13 FA 1999 which were relieved under s. 42 FA 1930 and leases which were relieved under s. 151 FA 1995.

[23] Para. 1(2)(a) of Sch. 7.

[24] An LLP does not qualify because it is treated as transparent for SDLT purposes: see para. 2(1) of Sch. 15 FA 2003.

[25] Last updated in March 2002.   [26] See *ibid.*, para. 6.124.

[27] Although strictly Revenue Interpretation 224 does not apply to SDLT.

[28] Sch. 7, para. 1(3)(a).

profits of the company.[29] On the old wording of section 42 FA 1930, it was held that the expression 'issued share capital' referred to the nominal value rather than the actual value of the shares.[30] Accordingly, it is thought that, for SDLT, the correct approach is to consider the nominal value of the ordinary share capital without regard to the market values of the different classes of share.

5.48   Beneficial ownership bears its ordinary meaning, and in most cases this will cause no difficulties. However, the test ceases to be met if, for example, the parent has agreed to sell the subsidiary under a specifically enforceable contract of sale. Problems also arise if a parent goes into liquidation because of the authorities indicating that a company loses beneficial ownership of its subsidiaries once it goes into liquidation.[31]

5.49   Ownership expressly includes indirect ownership by virtue of paragraph 1(4) of Schedule 7. Paragraph 1(4) provides that the rules for determining the amount of ordinary share capital owned through another company contained in section 838(5) to (10) ICTA 1988 are to apply here. Accordingly, the 75 per cent ownership test is met if a second subsidiary is interposed between the parent and its indirect subsidiary provided that the parent remains entitled to 75 per cent of the shareholding in the indirect subsidiary. The test will be satisfied where, for example, the parent owns all the shares in the immediate subsidiary which owns 75 per cent of the indirect subsidiary. However, if the parent owns 75 per cent of the immediate subsidiary, then any 75 per cent indirect subsidiaries will not qualify as members of the group. This is because the parent's indirect entitlement is only to 56.25 per cent[32] of the shares in the indirect subsidiary.

5.50   This can be represented diagrammatically in Figures 5.1 and 5.2.

5.51   Sub B is in the same group as Parent and Sub A, because Parent is indirectly entitled for 75 per cent of Sub B's shares.

5.52   Sub D is in the same group as Sub C but not Parent, because Parent is only indirectly entitled to a 64 per cent shareholding in Sub D.

5.53   The second condition is that the parent is entitled to not less than 75 per cent of the profits of the subsidiary available for distribution. The third and final limb of the 75 per cent test is that the parent must be entitled to at least 75 per cent of the assets of the subsidiary available for distribution on a winding up. The corporation tax rules for calculating who is entitled to profits and assets available for distribution contained in Schedule 18 ICTA 1988 are incorporated for the purposes of SDLT under paragraph 1(5) of Schedule

---

[29] Sch. 7, para. 1(5).
[30] See *Canada Safeway Ltd* v. *IRC* [1973] Ch 374; [1972] 1 All ER 666.
[31] See *Ayerst (Inspector of Taxes)* v. *C&K (Construction) Ltd* [1975] STC 345, HL; and *J. Sainsbury plc* v. *O'Connor (Inspector of Taxes)* [1991] 1 WLR 963; [1991] STC 318; 64 TC 208.
[32] I.e. 75 per cent of 75 per cent.

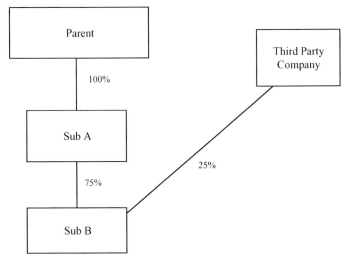

Figure 5.1

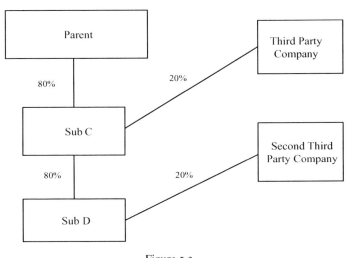

Figure 5.2

7 FA 2003.[33] The full details of Schedule 18 are outside the scope of this book, but most importantly it deems the equity holders to whom profits are available for distribution to include a loan creditor under a non-commercial loan.[34] Although it is not said so expressly, it is settled that the parent need

---

[33] With the omission of paras. 5(3) and 5B to 5E of Sch. 18 ICTA 1988.
[34] Sch. 18, para. 1(1)(b) ICTA 1988.

not be directly entitled to the income or the assets on a winding up. Entitlement through an intermediary company, as in the above examples, is again sufficient.

Restrictions on availability of group relief

5.54   Paragraph 2 of Schedule 7 contains anti-avoidance provisions which restrict the availability of group relief. The purpose of these provisions is to stop group relief being available where the intra-group transaction is a means of saving SDLT when the property, or an interest in it, moves outside the group. The most blatant example of this is of course to dispose of the purchasing company outside the group with the benefit of the land. Arguably, making the relief subject to strict conditions is now unnecessary because of the clawback provision.[35] The danger is that the provisions are drawn so widely that group relief will not be available on a transaction where the land does not end up being transferred out of the group. There are three circumstances in which group relief is prevented from applying under paragraph 2.

5.55   First, relief is not available by virtue of paragraph 2(1) if at the effective date of the transaction, arrangements are in existence for persons to obtain control of the purchaser but not of the vendor. In other words, group relief is not available if it is intended to sell the purchaser outside the group. Accordingly, a transfer of land into a group company as a prior step under an arrangement to sell that company on to a third party purchaser who wishes to acquire the land does not qualify for group relief.

5.56   Secondly, relief is barred under paragraph 2(2)(a) if there is an arrangement whereby the consideration is to be provided or received from outside the group. Paragraph 2(2)(a) should not apply to the situation where the purchaser obtains finance from a third party lender for the purchase of the asset provided that this is a genuine finance transaction and there is no arrangement in place for the third party to benefit from the land. This was the view of the Revenue for the equivalent stamp duty provision as stated in Statement of Practice 3/98 and it is anticipated that the Revenue will continue to apply it to SDLT. However, paragraph 2(2)(a) does not contain an express exemption for the situation where the consideration is provided by a bank, and accordingly the fear will remain that this may disqualify transfers from group relief until the Revenue confirms its practice for SDLT.

5.57   Thirdly, relief is not available under paragraph 2(2)(b) if there is an arrangement for the purchaser to cease being a 75 per cent subsidiary of the vendor or a third company. This is again designed to prevent group relief from being available where there is an arrangement for the transferor to leave the group holding the benefit of the land.

---

[35] Originally introduced for stamp duty by s. 111 FA 2002.

5.58   All the restrictions in paragraph 2 are widely drafted. An arrangement is defined under paragraph 2(5) to include 'any scheme, agreement or understanding whether or not legally enforceable'. The meaning of arrangement is discussed further at paragraph 4.99 above in the context of linked transactions. The concept of an arrangement is intended to be a much broader concept than a contract and to cover situations where agreement has yet to be fully reached. Nevertheless, two parties must still reach some sort of understanding for an arrangement to exist. Accordingly, if the transferor merely anticipates that the company will be sold on to an unspecified purchaser, there is no arrangement. The difficult issue is how definite the understanding must be in order to constitute an arrangement.

5.59   The definition of arrangement is intended to be as wide as possible in order to catch any situation which the Revenue believes is avoidance. The Revenue's view as stated in SP 3/98 on the equivalent stamp duty provision was that an arrangement existed where there was 'no likelihood in practice' that the plan would not be followed through. How far the new definition of an arrangement for the purposes of SDLT group relief widens the definition of arrangement will ultimately depend upon what limits the courts impose upon it. It is likely that the Revenue will argue strongly that the new definition will apply in circumstances which were outside the meaning of the equivalent stamp duty provision and SP 3/98.

5.60   An important question is whether an arrangement can exist before a third party purchaser for the land has been identified. For example, if land is transferred into a special purpose vehicle with the intention of being sold to the highest bidder, is that an arrangement? The better view is that it is not because there must be two parties for even an understanding to exist. To some extent, guidance can be gleaned from SP 3/93, which in conjunction with extra-statutory concession ESC C10 gives guidance about what constitutes arrangements for the purposes of corporation tax: see, in particular, section 410(1) and (2) ICTA 1988 regarding group and consortium reliefs. In essence, SP 3/93 confirms that negotiations for the disposal of shares will not give rise to the existence of arrangements before the point at which the offer is accepted. Where a disposal requires shareholder approval, things leading towards disposal will not give rise to arrangements before that approval is given or until the directors become aware that it will be given. However, this body of guidance goes on to say that arrangements may exist between parties even though they are not enforceable and even if they are not reduced to writing.

5.61   In summary, an arrangement requires some sort of an agreement between two or more persons. The group relief definition for SDLT is intended to be wider owing to the inclusion of the word 'understanding'. However, what amounts to an understanding is as equally uncertain and incapable of definition as is what amounts to an arrangement. Guidance from the courts is sorely needed. In the meantime, the key limit is that an arrangement cannot exist until a second party is in the picture. The chief difficulty is in determining at what point in a negotiation an arrangement comes into existence. See further the discussion at paragraph 4.99 above.

Group relief clawback

5.62   If the purchaser ceases to be a member of the same group as the vendor within three years of the original transfer, then, broadly speaking, group relief is withdrawn under paragraph 3. Relief is similarly withdrawn if the purchaser leaves the group as a result of arrangements made within that three-year period. For the clawback to apply, either the purchaser or a 'relevant associated company' must hold either the land acquired under the original sale or an interest derived from it. A 'relevant associated company' is defined in paragraph 3(4) of Schedule 7 as a company that 'is a member of the same group as the purchaser immediately before the purchaser ceases to be a member of the same group as the vendor' and 'ceases to be a member of the same group as the vendor in consequence of the vendor so ceasing'.

5.63   The wording in paragraph 3(4) and, in particular, 'relevant associated company' mirrors section 126 FA 2003 for stamp duty which itself was implemented with effect from 14 April 2003 and was specifically designed to catch a stamp duty planning technique known as 'double drop down' (or similar). This technique exploited a loophole in section 111 FA 2002 as originally enacted. It involved dropping the land down into a wholly owned subsidiary (the 'first purchaser') before there were arrangements, and in respect of which relief was claimed, and then again into a wholly owned subsidiary of the first purchaser (the 'second purchaser'), again in respect of which transfer relief was claimed. The first purchaser was then sold out of the group, owning the second purchaser which itself owned the land. The Revenue was unable to apply section 111 FA 2002 as originally enacted to clawback the relief in respect of either of the two applications because at the time of its exit from the vendor's group the first purchaser did not hold the land and the second purchaser remained grouped with the first purchaser. This technique is no longer effective for SDLT because of paragraph 2(2)(b) and the inclusion of the concept of a 'relevant associated company' in the clawback provision under paragraph 3. However, it is unclear whether the legislation is entirely effective in achieving its purpose. See further paragraph 7.38 below.

Limitations on clawback

5.64   The clawback will not apply to an interest derived from the original land if the new interest was acquired at market value on a transaction on which group relief has not been claimed. The amount of tax chargeable under paragraph 3 is the market value of the property. Where only part of the property is subject to the recovery charge, then only an appropriate proportion of the tax is chargeable.

5.65   The clawback is subject to three exceptions provided for in paragraph 4 of Schedule 7. The first situation where it does not apply is where the purchasing company which claimed the group relief ceases to be in a group with the vendor because the vendor leaves the group. The vendor is regarded as leaving the group if the group relationship is brought to an end by a transaction relating to shares in either the vendor or another company that as a result of the transaction ceases to be a member of the same group as the purchaser.

5.66   The second situation is where the de-grouping arises because of the winding up of the vendor or another company that is above the vendor in the group structure.[36] A company is above the vendor in the group structure if the vendor or another company above the vendor is a 75 per cent subsidiary of the vendor.[37]

5.67   The third situation is where the purchaser ceases to be a member of the same group as the vendor as a result of a transaction on which stamp duty acquisition relief is claimed under section 75 FA 1986.[38] However, this exception is, in turn, subject to a further clawback provision[39] if the purchaser de-groups from the acquiring company within three years of the original transaction.

Compliance and enforcement aspects of group relief
Duty to make returns

5.68   A transfer of freehold land on which group relief is claimed will always be a notifiable transaction under section 77 FA 2003 requiring a return to be sent in. Where relief is subsequently withdrawn under the clawback provision, then a further return must be made to the Revenue within thirty days of the disqualifying event by virtue of section 81 FA 2003. If such a further return is not made, the interest and penalties become due in the normal way.

Recovery of group relief from other group companies and controlling directors

5.69   Paragraph 5 of Schedule 7 provides that, where the clawback charge under paragraph 3 has not been paid within six months of its having been finally determined, the Revenue may look elsewhere for the tax. The vendor, other group companies and any person who at any relevant time was a controlling director of the purchaser or a company which it controlled may be required to pay the tax. The Revenue may serve a notice on any such person requiring them to pay the tax. These provisions apply to a person who was a controlling director or company that was in the same group during the three-year period following the original transfer on which group relief was claimed.[40] A person made liable under paragraph 6 can recover the tax from the purchaser under paragraph 6(5). Nevertheless, in theory, taxpayers who had nothing to do with any tax avoidance may be caught by these provisions, for example someone who was a director for a short time.[41]

---

[36] Para. 4(4) of Sch. 7.   [37] Para. 4(5) of Sch. 7.   [38] Para. 4(6).   [39] Para. 4(7).
[40] See para. 5(3).
[41] Depending on the circumstances, such a person might have a defence under the Human Rights Act 1998. In practice, the Revenue is likely to apply these provisions sparingly.

Reconstruction and acquisition reliefs

Introduction

5.70 Reconstruction and acquisition reliefs are dealt with in Part 2 of Schedule 7. These are separate reliefs. However, both apply in circumstances in which a purchaser company acquires land as part of the undertaking of the vendor company in return for shares. Reconstruction relief provides total exemption from SDLT. Acquisition relief reduces the rate of tax to 0.5 per cent.

5.71 These provisions are designed to replicate the old stamp duty reliefs in sections 75 and 76 FA 1986, so the Revenue's *Stamp Office Manual* is a good source of guidance. However, an important change is that it is no longer a requirement for either of these reliefs that the registered office of the acquiring company be in the UK, as was formerly the case with stamp duty.

5.72 Before discussing the provisions in more detail, it is worth noting some of the potential difficulties. Unsurprisingly, a strict set of conditions has to be met before either relief can apply. Both reliefs are now subject to clawback provisions in the same way as group relief. Finally, these SDLT reliefs are not aligned with the equivalent capital gains reliefs. Accordingly, the SDLT position has to be considered independently of other taxes and *vice versa*.

Availability of reconstruction relief

5.73 Reconstruction relief provides relief for land transferred as part of a company reconstruction. Under paragraph 7(1), relief is available where the purchaser acquires the whole or part of a scheme of reconstruction of the target company. The meanings of 'undertaking' and 'scheme of reconstruction' are not defined in the Act but are the subject of case law. The relief potentially applies to all land transactions not just the transfer of a freehold or other existing interest.

5.74 A reconstruction essentially involves the transfer of a company's undertaking or part of that undertaking as a going concern to another company under substantially the same ownership. An important limitation on the availability of relief is that the acquiring company must be owned by the same persons in the same proportions as before. Importantly, this means that a partition reconstruction, where a company is split in two parts each owned by separate shareholders, does not count as a scheme of reconstruction for SDLT purposes. This is so even though partition reconstructions qualify for capital gains tax relief under Schedule 5AA TCGA 1992. In a partition reconstruction, it will be necessary to claim acquisition relief. Accordingly, in practice SDLT reconstruction relief is available when a company's undertaking is transferred to another company or divided between two companies with the same shareholders.

5.75 The meaning of undertaking is also the subject of discussion in the case law. Essentially, the undertaking of a company simply means its business. Both trading and actively managing investments amount to a business. The concept of a business requires there to be some activity on the part of the person who carries it on.[42] However, in *Jowett* v. *O'Neill*,[43] Park J decided that a company was not carrying on a business by having money in its current account earning interest.[44] Accordingly, if the company has cash in a current account which is not used for the purposes of its business, then that cash may not form part of the company's undertaking. However, if the company also holds land, even as an investment, then there should always in practice be an undertaking.

5.76   For reconstruction relief to apply, three further conditions must be satisfied. First, the consideration must consist wholly or partly of the issue of non-redeemable shares by the purchaser to the target company or its shareholders.[45] If the consideration consists only partly of the issue of shares, then the only other type of permitted consideration is the assumption or discharge of liabilities of the target company. Accordingly, if the purchaser also pays cash to the shareholders of the target, then reconstruction relief is not available.

5.77   Secondly, following the reconstruction, each of the two companies must be owned by the same persons in the same proportions.[46] In other words, the share-holdings in the two companies should reflect a mirror image of one another. The only permitted difference is that it does not matter how many shares are issued by each company provided that they are owned in the same proportions.

5.78   The third condition[47] is that the reconstruction is for *bona fide* commercial reasons and does not form part of an arrangement of which the main purpose, or one of the main purposes, is the avoidance of tax. So, for example, this might apply if the aim of the arrangement is to sell the land through the company where a company is partitioned and the company holding the land is then sold. Taking advantage of the reliefs provided by SDLT and other taxes is not tax avoidance, and neither is partitioning a company to allow two businesses to operate separately. For this purpose the relevant taxes are stamp duty, income tax, corporation tax, capital gains tax and SDLT. Inheritance tax is not one of the relevant taxes for these purposes, so a reconstruction undertaken for inheritance tax purposes, for example to ensure the availability of inheritance tax business property relief, is permitted.

Availability of acquisition relief

5.79   Acquisition relief operates to reduce the rate of tax to 0.5 per cent where a company acquires the whole or part of an undertaking of another company

---

[42] See *American Leaf Blending Co.* v. *Directors General of Inland Revenue* [1979] AC 676 at 684 *per* Lord Diplock.

[43] *Jowett (Inspector of Taxes)* v. *O'Neill & Brennan Construction Ltd* [1998] STC 482; 70 TC 566.

[44] See also *Land Management* v. *Fox* [2002] STC (SCD) 152 at 160.

[45] See para. 7(2).

[46] See para. 7(14) of Sch. 7.   [47] See para. 5 of Sch. 7.

(the 'target') and the conditions of paragraph 8 are satisfied. The relief applies in similar situations to reconstruction relief although it is less generous and the conditions for its application are less onerous. In particular, it does not require a scheme of reconstruction or an identity of shareholders, and there is no requirement that the transaction be carried out for *bona fide* commercial reasons. Again, acquisition relief is only available where an undertaking is transferred. Accordingly, the discussion at paragraph 5.75 above applies here. There are two further conditions for acquisition relief to apply.

5.80   First, the consideration must consist wholly or partly of the issue of non-redeemable shares by the purchasing company to the target or its shareholders.[48] If the consideration is only partly non-redeemable shares, then the only other types of consideration permitted are the assumption of liabilities and cash up to 10 per cent of the nominal value of the shares.

5.81   The second condition is an anti-avoidance provision. Paragraph 8(4) provides that the purchaser must not be associated with another company that is party to arrangements with the target relating to the shares issued by the purchaser in connection with the transfer. Companies are associated if one controls the other or if they are under common control within the meaning of section 416 ICTA 1988. The purpose of paragraph 8(4) is to prevent the relief applying where there is a pre-existing arrangement to sell to the purchaser with the benefit of the land.

Clawback of reconstruction and acquisition reliefs

5.82   Both reconstruction and acquisition reliefs are subject to a clawback provision similar to that for group relief. If control of the purchaser company changes within a three-year period from the effective date or under arrangements made within that period, then relief is retrospectively withdrawn under paragraph 9 of Schedule 7. At the time when control changes, the purchaser or a relevant associated company must still own the land or an interest derived from it. Where relief is withdrawn, tax is charged as if the original transaction had taken place at market value with no relief available. As with the group relief clawback, an appropriate proportion of the tax will be charged if only part of the land is transferred with the purchaser.

5.83   The reconstruction and acquisition relief clawback charge is subject to five exceptions provided for in paragraph 10 of Schedule 7. The first is where control of the purchaser changes as a result of a transaction connected with divorce under paragraph 3 of Schedule 3. The second is where control changes as a result of a variation of the dispositions taking effect on death under paragraph 4 of Schedule 3.

5.84   The third case, under paragraph 10(4), is where control of the purchaser changes as a result of a transfer of shares within the group which qualifies

---

[48] See para. 8(2) of Sch. 7.

for exemption from stamp duty under section 42 FA 1930. The fourth case, under paragraph 10(5), is where control changes owing to a transfer of shares to another company to which share acquisition relief from stamp duty under section 77 FA 1986 applies.

5.85   However, the third and fourth case exceptions are themselves subject to another anti-avoidance clawback provision contained in paragraph 11 of Schedule 7. Paragraph 11 disapplies these exceptions where, subsequent to the exempt transfers, another transaction occurs which effectively changes the ultimate ownership of the land. Paragraph 11(1)(a) withdraws the third case exception where, following an exempt transfer of shares between group companies, a company holding shares in the purchaser leaves the group. Similarly, relief under case four, under paragraph 10(5), is withdrawn where control of the company which took control of the purchaser under an exempt transfer again changes. For paragraph 11 to apply, the chargeable event must again occur within three years of the original sale of the land or under arrangements made within that period. The original purchaser or an associated company[49] must continue to hold the land.

5.86   The fifth exception to the clawback is where control of the purchaser changes as a result only of a loan creditor ceasing to be treated as having control of the purchaser. Finally, the Chief Secretary to the Treasury gave an assurance in Standing Committee that the clawback would not be triggered by a change of control of a public company arising from an ordinary market transfer of its shares.

Compliance and enforcement of reconstruction and acquisition reliefs

5.87   Reconstruction and acquisition reliefs are subject to the same compliance regime as group relief. A transaction in which relief is claimed will always be notifiable where freehold land is being transferred. Where the clawback is triggered, the purchaser must make a further return within thirty days under section 81(1)(b). Where reconstruction and acquisition reliefs are withdrawn under the clawback provisions, the tax can be recovered from controlling directors and other group companies under paragraphs 12 and 13 of Schedule 7. The provisions are identical to those for group relief.

Compulsory purchase

5.88   Section 60 FA 2003 contains a relief to prevent a double charge to SDLT in situations where the person acquiring the property is not the ultimate developer. In practice, the person acquiring the property from the original owner will usually be a local planning authority which acquires the land under a compulsory purchase order and then sells it on to a developer. If the local authority is itself the developer or the property is conveyed directly by the original owner to the

---

[49] Defined in para. 11(5) of Sch. 7.

developer, then relief does not apply. In this instance, SDLT will still be charged in the normal way because the relief only prevents double charges to SDLT.

Compliance with planning obligations

5.89   Land transactions entered into to comply with planning obligations where the purchaser is a public authority are exempted from charge by section 61 FA 2003. This relief is intended to apply in the situation where a developer is granted planning permission conditional upon providing something, a community centre for example, to a public authority. This agreement would normally be made under section 106 of the Town and Country Planning Act 1990 (or section 75 of the Town and Country Planning (Scotland) Act 1997 or Article 40 of the Planning (Northern Ireland) Order 1991). Section 61 contains a list of public bodies, but the essential idea is that any public authority that might enter into a section 106 agreement should be exempt.

5.90   SDLT is payable on the acquisition of the land by the developer, but the sale on to the public authority is exempt. Although the SDLT that would have been chargeable on the second transaction would have been payable by the local authority, it would have wanted, in practice, to pass this on to the developer. For example, a developer is granted planning permission to build a housing estate by Rotten Borough Council. Planning permission is granted subject to a section 106 agreement that A Ltd builds and gives back to Rotten Borough Council a community centre. A Ltd will pay SDLT on the land it acquires to build the community centre but no SDLT is chargeable on the transfer by A Ltd to Rotten Borough Council. If the developer buys the site from Rotten Borough Council, the value of the building works will not count as chargeable consideration owing to the operation of paragraph 10 of Schedule 4 (see paragraph 4.42 above).

Statutory reorganisation of public bodies

5.91   A land transaction is exempt from charge by virtue of section 66 FA 2003 if both the vendor and purchaser are public bodies and the reorganisation is effected under a statutory provision. A list of what counts as a public body for these purposes is contained in section 66(4). It includes local councils, NHS trusts and bodies other than companies established under statute for the purposes of carrying out statutory functions. Accordingly, private companies involved in PFI projects and, for example, Network Rail, a company established by statute, are not public bodies. However, the Treasury has the power to prescribe that anyone is a public body, and it may be that this will be used to exempt specific transactions with a public element. A reorganisation is defined under section 66(3) as including the creation or abolition of a public body, the creation of functions to be discharged by a public body and the transfer of functions from one public body to another.

5.92   There is no general relief for transfers where the purchaser is a public body. However, as has been mentioned at paragraph 5.2 above, a transaction where the purchaser is a government minister or a parliamentary body is exempt from charge under section 107(2) FA 2003 and no tax is payable by public offices or departments of the Crown where it would ultimately be borne by the Crown under section 107(1).

Charities relief

5.93   Acquisitions of land by charities are exempt from SDLT by virtue of section 68 and Schedule 8 FA 2003. A charity is defined as a body of persons or trust established for charitable purposes only and follows the general law meaning. Schedule 8 also contains anti-avoidance provisions in order to prevent the charities exemption being exploited for tax planning purposes. For the exemption to apply, the charity must intend to hold the land either in furtherance of its own charitable purposes or those of another charity or as an investment the profits of which are applied towards its own charitable purposes.

5.94   If the transaction is entered into for the purpose of avoiding SDLT, then the exemption does not apply. The reason for these anti-avoidance provisions is that the Revenue believed that the charity exemption in the old stamp duty regime, which simply exempted purchases by charities, was being exploited for tax planning purposes. There were differing variations on this theme depending upon how the property was conveyed to the true purchaser but all involved the initial purchase being made by the charity. There is some doubt as to whether these structures would have been effective to save stamp duty had their effectiveness been tested in court.

5.95   Structures exploiting the charities exemption will not be effective for SDLT. In particular, if a charity acquires a property intending to sell it on to a particular purchaser as part of an arrangement designed to save SDLT, then the exemption does not apply by virtue of paragraph 1(3) of Schedule 8. Moreover, even if it could be said that the charity was entering into the transaction for purely commercial reasons it would still not be exempt because it does not intend to hold the property either for charitable purposes or as an investment.

5.96   Paragraph 2 of Schedule 8 contains a clawback provision which applies where a disqualifying event occurs either within three years of the transaction or in pursuance of arrangements made within three years of that transaction. A disqualifying event occurs when either the purchasing charity ceases to be established for charitable purposes only or the land is used by the charity otherwise than for qualifying charitable purposes. Accordingly, if the charity resells the property within three years for reasons other than as part of its charitable purposes, the relief is retrospectively withdrawn.

5.97   Where the clawback applies, the charity becomes liable to make a return under section 81 and to pay the tax that would have been chargeable on the original purchase. Where only part of the land is disqualified, only the appropriate proportion is payable. Charities and their advisers need to be aware of these ongoing compliance obligations.

Bodies established for national purposes

5.98   Land transactions where the purchaser is one of certain specified institutions established for national purposes are granted exemption from tax under section 69 FA 2003 in the same way as charities. The institutions to which the exemption applies are the National Heritage Memorial Fund, the Historic Buildings and Monuments Commission for England, the Trustees of the British Museum and the Trustees of the Natural History Museum. Specific exemption is needed for these bodies because they do not qualify as charities.

Conversion of partnership to limited liability partnership

5.99   Exemption is given for the transfers of land to a limited liability partnership (LLP) in connection with its incorporation under section 65 FA 2003. This is intended to re-enact, with minor amendments, the relief from stamp duty in section 12 of the Limited Liability Partnerships Act 2000. Three conditions must be met for the relief to apply. First, the transfer must take place within one year of the LLP's incorporation. Secondly, the transfer must be made by a partner in a partnership comprised of all the persons who are to become partners in the LLP and no one else or a bare trustee or nominee for such a partner. Accordingly, if two partnerships merge to form an LLP, then section 65 relief is not available. The third condition is that either the shares of the partners in the LLP must be the same as under the original partnership, or, alternatively, any differences in those shares must not have arisen for tax-avoidance reasons.

5.100   However, the legislation contains a technical defect in the situation where the members of the LLP change between the date on which it is established and the date the business is transferred. The problem arises because for the second condition to be satisfied, the partner making the transfer must 'at the relevant time' be a partner in a partnership comprised of all the persons who are to be members of the LLP and no one else. The relevant time under section 75(5) is the moment immediately before the incorporation of the LLP, unless the partner acquired his interest in his partnership interest after the incorporation of the LLP. Accordingly, if a new partner joins the LLP after its incorporation then the transferor was not at the relevant time in partnership with all the persons who were to be members of the LLP and no one else and the second condition is not met. This defect is contained in the old stamp duty provisions and has been re-enacted.

Alternative finance arrangements between individuals

5.101   Sections 72 and 73 provide exemption for certain types of financing arrangement between individuals and banks or building societies. Although located in a different part of the Act, the purpose of these provisions is to exempt other finance transactions from SDLT in the same way as a standard mortgage, which is exempted from the definition of chargeable interest under section 48. The word 'alternative' in the section heading means an alternative to a straightforward mortgage or loan secured by a legal charge.

5.102   Section 72 applies where the individual enters into a sale-and-leaseback arrangement with the lender. The financial institution must acquire a major interest in the land[50] and then grant a lease back to the individual. In addition, the individual must be able to repurchase the interest acquired by the institution. Provided that the other conditions of section 72 are satisfied, the sale, leaseback and any repurchase of the institution's interest by the individual or transfer to a third party at his direction are all exempt from charge.

5.103   Section 73 applies where the bank purchases the property (which transaction is chargeable to SDLT unless the vendor will re-purchase the property from the bank) and sells it to the purchaser, taking a legal mortgage under section 205(1)(xvi) of the Law of Property Act 1925 over the property.[51] This is aimed at the situation where the purchaser buys the property from the lender in instalments, although that is not actually a requirement of section 73.

5.104   The arrangements provided by sections 72 and 73 are important for Muslims because Shariah law forbids the charging of interest on loans. However, the exemption is not restricted to so-called Islamic mortgages. Nor is there any restriction on what the money can be used for. Accordingly, individuals and partnerships can, for example, enter into sale-and-leaseback arrangements to obtain business finance without triggering a charge to SDLT.

5.105   However, the relief is restricted to arrangements between individuals and banks and building societies. Companies are not eligible for relief, and both sections contain an anti-avoidance provision designed to prevent companies taking advantage of the relief by having an individual acquire the property as trustee or a partner where a beneficiary or another partner is a company.[52] The position of more complicated financing arrangements entered into by companies is discussed further at paragraph 9.41 below.

Demutualisation of insurance company

5.106   When land is transferred as part of the demutualisation of an insurance company, that transfer is exempt from charge under section 63 FA 2003. The

---

[50] A freehold or a term of years absolute as defined in s. 117 FA 2003. See para. 4.54 above.

[51] Or, in Scotland, a standard security and, in Northern Ireland, a mortgage by conveyance of a legal entity or by demise or sub-demise or a charge by way of legal mortgage.

[52] See ss. 72(6) and 73(4).

relief applies to a land transaction for the purposes of or in connection with the transfer of the business of a mutual insurance company to a company with issued share capital. Shares in the new company must be offered to at least 90 per cent of the persons who were members of the mutual immediately before the transfer. All shares to be issued in the new company, other than those offered to the public, must be offered to members of the mutual, persons entitled to become members of the mutual or past and present employees of the mutual.

5.107   Two types of transfer of an insurance business qualify under section 63(2): first, a transfer under an insurance business transfer scheme, as defined in Part 7 of the Financial Services and Markets Act 2000; secondly, a transfer of the business of a general insurance company in accordance with either the Life Assurance Directive or the Third Non-life Assurance Directive. The shares may be issued by a parent and the business acquired by a subsidiary. The Treasury has power to amend this section by regulations to relax the shareholding requirements for the new company. Section 63 is designed to replicate the former stamp duty relief contained in section 96 FA 1997.

Demutualisation of a building society

5.108   A land transaction on the demutualisation of a building society effected under section 97 of the Building Societies Act 1986 (BSA 1986) is exempt from SDLT by virtue of section 64 FA 2003. Section 97 BSA 1986 provides for the demutualisation by a building society by the transfer of its business to a commercial company. Accordingly, anyone advising on a demutualisation needs to refer back to the BSA 1986.

5.109   Section 64 is more controversial for what is missing from it. The general relief for transactions involving building societies under section 109 BSA 1986 is not incorporated into SDLT. At present, SDLT provides no specific relief on the merger of two building societies. However, section 109 BSA 1986 provides exemption from 'stamp duties'. Accordingly, the issue arises of whether SDLT is a stamp duty for the purposes of section 109 BSA 1986. If SDLT is a stamp duty then section 64 FA 2003 is perhaps unnecessary.

Collective enfranchisement by leaseholders

5.110   Section 74 FA 2003 operates to prevent the chargeable consideration being aggregated on the purchase of the freehold of a flat by two or more leaseholders. Where a freehold is purchased by an RTE company, as defined in section 4A of the Leasehold Reform, Housing and Urban Development Act 1993, in pursuance of a right of collective enfranchisement, then, under section 74(2), the consideration is divided by the number of flats. The rate of tax is then determined by reference to that fraction of the total consideration. In other words, tax will be charged as though each of the leaseholders acquired their share of the freehold separately.[53] The rights of collective enfranchisement are those exercisable by an RTE company, a company limited by guarantee whose objectives include the exercise of the right of collective enfranchisement with respect to the premises under Part I of the Landlord and Tenant Act 1987 or Chapter 1 of Part 1 of the Leasehold Reform, Housing and Urban Development Act 1993.[54] These provisions require the use of such a company, and section 74 compensates for this requirement.

Crofting community right to buy

5.111 Section 75 FA 2003 applies in the same way as section 74 where two or more crofts are being bought. For crofters to exercise their right to buy under the Land Reform (Scotland) Act 2003, the purchase must be made together with other crofters. Accordingly, section 75 operates to ensure that this does not produce a detrimental effect for SDLT through the consideration being aggregated. As under section 74, the consideration is divided by the number of crofts bought so that, provided all the crofts are of equal value, SDLT is payable in the same way as if each crofter were to purchase his land separately.

Transfer in consequence of reorganisation of parliamentary constituencies

5.112 This exemption, contained in section 67, applies to a transfer of land by a local constituency organisation to its successor which occurs as a result of a boundary change to parliamentary constituencies. Accordingly, it is of limited interest.

---

[53] Although this may not be true if one flat has a much larger value.
[54] As amended by the Commonhold and Leasehold Reform Act 2002.

6

SDLT and leases

Introduction

6.1 The purpose of this chapter is to discuss the application of SDLT to leases on which rent is payable. One of the major changes introduced by SDLT is the introduction of a complicated new formula for calculating the amount of tax chargeable on a lease for a rent. The principle is now that leases at a rent will be subject to an upfront charge on the value of the rental stream in a similar way to a sale of freehold land. SDLT is expected to raise some £250 million of revenue every year from lease rents, an increase of some £200 million on the amount raised by stamp duty. Accordingly, the charge to SDLT on the grant of a lease is now a much more important issue to consider than the former stamp duty charge. Levying an upfront charge is a pragmatic way of securing extra tax while requiring minimal extra compliance work on the part of the Revenue. The provisions for taxing leases at a rent, sometimes referred to as lease duty,[1] are located in section 56 and Schedule 5 FA 2003.

Ongoing consultation

6.2 The charge to SDLT on leases is one of the areas in which the government in-troduced ongoing consultation in the 2003 Budget. This consultation continues notwithstanding that the Finance Act 2003, including the lease duty provisions and the complex new formula contained in Schedule 5, has received Royal As-sent. Section 112(1)(a) FA 2003 gives the Treasury a specific power to amend Schedule 5 by making regulations.[2] The outcome of this consultation will al-most certainly be that both the form and the effect of the provisions that have been enacted in Schedule 5 FA 2003 will remain substantially the same. In particular, there will be a formula[3] for calculating the present value of the lease on grant and that formula will be the same as or a variation on the one which has been enacted. However, the government is likely to make some concessions

---

[1] Strictly, the term 'lease duty' is now incorrect because SDLT is a tax: see s. 121 FA 2003.
[2] The statutory instrument containing the regulations must be debated and approved by the House of Commons under an affirmative resolution procedure. See s. 112(3) FA 2003.
[3] See para, 6.13 below.

as a political gesture and in order to appease those who have been lobbying on behalf of taxpayers. These concessions are unlikely to be particularly generous because the government is determined to raise the additional revenue. See the bulletin board for the book at www.cambridge.org/sdlt/ for confirmation of the formula.

6.3   Nevertheless, the principles upon which the new charge on rental lease is founded are most unlikely to change.

6.4   The Revenue has promised that a mechanism for calculating the new formula will be available online in order to calculate the duty payable. Accordingly, calculating the tax in practice will simply be a matter of visiting the Revenue's website at www.inlandrevenue.gov.uk. Whatever formula is used will require considerable effort in order to perform the tax calculation manually.

Overview of the tax charge on the grant of a lease

6.5   The charge to tax under Schedule 5 applies to leases where rent is payable. If the lease is granted solely for a premium, then tax is chargeable in the normal way under Schedule 4 and Schedule 5 is not in issue. Where the consideration consists of both rent and premium, then the rules in paragraph 9 of Schedule 5 apply; these are discussed at paragraph 6.34 below.

6.6   The principle behind the tax charge on leases is that the grant of a lease should be subject to an upfront charge on the value of the rent over the life of the lease in a similar way to the sale of freehold land. This principle is extremely controversial because the essence of a lease is that it involves temporary rather than outright ownership of land and rent is an ongoing payment for use over time rather than an instalment payment towards acquiring the property outright. The government's reluctance to alter its stance is undoubtedly influenced by the fact that an upfront charge makes it easy to administer the tax and there was a charge on the grant of a lease under stamp duty. Nevertheless, the result is that lease duty is something of an attempt to put a square peg in a round hole.

6.7   Tax is charged at 1 per cent on the 'net present value of the rent payable over the term of the lease'.[4] There is a nil-rate band of £60,000 where the land is residential property and £150,000 where the land is non-residential or mixed-use. The net present value is calculated according to the formula contained in paragraph 3 of Schedule 5. The formula operates by aggregating the rent for the entire period of the lease but with a discount for the value of future rents calculated by applying a temporal discount rate. The nil-rate band, the rate of tax and the discount rate may be altered as a result of the consultation, but the principles behind the charge are unlikely to change.

---

[4] Para. 2(2) of Sch. 5 FA 2003.

Background

6.8   To understand the importance of the SDLT charge on leases, it is necessary to revisit the old stamp duty position. Stamp duty on leases at a rent was chargeable as a percentage of the average annual rent at the rates set out in Table 6.1.[5]

Table 6.1 Rates of the former stamp duty on leases	
Length of term	*Rate of tax*
Term not more than seven years or indefinite:	
• if the rent is £5,000 or less	nil
• if the rent is more than £5,000	1 per cent
Term more than seven years but not more than thirty-five years	2 per cent
Term more than thirty-five years but not more than 100 years	12 per cent
Term more than 100 years	24 per cent

6.9   The result was certainly that the charge to stamp duty on the grant of a lease at a rent was less onerous than it was on the purchase of a freehold. The government formed the view that this was distortive and identified it as an area where they could raise more revenue while claiming that they were simply bringing the charge on leases into line rather than setting out to raise taxes. It is thought that a small number of taxpayers were using the difference in treatment between a freehold sale and the grant of a lease at a rent as a basis for stamp duty planning. For example, instead of buying the freehold, the taxpayer would purchase a 999-year lease with high rental payments payable for the first few years of the term and a peppercorn rent payable thereafter. Although the 24 per cent rate applied to the average annual rent payable over the term of the lease, the tax charge would be small owing to the length of the lease.

6.10   The Chief Secretary to the Treasury gave the following statement in *Hansard*:

> Stamp duty payable on the rental element of leases, which is often called lease duty, has long been out of step with the duty payable on purchases, and the existing structure of lease duty distorts commercial decision-making. The current charge is on just one year's rent, at rates that vary according to the length of the lease. A lease of thirty-five years is charged at 2 per cent, whereas one of thirty-six years is charged at 12 per cent. The government believe that the decision to own a property leasehold or freehold, or on what type of lease to take, should be business led, not tax led.
>
> After extensive consultation, we now propose a new lease duty structure to reduce such distortions while securing a fair amount of tax from those transactions. The government are still open to comment on the proposals. My officials have recently had positive and constructive meetings with interested parties. We are perfectly prepared to consider an alternative

---

[5] Para. 12(3) of Sch. 13 FA 1999.

structure that meets the government's objectives equally well. Under the proposals, lease duty will, as now, be a one-off, up-front charge on rents, but based instead on the value of the lease over its term, using total rent discounted to net present value. That approach surely better captures the value of a lease to the lessee and reflects modern commercial practice in the treatment of future payments.

The £150,000 zero rate threshold for purchases will apply equally to the value of rents on commercial leases, so that leases where the net present value of rent over the term is less than £150,000 will be exempt. That will take 60 per cent of all commercial leases out of the charge completely; and businesses that do pay more under the proposals will pay at a flat rate of 1 per cent, which is still considerably less than the 4 per cent on an equivalent purchase. That decision was welcomed by the industry.

The structure narrows the gap between charges on leasehold and freehold transactions without imposing an unfair burden on large businesses, and removes the burden completely for smaller leases such as those typically used by small businesses and start-ups, where help is most needed... Most residential rental leases are currently liable to lease duty, but under the proposals the vast majority will fall below the £60,000 threshold. A small number of residential leases, about 5,000 per year, will be liable – broadly those with the very highest rents. The proposals thus reflect the government's commitment to fairness, to encouraging enterprise and to reducing regulatory burdens.

6.11   This passage gives a good insight into the thinking behind the charge on leases, and any changes will follow from the principles which it contains. However, even the assumptions on which the reform of the charge on leases is founded are controversial. The claim that 60 per cent of all commercial leases will be taken out of the charge completely is treated with scepticism by some commentators because many leases not owned by large businesses will remain within the charge.[6] Similarly, it is doubtful whether the stamp duty consequences had much impact on the length of leases taken out because this remained a commercial decision.[7]

The effect of the change in practice

6.12   The examples contained in Table 6.2 illustrate how the new formula will affect the amount of tax payable in practice. The table shows the impact of the change

---

[6] The British Retail Consortium, for example, estimates that only 30 per cent of leases taken out by their members, the majority being small and medium-sized retailers, will be exempt if a threshold of £150,000 applies.

[7] As borne out by the Revenue's own statistics which showed that there were fewer leases for seven years than for eight years – the opposite effect from a tax-driven reaction to the 1 per cent rate jumping to 2 per cent. And longer lease lengths tended to be at round figures such as multiples of five years, including thirty-five years where the tax rate jumped but also at twenty, twenty-five and thirty years where there was no tax change.

on commercial leases of terms of multiples of five years between five and thirty-five years with various rents. The charges under stamp duty and SDLT are compared. The SDLT charge is at a multiple of between four and ten times the former charge under stamp duty. Although the formula may change, the differences are likely to remain substantial.

Table 6.2 SDLT on rent as calculated under FA 2003 compared with stamp duty (illustrative figures for commercial leases)

Term (years)	Annual rent (including VAT)	Stamp duty pre-1 December 2003	Total rent	Value of rent	SDLT	SDLT as multiple of stamp duty
5	£20,000	£200	£100,000	£90,301	£0	0.0
5	£100,000	£1,000	£500,000	£451,505	£4,515	4.5
10	£14,000	£280	£140,000	£116,432	£0	0.0
10	£50,000	£1,000	£500,000	£415,830	£4,158	4.2
15	£250,000	£5,000	£3,750,000	£2,879,353	£28,794	5.8
20	£100,000	£2,000	£2,000,000	£1,421,240	£14,212	7.1
25	£1,500,000	£30,000	£37,500,000	£24,722,272	£247,223	8.2
30	£10,000	£200	£300,000	£183,920	£1,839	9.2
35	£20,000	£400	£700,000	£400,013	£4,000	10.0

Calculating the charge to SDLT on the grant of a lease at a rent

Charge on net present value

6.13   SDLT is chargeable under paragraph 2(2) of Schedule 5 as a percentage of the net present value of the rent payable over the term of the lease. The following formula is contained in paragraph 3:

The net present value (v) of the rent payable over the term of a lease equals

$$\sum_{i=1}^{n} \frac{r_i}{(1+T)^i}$$

where:
r_i is the rent payable in year i,
i is the first, second, third, etc. year of the term,
n is the term of the lease, and
T is the temporal discount rate.

6.14   The first point to note about this formula, or any substitute, is that, in practice, it should not be necessary to calculate it manually because the Revenue has promised that an electronic facility will be made available online to perform the calculation. Translated from mathematics into English, the formula means that the net present value of the lease is the sum of the rent over the entire duration of the lease but with a discount applied to determine the value of rents payable in future years. Accordingly, in order to apply the formula, it is necessary to work out the term of the lease and the rent payable for each year of that term according to the rules contained in Schedule 5. The temporal discount rate applied to future rents is currently 3.5 per cent under paragraph 8(1), although the Revenue has the power to vary it and may do so. The current rate of 3.5 per cent is not generous: it takes no account of inflation and assumes minimal other risks.[8]

Rent payable

6.15   The rent payable is determined according to the rules contained in paragraphs 4 and 5. A single sum expressed to be payable in respect of rent and other matters, for example service charges, is treated as being entirely rent under paragraph 4(1) and apportionment is not allowed even though part of the sum is genuinely payable for other matters. However, the same does not apply the other way around: paragraph 4(1) goes on to provide that, if the taxpayer does apportion the consideration, it must be on a just and reasonable basis under paragraph 4 of Schedule 4.

6.16   Paragraph 4(1) is so busy with introducing these rules on apportionment that it does not say what the position is if no sum is expressed to be payable as rent and everything is attributed to service charges. However, there cannot be any serious doubt that sums that are in substance rent will be taxed as rent whatever label is attached to them. Moreover, a sum that is not rent but is paid for the land element of a lease rather than ancilliary services is potentially chargeable under the general charge as deferred consideration.

6.17   One area where these rules will be important in practice is in Private Finance Initiative (PFI) transactions. Often under a PFI transaction a private sector

---

[8] The 3.5 per cent rate, and indeed the net present value formula, have been borrowed from the mechanism used by the Treasury to calculate comparable costs for public expenditure projects where expenditure occurs over an extended period. For example, a contract for a large civil engineering project might specify stage payments of £10 million for each of the next ten years. A rival contract might require no stage payments but have a single payment of £105 million at the end of the ten-year period. Whether the total £100 million phased over ten years is cheaper to finance than the £105 million payment after ten years will depend on the interest rate for capital borrowing. If, say, the annual interest rate is 5 per cent, then a payment of £10 million now equates to a payment of £10.5 million in one year's time. Putting this another way, a payment of £10.5 million next year should be divided by 1.05 to produce a figure corresponding to expenditure now. A comparison of net present values, with an appropriate discount rate, is an accepted method for making a fair comparison between the expenditure flows. The Treasury specifies 3.5 per cent as a standard rate to use for public-sector projects. The use of a 3.5 per cent risk-free rate might be appropriate for government. But commercial tenants cannot borrow at risk-free rates and argue that their cost of capital is much higher than 3.5 per cent.

company will acquire the land and lease it back to the public sector operator while also providing ancillary services. The Revenue has indicated that the impact of the SDLT rules on PFI transactions will be considered and that special provisions may have to be made for them. PFI transactions are discussed further at paragraph 3.53 onwards above.

6.18   Paragraph 4(2) provides that, subject to the rules on rent reviews contained in paragraph 5, section 51 FA 2003 applies to contingent and uncertain consideration. Accordingly, where the consideration is contingent on, for example, the lessee reaching a certain level of turnover, SDLT will be calculated on the basis of the maximum possible rent. Tax may be reclaimed under section 80 if the actual rent payable turns out to be less. Where the rent is uncertain, a reasonable estimate must be made in accordance with section 51(2) (see paragraph 6.23 for further discussion of this in relation to turnover-based rents). No application may be made to defer payment of tax under section 90 FA 2003 where the rent is contingent or uncertain.[9] This could result in some difficult ongoing annual compliance work for the taxpayer in order to reclaim a sum which may be less than the value of the time spent reclaiming it.

6.19   In calculating the amount of the rent, any VAT chargeable on that rent where the landlord has elected to charge VAT under Schedule 10 VATA 1994 on or before the effective date of the transaction is also taken into account owing to the operation of paragraph 2 of Schedule 4 FA 2003. It appears that paragraph 2 of Schedule 4 contains a general principle of SDLT which must apply equally to Schedule 5, and this interpretation is supported by the statement made by the Chief Secretary to the Treasury in Standing Committee concerning the operation of paragraph 2 of Schedule 4 in which he specifically referred to leases. Similarly, the value of the covenants given by the tenant on the grant of a lease other than the obligation to pay rent will not count as chargeable consideration owing to paragraph 13 of Schedule 4.

Rent reviews

6.20   In calculating the value of the rent, no account is taken of a provision for the adjustment of the rent in line with inflation by virtue of paragraph 4(3) of Schedule 5. The position of rent reviews is dealt with by paragraph 5. A rent review is defined as a 'provision for adjustment of the rent, as from a specified date or dates, to reflect current market values'. Where the lease provides for a rent review on or before the end of the second year, then the rules contained in section 51 for valuing contingent and uncertain consideration again apply in relation to the effect of that review by virtue of paragraph 5(3).

6.21   If the lease provides for a rent review after the end of the second year, then in determining the rent payable after that rent review, the effect of the rent review

---

9   By virtue of para. 4(2) of Sch. 5.

is ignored under paragraph 5(4)(a). Bizarrely, paragraph 5(4)(b) then provides that the rent payable after that review 'is assumed to be the same as the annual rent payable over the year preceding the first rent review, or if the period from the beginning of the lease to the date of the first rent review is less than a year, over that period'. There appears to be a mistake in the drafting here, but nevertheless the effect is clear: the rent payable after a second rent review taking place after two years is deemed to be the rent which was payable before the first rent review.

6.22   For example, suppose that a lease provides for a one-year rent holiday with a rent of £10,000 payable in year two, £20,000 in year three and the rent thereafter to be fixed according to a series of rent reviews, the first of which takes place after the end of the third year of the lease. The rent for the first year of the lease will be nil, for the second year £10,000 and for the third year £20,000. However, after the rent review something very odd happens. Not only is the effect of that rent review ignored under paragraph 5(4)(a) but the rent is assumed to be the same as that payable in the year preceding the first rent review, which is £20,000 under paragraph 5(4)(b). The same applies for every subsequent rent review. Accordingly, in this example, the rent taken into account for every year after the rent review for the purposes of the SDLT calculation is £20,000. It does not appear to matter that the rent review may have fixed the actual rent at, for example, £100,000 per year. Similarly, if the lease provides for a one-year rent holiday with the rent thereafter to be determined according to a bi-annual rent review, it seems that the rent taken into account after the second rent review (at the end of year 3) would be nil.

Rents dependent on turnover or other factor

6.23   Where the rent, or part of the rent, is dependent on turnover, then the taxpayer is placed in a difficult position. This might apply, for example, to turnover rent leases which are particularly common in shopping centres, minerals leases where the rent depends on the amount of aggregate removed by the tenant, and leases of windfarm sites where the rent depends on the energy generated by the turbines on the site. The rules on rent reviews do not apply to turnover-based rents because an adjustment to take into account turnover does not fall within the definition of a rent review. Accordingly, it is simply a matter of applying section 51 and making a reasonable estimate, subject to adjustment under section 80 on each occasion when the rent, or an element or instalment of it, becomes known (and remember it is not possible to apply under section 90 for deferral of tax on rents[10]). The problem for the taxpayer is that, if the estimate is too low, the Revenue may challenge it and even claim that it was a negligent estimate so that the usual time limits do not apply. On the other hand, if the estimate is too high, not only is there additional tax to pay but the taxpayer has to go to the trouble of reclaiming it on an ongoing basis. In addition, by a strict

[10]   Sch. 5, para. 4(2).

reading of section 80, a fresh land transaction return requires to be submitted, and the SDLT recalculated and any underpayment made up by the tenant, at the end of each turnover period – which might be perhaps monthly or quarterly in the case of a typical turnover lease of a retail unit. Clearly, this results in a significant compliance burden on the tenant. These are areas that are being considered in the consultation and it is likely that there will be some Revenue guidance forthcoming and possibly a relaxation of the rules.

Rent increases not provided for in lease

6.24   A rent increase otherwise than in pursuance of a provision already contained in a lease is treated as the grant of a new lease in consideration of the additional rent payable under paragraph 10 of Schedule 5. For example, if halfway through a ten-year lease the rent is increased, then tax is payable by reference to the value of the additional rent over the next five years.

6.25   The relief for surrender and regrant of a lease contained in paragraph 14 of Schedule 4 may be useful in this situation. However, it is subject to strict limitations so that it is no use where, for example, the tenant also wishes to lease a smaller area or to extend the term. This is discussed further at paragraphs 3.29, 4.65, 6.37 and 7.41.

Term of lease

6.26   The second piece of information required for calculating the charge to SDLT is the term of the lease. The term of a lease is determined according to the rules in paragraph 6. Under paragraph 6(2), it is the shorter of the term specified in the lease or the period from the date of grant until the end of the lease. In other words, where the term of the lease is backdated from the date of grant no account is taken of that period. No account of break or renewal clauses is taken in calculating the term by virtue of paragraph 6(5).

6.27   Where there is a contract for a lease, then the term of the lease is deemed to begin from the date on which the contract is substantially performed if that date is before the grant of the lease itself. This follows the rule for freehold land contained in section 44 and substantial performance has the same definition. For example, if A enters into an agreement to grant B a ten-year lease of premises and B immediately takes possession of the premises, then the term of the lease is deemed to begin from that date because the contract has been substantially performed. It does not matter that no rent has been paid and the lease itself has not been granted.

6.28   A lease for an indefinite term is treated as a lease for twelve years under paragraph 7. This expressly includes a lease which is expressed to be perpetual, a lease for life and a lease which is determinable on the marriage of the lessee, by virtue of paragraph 7(2). Paragraph 7(2) provides that no account is to be taken of any other statutory provision deeming the lease to be for a longer and definite term.

6.29   Where a lease is granted on the renewal of a previous lease, then the lease is treated as if it begins on the expiry of the previous lease under paragraph 6(4). Finally, the rules for determining the term of a lease will also be used in deciding whether a rent review falls within the first two years of the lease under paragraph 5.

Rates of tax

6.30   Having calculated the net present value by applying the formula in paragraph 3 of Schedule 5, the next step is to apply the rates of tax contained in paragraph 2. These are set out in Tables 6.3 and 6.4.

Table 6.3 Rates of SDLT on leases of residential property

Relevant rental value	Percentage
Not more than £60,000	0 per cent
More than £60,000	1 per cent

Table 6.4 Rates of SDLT on leases of non-residential or mixed-use property

Relevant rental value	Percentage
Not more than £150,000	0 per cent
More than £150,000	1 per cent

6.31   Whether or not property is residential property is again determined according to the rules contained in. section 116 FA 2003. Mixed-use property is taxed at the commercial rate even though it may contain a residential element.

6.32   The rate of tax is determined under paragraph 2(3) by reference to the net present value of the rent given for the 'relevant land'. The relevant land means the land which is the subject of the lease and any linked transactions where the consideration also consists of rent. The meaning of linked transactions is discussed further at paragraph 4.92 onwards above.

6.33   The linked transactions rules are applied separately for rent and for other consideration as paragraph 9(5) of Schedule 5 expressly makes clear. This follows the rule that rent and other consideration are treated separately. For example, if A buys the freehold of Blackacre and leases Whiteacre from B for a rent under the same contract, then, although the transactions will be linked, tax will be charged as if they were entered into separately. However, if A were to pay a premium for the lease of Whiteacre, then that premium would be aggregated with the price paid for the freehold of Blackacre. In the same way, if A were to lease both Whiteacre and Blackacre at a rent, then the consideration would again be aggregated. This rule seems to be founded on pragmatism rather than principle on the basis that aggregating rent and other consideration would be very complicated. The rules for determining when transactions are linked under section 108 are discussed at paragraph 4.94 above.

Leases for both rent and other consideration

6.34   Where a lease is granted for both rent and other consideration, then both elements remain chargeable in the normal way. In addition, if the average annual rent exceeds £600 per year, then the nil-rate band that would otherwise apply to the premium under section 55(2) ceases to apply. and any premium falls within the 1 per cent band. So, for example, if a ten-year lease is granted for a £50,000 premium, then the premium is not chargeable if the rent is £500 per year but tax of £500 is payable if the rent is £700 per year. It does not matter that no tax is payable on the rent in this situation because its net present value is nowhere near £60,000. This rule is arbitrary.

Surrenders, assignments and variations of leases

Introduction

6.35   This section is concerned with events involving a lease that can trigger a tax charge other than the initial grant. The SDLT treatment of these events has been discussed in detail in the preceding chapters; however, for convenience, the position is summarised here together with reference to the earlier discussion. Although stamp duty was chargeable both on the assignment and on the surrender[11] of a lease,[12] there was no requirement to stamp such an agreement. Under SDLT, the charge is wider because the concept of a land transaction under section 43 includes a surrender which takes place by operation of law. Moreover, the taxpayer is required to file a return not only on every occasion when tax is payable on an assignment or a surrender but also in certain circumstances when it is not. See paragraph 8.6 onwards below.

Surrender

6.36   Where the tenant pays a reverse premium in order to be allowed to surrender his lease, that reverse premium is excluded from the definition of chargeable consideration by paragraph 15 of Schedule 4 FA 2003. No SDLT is payable on the surrender of a lease in consideration of a reverse premium paid

---

[11] Subject to a limited exception contained in s. 77(1) of the Stamp Act 1891 where a lease was granted in consideration only of the surrender of an existing lease of the same property.

[12] See especially s. 243 FA 1994 and *Tax Bulletin* No. 18, August 1995.

by the tenant. However, any payment made by the landlord to the tenant on a surrender is chargeable to SDLT in the normal way. See the discussion at paragraph 4.64 above. The surrender of a lease for a reverse premium is not for chargeable consideration under paragraph 1 of Schedule 3 FA 2003, and accordingly the transaction is not a notifiable transaction under section 77(3) FA 2003. However, the surrender of a lease for consideration paid by the landlord is always notifiable under section 77(3) no matter how small the consideration, and, accordingly, a return must always be made. For a more detailed discussion of the concept of 'notifiable transaction' and the rules as to when a land transaction return must be made see Chapter 8 and especially paragraph 8.12 below.

Surrender and regrant

6.37   Paragraph 14 of Schedule 4 FA 2003 provides a very narrow exemption from tax on the grant of a new lease following the surrender of an existing one. The exemption operates by excluding both the surrender and the grant of the new lease from the definition of chargeable consideration. But it only applies where the new lease is of substantially the same premises for substantially the same duration and on substantially the same terms. Paragraph 14 of Schedule 4 is discussed in more detail at paragraph 4.65 above.

6.38   Where paragraph 14 of Schedule 4 does not apply, then the surrender and regrant of the lease will be chargeable under the general rules for exchanges contained in section 47 FA 2003. A lease of whatever duration is always a major interest in land under section 117(2)(b) FA 2003 so that both the landlord and the tenant will each be chargeable on the value of the interests which he acquires under paragraph 5(3) of Schedule 4. Care must also be taken to ensure that a surrender and regrant does not take place by operation of law on the variation of a lease. In practice, it may be better to vary the terms of the existing lease prior to surrender, or to grant an overriding lease. For example, if the parties wish to extend the term of the lease, the landlord might make a grant of an overriding reversionary lease to take effect within twenty-one years. The tax consequences of a surrender and regrant are discussed at paragraphs 3.29 above and 7.41 below.

Assignment

6.39   A payment made by an existing tenant in order to induce a third party to take an assignment of his lease is included within the definition of a reverse premium under paragraph 15(2)(b) of Schedule 4 and is therefore exempt from SDLT in the same way as a reverse premium paid to the landlord. Conversely, a payment made by the assignee to the assignor is chargeable to tax in the normal way as the sale of a chargeable interest. The agreement by the assignee to assume the burden of the obligation to pay rent should not form part of the chargeable consideration following *Swayne* v. *IRC*[13] on the basis that the liability to pay rent is inherent in the nature of a lease. The application of the rule in *Swayne* v. *IRC* to the new SDLT rule on the assumption of debt contained in paragraph 8 of Schedule 4 is discussed at paragraphs 4.24 and 4.25 above. Finally, the assignment of a lease for chargeable consideration is always a notifiable transaction under section 77(3) FA 2003. See further paragraph 8.14 below.

Variation

6.40   The variation of a lease for consideration will almost always be within the charge to SDLT because even if it is not itself a right over land it will normally affect the value of both the lease and the reversion and therefore fall within the definition of chargeable interest under section 48(1)(b) FA 2003. It is important to ensure that any variation is not treated as the grant of a new lease, as discussed at paragraph 3.29 above.

6.41   This is also an area where particular vigilance is needed to ensure that notifiable variations are properly covered by compliance systems. Most lease variations had no stamp duty implications. Under SDLT, many of them will trigger a tax charge. Inadvertent non-compliance will be a distinct new risk where neither taxpayers nor their advisers automatically think that there may be tax to pay.

Scottish missives of let

6.42   In Scotland, where conclusion of missives of let which themselves constitute a lease results in SDLT being paid, and a lease is subsequently granted which either is in conformity with the missives of let or relates to substantially the same property and period as the missives of let, the SDLT that would otherwise be chargeable on that subsequent lease is reduced by the amount of tax paid on the land transaction which was constituted by the original missives of let under section 120(5) FA 2003.

---

[13] [1899] 1 QB 341.

7

Structuring transactions and planning

Introduction

7.1   The preceding chapters have focused on how SDLT applies to different types of transaction with reference to practical examples. This chapter is concerned with how transactions might best be structured in order to obtain the most favourable SDLT treatment. As has already been discussed, a large part of the SDLT legislation is taken up with what are essentially anti-avoidance provisions designed to put an end to various techniques which were being used in stamp duty planning. However, the introduction of SDLT means the end of stamp duty planning but only the beginning of SDLT planning. The more money a tax is intended to raise, the more effort taxpayers may be prepared to make in order to try and save it. SDLT is intended to raise some £5 billion.

7.2   Nevertheless, SDLT planning will be markedly different to stamp duty planning. Not only have the old planning techniques been swept away but the new tax is based on fundamentally different concepts. The best tax planning involves using the legislation to the taxpayer's advantage by ensuring that he falls squarely outside the charge or within a relief rather than trying to avoid the tax artificially. Accordingly, SDLT planning is founded upon the rules and principles of the tax itself which have been discussed in the preceding chapters.

Modern tax planning

7.3   SDLT is a modern tax enforced by a self-assessment regime, in stark contrast to stamp duty which was hopelessly outdated and not directly enforceable. Accordingly, the changes introduced by SDLT affect the whole way in which planning must be approached rather than just the concepts which underpin it. Stamp duty was something of a special case as far as tax planning was concerned. Before the rate increases of the last few years the legislation had scarcely changed in decades. The result was that it was relatively easy to plan around the charge to duty. From the Revenue's viewpoint stamp duty was full of loopholes which were being exploited by well-advised taxpayers. Piecemeal anti-avoidance legislation existed, such as the provisions in the Finance Act 2000[1] which prevented land being first transferred to a connected company with that company

---

[1] Ss. 119 and 120 FA 2000.

then being sold on to a purchaser with stamp duty payable at 0.5 per cent on the sale of the shares. That simple planning such as this, or resting on contract, has continued into the twenty-first century says everything about how far stamp duty was lagging behind other taxes.

7.4   The introduction of SDLT removes most of the so-called loopholes and generally makes tax planning much more difficult. Accordingly, SDLT planning will focus increasingly on structuring transactions in the most favourable way rather than in trying to find a loophole or a magic solution in order to escape tax altogether. In this way SDLT will follow the pattern of other taxes. There will sometimes be a loophole which can be taken advantage of, but these will be increasingly fewer and further between. More often it will be a case of ensuring that the elements of a transaction are arranged in the most favourable way taking account of commercial considerations and other taxes apart from SDLT. Putting a structure in place well in advance of any sale will generally help minimise the chances of suffering an unnecessary tax charge. For example, if land is purchased at the outset by a company which can then simply be sold on in due course, there will never be any need to transfer the land into a special purpose vehicle so as to incur a charge to tax under section 53 FA 2003.

7.5   The second major way in which SDLT planning must be approached differently arises from the introduction of self-assessment. Self-assessment is founded on openness between the taxpayer and the Revenue. The burden is on the taxpayer to provide the Revenue with all the relevant facts, including those which may allow the Revenue to reach a different conclusion as to the taxpayer's liability. Importantly, the general rule for SDLT is that, in any transaction where the taxpayer claims that no tax is payable because of the operation of a relief, a return must still be made because the transaction will be a notifiable transaction under section 77 FA 2003. These points are discussed further at paragraphs 8.23 onwards below. For present purposes, the important point is that SDLT planning will be scrutinised by the Revenue with full knowledge of the facts, including any unfavourable to the taxpayer.

Interpreting tax legislation and the approach of the courts to tax planning

7.6   If the Revenue and the taxpayer cannot agree on the correct application of the law to a transaction, then the taxpayer will have to appeal to the Commissioners and, ultimately, to the courts. Accordingly, it is necessary to consider how the courts are likely to react to any tax planning from the earliest stage because it is their view which is ultimately decisive.

7.7   The issue in a tax case is always whether or not the facts as found fall within the meaning of the statutory provision, be that a relief or a charging provision. Statutes may be given a narrow technical construction or a broader and more purposive construction. Where a judge finds that steps have been taken for tax planning purposes, he is more likely to construe the statute against the taxpayer.

7.8   The question of how the courts should interpret tax statutes in situations where the taxpayer has undertaken planning has a long and difficult history. The traditional approach was to interpret tax legislation fairly strictly.[2] This helped some very artificial tax planning schemes to become fashionable in the 1970s. The limits of this sort of tax planning were exposed by the House of Lords judgment in *W.T. Ramsay* v. *IRC*.[3] *Ramsay* concerned a tax-avoidance scheme designed to create an artificial loss through a series of pre-planned paper transactions which could then be set against the taxpayer's chargeable gains. Their lordships decided that this was not the sort of loss which Parliament intended to be made available to relieve chargeable gains. Lord Wilberforce set out the following principle:[4]

> Given that a document or transaction is genuine, the court cannot go behind it to some supposed underlying substance. This is the well-known principle of *Inland Revenue Commissioners* v. *Duke of Westminster* [1936] AC 1. This is a cardinal principle but it must not be overstated or overextended. While obliging the court to accept documents or transactions, found to be genuine, as such, it does not compel the court to look at a document or a transaction in blinkers, isolated from any context to which it properly belongs. If it can be seen that a document or transaction was intended to have effect as part of a nexus or series of transactions, or as an ingredient of a wider transaction intended as a whole, there is nothing in the doctrine to prevent it being so regarded: to do so is not to prefer form to substance, or substance to form. It is the task of the court to ascertain the legal nature of any transaction to which it is sought to attach a tax or a tax consequence and if that emerges from a series or combination of transactions, intended to operate as such, it is that series or combination which may be regarded. For this there is authority in the law relating to income tax and capital gains tax: see *Chinn* v. *Hochstrasser* [1981] AC 533 and *Inland Revenue Commissioners* v. *Plummer* [1980] AC 896.
>
> For the commissioners considering a particular case it is wrong, and an unnecessary self-limitation, to regard themselves as precluded by their own finding that documents or transactions are not 'shams', from considering what, as evidenced by the documents themselves or by the manifested intentions of the parties, the relevant transaction is. They are not, under the *Westminster* doctrine or any other authority, bound to consider individually each separate step in a composite transaction intended to be carried through as a whole. This is particularly the case where (as in *Rawling*) it is proved that there was an accepted obligation once a scheme is set in motion, to carry it through its successive steps. It may be so where (as in *Ramsay* or in *Black Nominees Ltd* v. *Nicol* (1975) 50 TC 229) there is an expectation that it will be so carried through, and no likelihood in practice that it will not. In such cases (which may vary in emphasis), the commissioners should find the facts and then decide as a matter (reviewable) of law whether what is in issue is a composite transaction, or a number of independent transactions.

---

[2] See especially *IRC* v. *Duke of Westminster* [1936] AC 1.
[3] [1982] AC 300 at 326.   [4] [1982] AC 300 at 323a–324d.

7.9   His lordship continued on the same theme:

> I have a full respect for the principles which have been stated [for the taxpayer] but I do not consider that they should exclude the approach for which the Crown contends. That does not introduce a new principle: it would be to apply to new and sophisticated legal devices the undoubted power and duty of the courts to determine their nature in law and to relate them to existing legislation. While the techniques of tax avoidance progress and are technically improved, the courts are not obliged to stand still. Such immobility must result either in loss of tax, to the prejudice of other taxpayers, or to parliamentary congestion or (most likely) to both. To force the courts to adopt, in relation to closely integrated situations, a step by step, dissecting approach, which the parties themselves may have negated, would be a denial rather than an affirmation of the true judicial process. In each case the facts must be established, and a legal analysis made: legislation cannot be required or even be desirable to enable the courts to arrive at a conclusion which corresponds with the parties' own intentions.
>
> The capital gains tax was created to operate in the real world, not that of make-belief. As I said in *Aberdeen Construction Group Ltd* v. *Inland Revenue Commissioners* [1978] AC 885, it is a tax on gains (or I might have added gains less losses), it is not a tax on arithmetical differences. To say that a loss (or gain) which appears to arise at one stage in an indivisible process, and which is intended to be and is cancelled out by a later stage, so that, at the end of what was brought as, and planned as, a single continuous operation, there is not such a loss (or gain) as the legislation is dealing with, is in my opinion well and indeed essentially within the judicial function.

7.10   What is commonly referred to as the *Ramsay* principle was born. It was viewed as a special rule aimed at combating tax avoidance, and provided that, if certain conditions were met, the tax planning would fail. For the next few years the courts attempted to lay down a definitive principle as to when it would apply. The most authoritative statement of principle was laid down by Lord Brightman in *Furniss (Inspector of Taxes)* v. *Dawson*:[5]

> First, there must be a pre-ordained series of transactions; or, if one likes, one single composite transaction. This composite transaction may or may not include the achievement of a legitimate commercial (i.e. business) end. The composite transaction does, in the instant case . . . It did not in *Ramsay*. Secondly, there must be steps inserted which have no commercial (business) *purpose* apart from the avoidance of a liability to tax – not 'no business *effect*'. If those two ingredients exist, the inserted steps are to be disregarded for fiscal purposes. The court must then look at the end result. Precisely how the end result will be taxed will depend on the terms of the taxing statute sought to be applied.

7.11   Lord Brightman's speech sets out the two requirements for the *Ramsay* principle to apply: a pre-ordained series of transactions with steps inserted which have no

---

[5] [1984] AC 474 at 527.

commercial purpose other than avoiding tax. Accordingly, the limits of *Ramsay* depended upon the concept of pre-ordainment and when it was possible to say that a step had no purpose other than avoiding tax. The limits of these concepts are the subject of lengthy discussion in the judgments given by the House of Lords in *Craven* v. *White*,[6] where the majority decided that there was insufficient certainty that the transactions would be entered into to conclude that they were pre-ordained.[7] Although not decisive, it is apparent from *Craven* v. *White*[8] that it is much harder to apply *Ramsay* if a significant period of time has elapsed between the different steps because in practice that makes it much harder for the Revenue to argue that the end result was pre-determined at the outset. Similarly, it is extremely unlikely that a court would decide that part of a transaction has no commercial purpose if it has tax consequences of its own.[9]

7.12   During this time, it was confirmed that the *Ramsay* principle did apply to stamp duty when Vinelott J rejected the taxpayer's argument to the contrary in *Ingram* v. *IRC*.[10] However, that rarely made any difference in practice because stamp duty was a tax on instruments and an instrument simply does what it says. Moreover, not everyone accepted that *Ramsay* did apply to stamp duty and support for this view can be found in Lord Hoffmann's speech in *MacNiven* v. *Westmoreland* where he gave the phrase 'conveyance or transfer on sale' as an example of a term to be construed narrowly:[11] Lord Hoffmann's views on this are set out at paragraph 7.15 below.

7.13   Exactly how far the *Ramsay* principle applied to stamp duty is a moot point.

7.14   Following *Craven* v. *White* it became apparent that there was no one rule for deciding when the courts would find against a tax-avoidance scheme. The House of Lords' most recent decision on the subject, *MacNiven* v. *Westmoreland*,[12] recognises this and marks a change of approach. *Westmoreland* reaffirms that all the courts are doing in a tax case is interpreting the statute and applying it to the particular facts. Lord Hoffmann considered the *Ramsay* principle and stated that:[13]

> I am bound to say that [Counsel for the Revenue's formulation of the *Ramsay* principle] does not look to me like a principle of construction at all. There is ultimately only one principle of construction, namely, to ascertain what Parliament meant by using the language of the statute. All other

---

[6] [1989] AC 398.

[7] See especially *per* Lord Keith. Note that *Craven* v. *White* was heard together with *IRC* v. *Bowater Property Developments Ltd* and *Bayliss* v. *Gregory*, where the House of Lords unanimously decided that *Ramsay* did not apply.

[8] And see also *Piggott (Inspector of Taxes)* v. *Staines Investments Ltd* [1995] STC 114; 68 TC 342.

[9] See *Countess Fitzwilliam* v. *IRC* [1993] 1 WLR 1189; [1993] 3 All ER 184; [1993] STC 502; 67 TC 614.

[10] [1986] Ch 585; [1986] 2 WLR 598; [1985] STC 835.   [11] [2001] STC 237 at 256a–b.

[12] [2001] STC 237.   [13] [2001] STC 237 at 248a, para. 29.

'principles of construction' can be no more than guides which past judges have put forward, some more helpful or insightful than others, to assist in the task of interpretation. But Mr McCall's [counsel for the Revenue] formulation looks like an overriding legal principle, superimposed upon the whole of revenue law without regard to the language or purpose of any particular provision, save for the possibility of rebuttal by language which can be brought within his final parenthesis. This cannot be called a principle of construction except in the sense of some paramount provision subject to which everything else must be read, like section 2(2) of the European Communities Act 1972. But the courts have no constitutional authority to impose such an overlay upon the tax legislation and, as I hope to demonstrate, they have not attempted to do so.

7.15   Lord Hoffmann proceeded to explain the earlier case law, including *Furniss* v. *Dawson*, as providing guidance on how the courts will apply tax statutes. His Lordship then went a stage further and set out the basis for interpreting some statutory provisions more broadly and others more narrowly. He stated that sometimes the legislation incorporates 'commercial concepts' which are to be understood in a broader sense than 'legal concepts':[14]

> For present purposes, however, the point I wish to emphasise is that Lord Brightman's formulation in *Furniss (Inspector of Taxes)* v. *Dawson*, like Lord Diplock's formulation in *IRC* v. *Burmah Oil Co. Ltd*, is not a principle of construction. It is a statement of the consequences of giving a commercial construction to a fiscal concept. Before one can apply Lord Brightman's words, it is first necessary to construe the statutory language and decide that it refers to a concept which Parliament intended to be given a commercial meaning capable of transcending the juristic individuality of its component parts. But there are many terms in tax legislation which cannot be construed in this way. I refer to purely legal concepts which have no broader commercial meaning. In such cases, the *Ramsay* principle can have no application. It is necessary to make this point because, in the first flush of victory after *Ramsay*, *IRC* v. *Burmah Oil Co. Ltd* and *Furniss (Inspector of Taxes)* v. *Dawson*, there was a tendency on the part of the Revenue to treat Lord Brightman's words as if they were a broad spectrum antibiotic which killed off all tax-avoidance schemes, whatever the tax and whatever the relevant statutory provisions.

And he continued:[15]

> The limitations of the *Ramsay* principle therefore arise out of the paramount necessity of giving effect to the statutory language. One cannot elide the first and fundamental step in the process of construction, namely, to identify the concept to which the statute refers. I readily accept that many expressions used in tax legislation (and not only in tax legislation) can be construed as referring to commercial concepts and that the courts are today

---

[14] [2001] STC 237 at 253, para. 49.   [15] [2001] STC 237 at 255, para. 58.

readier to give them such a construction than they were before *Ramsay*. But that is not always the case. Taxing statutes often refer to purely legal concepts. They use expressions of which a commercial man, asked what they meant, would say 'You had a better ask a lawyer.' For example, stamp duty is payable upon a 'conveyance or transfer on sale' (see paragraph 1(1) of Schedule 13 FA 1999). Although slightly expanded by a definition in paragraph 1(2), the statutory language defines the document subject to duty essentially by reference to external legal concepts such as 'conveyance' and 'sale'. If a transaction falls within the legal description, it makes no difference that it has no business purpose. Having a business purpose is not part of the relevant concept. If the 'disregarded' steps in *Furniss (Inspector of Taxes)* v. *Dawson* had involved the use of documents of a legal description which attracted stamp duty, duty would have been payable.

Even if a statutory expression refers to a business or economic concept, one cannot disregard a transaction which comes within the statutory language, construed in the correct commercial sense, simply on the ground that it was entered into solely for tax reasons. Business concepts have their boundaries no less than legal ones. Thus in two of the cases considered in *Craven (Inspector of Taxes)* v. *White* [1988] STC 476, [1989] AC 398 the House was unanimously of the view that, although there had been an initial disposal with no commercial purpose, except to lay the ground for an avoidance of tax if and when there should be a further disposal to a third party, the transactions were so separate in fact as well as in law as to make it impossible to treat them, even in a commercial sense, as a single disposal to a third party. The lapse of time between the two transactions, the lack of contemplation of any specific later disposal at the time of the first transaction, were commercial realities. The division of opinion in the House over how the third transaction should be categorised did not detract from the agreement that it had to fall within the statutory language.

7.16   The problem with Lord Hoffmann's distinction is that it is often extremely difficult to distinguish a narrow legal concept from a broad commercial one. In hard cases the court will simply want to interpret the statute. Nevertheless, the distinction does at least give some guidance as to when the courts are likely to construe a statute more broadly.

7.17   Lord Hoffmann then proceeded to explain that the term 'tax avoidance' was a source of confusion and best avoided:

> It has occasionally been said that the boundary of the *Ramsay* principle can be defined by asking whether the taxpayer's actions constituted (acceptable) tax mitigation or (unacceptable) tax avoidance. In *IRC* v. *Willoughby* [1997] STC 995 at 1004, [1997] WLR 1071 at 1079 Lord Nolan described the concept of tax avoidance as 'elusive'. In that case, the House had to grapple with what it meant, or at any rate what its 'hallmark' was, because the statute expressly provided that certain provisions should not apply if the taxpayer could show that he had not acted with 'the purpose of

avoiding liability to taxation'. The same question arises on the interpretation of the anti-avoidance provisions to which Lord Cooke referred in *IRC*
v. *McGuckian* [1997] STC 908 at 921, [1997] NI 157 at 172. But when the
statutory provisions do not contain words like 'avoidance' or 'mitigation',
I do not think that it helps to introduce them. The fact that steps taken for
the avoidance of tax are acceptable or unacceptable is the conclusion at
which one arrives by applying the statutory language to the facts of the
case. It is not a test for deciding whether it applies or not.

7.18   In other words, there is really no such thing as tax avoidance. Successful tax
planning is not avoidance because Parliament has not provided for a charge to
tax in those circumstances. Unsuccessful tax planning is simply chargeable to
tax. However, in practice the system works differently because, as a matter of
fact, the Revenue will persuade Parliament to change the law where the courts
uphold tax planning and decide that no tax is chargeable in a situation where the
Revenue believes that it should be. On this view, avoidance means tax planning
of which the Revenue does not approve which will eventually be countered by
a change in the law.

7.19   Returning to SDLT, it is difficult to see why the principles of statutory interpretation as laid down in *MacNiven* v. *Westmoreland* should not apply to a
transaction tax of the species of SDLT. Assuming that this view is correct, then
the *Ramsay* principle, as modified by the subsequent case law including *Furniss*
v. *Dawson*, also applies to SDLT. The *Ramsay* principle is more easily applied
to SDLT than it was to stamp duty because SDLT is a tax on land transactions
rather than a charge on documents. Accordingly, there is much more scope for
the courts to look at all the facts in order to determine the true nature of the land
transaction that is taking place. The argument that *Ramsay* does not apply to a
charge on instruments cannot be applied to SDLT.

7.20   The SDLT charging provisions are drafted in very wide terms and will undoubtedly be construed widely. Whether the courts decide they are legal or
commercial concepts may not matter very much. Perhaps a more interesting
question is how both the reliefs and the anti-avoidance provisions will be construed. Both of these sets of provisions are much more targeted, which lends
itself towards a narrow legal construction. However, as the more relaxed approach in *MacNiven* v. *Westmoreland* makes clear, each piece of the legislation
has to be construed by itself according to what Parliament intended.

Principles of planning

7.21   The best tax planning aims to make the legislation work in the taxpayer's
favour. The following section of this chapter will aim to identify areas where
the SDLT legislation itself provides the opportunity for taxpayers to turn it to
their advantage.

7.22   Tax planning is constantly changing as taxpayers develop new ideas and the Revenue reacts by forcing taxpayers to appeal and enacting anti-avoidance legislation. Under the SDLT regime, the Revenue is given the power to amend the legislation by making regulations which allows them to react particularly quickly to tax planning. Moreover, at the time of writing, the introduction of SDLT is four months away. SDLT planning is still at an embryonic stage as advisers concentrate their energies on stamp duty planning and taking full advantage of the transitional provisions.

7.23   The approach of this chapter is to identify possible planning techniques rather than to set out comprehensive structures. Any suggested structure will, in any event, need to be modified in order to fit the particular facts. It is important to bear in mind when considering these structures that, although they are designed to save SDLT, they will also have consequences for other taxes which need to be considered.

Suggested SDLT planning techniques

Keep outside the charge to SDLT

7.24   The charge to SDLT is drafted very widely, which leaves little scope for staying outside it. However, the exception of licences, tenancies at will and security interests from the definition of chargeable interest in section 48 FA 2003 may be useful in some situations.

Acquisition of a licence or tenancy at will

7.25   If the taxpayer buys a contractual licence rather than a lease, then the transaction is outside the scope of SDLT. There are two difficulties with this idea. First, the purchaser has to be content as a matter of general law with the lesser protection provided by a licence: if not then the idea is a non-starter. Secondly, it is not enough for the parties simply to label their contract a licence rather than a lease. Its effect must actually be to create what is in substance a licence rather than a lease. The lease/licence distinction is discussed further at paragraph 2.11 onwards above. The key test is that of 'exclusive possession'. The challenge for those wishing to take advantage of the exemption for licences is to ensure that, on the particular facts, what is created is a licence. If the purchaser in reality requires exclusive possession, then this will be extremely difficult. One suggestion is to provide that the vendor can move the licensee between different premises or insert additional tenants. Licences are also likely to be useful when the occupation is only temporary or the vendor and the purchaser are closely connected.

7.26   One area where licences may be useful is that of developments. Suppose the deal is that a developer will build ten houses on land currently belonging to a farmer and the profits will be shared between them. Under stamp duty, the developer might have bought the land but the sale would not have been completed and instead the farmer would have granted conveyances of the newly completed houses to the ultimate purchasers. The abolition of resting on contract and the restriction of sub-sale relief under sections 44 and 45 FA 2003 now makes this impossible. If the developer buys land from the farmer, then SDLT will be payable on that sale. If the farmer grants the builder a licence to enter upon the land then that will amount to substantial performance of any contract to sell under section 44(5)(a). However, it may be worth considering an arrangement where there is no contract of sale between the farmer and the developer but instead the developer is to enter onto the land as licensee and to build the development in consideration of being entitled to receive a sum of money equal to a proportion of the sale proceeds from the completed development.

7.27   Finally, where a licence is not possible because exclusive possession is required, then it may be worth considering a tenancy at will. It is possible to create a tenancy at will expressly with rent payable.[16] The downside is that a tenancy at will is terminable by either party without prior notice. Accordingly, it is no use if the purchaser requires any security of tenure.

Security interests

7.28   If a bank assigns its charge on a property to another bank, that is undoubtedly an acquisition of an exempt security interest under section 48(2)(a) FA 2003. The position where the bank assigns its obligation to another individual or a company is less clear. Arguably, that is also an acquisition of an exempt security interest. Accordingly, suppose A wishes to acquire land belonging to B which is subject to a mortgage. It may be that, instead of buying the property directly from B, A could purchase the mortgagee's security interest and then enforce it against A. The end result is that B will end up owning the property without having to pay SDLT except on the value of the property subject to the mortgage. It is not possible simply to buy a property by paying the mortgagee to take over the mortgage and the owner for the value of the equity because if the purchaser proceeds to release the original owner from the debt that debt becomes chargeable consideration under paragraph 8 of Schedule 4. However, if the debt is actually enforced, then such an arrangement might be possible. The problem is that there cannot be any arrangements to let the vendor off the debt. Nevertheless, this technique might be of use where, for example, the vendor is insolvent and the mortgagee is preparing to enforce its charge in any event. In other words, the purchaser will not have to pay SDLT if he acquires the benefit of the bank's interest as mortgagee directly from the bank and enforces the charge himself rather than waiting for the bank to first repossess the property.

---

[16] *Hagee (London) Ltd* v. *AB Erikson and Larson* [1976] 1 QB 209.

Keeping the transaction within the stamp duty regime

Transitional provisions

7.29   Transactions completed before 1 December 2003 remain within the stamp duty regime. The advantage of remaining within stamp duty is that the wider opportunity for planning which it offers will be available.

Partnerships

7.30   Transactions involving transfers of land into and out of a partnership by a partner and transfers of partnership interests are not due to be brought within the SDLT regime until the time of Budget 2004. Accordingly, in the meantime, it will be possible to take advantage of the old stamp duty planning techniques involving partnerships until that time unless, of course, the Revenue announces that this will be changed. See further paragraphs 3.44 above and 9.40 below.

7.31   For example, if land free of charge is contributed to a Jersey partnership, then a sale of an interest in that partnership will be outside the scope of UK stamp duty if executed outside the UK. Such simple tax planning will not be available under SDLT, but nevertheless it arguably remains effective for stamp duty and the authors are aware of these structures being approved by the Revenue on adjudication. However, two notes of caution should be sounded. First, it is important that a partnership is created not just in the foreign jurisdiction but, arguably, also as a matter of UK law. In other words, there is a Conflict of Laws question as to the meaning of the word 'partnership', and the safe course is to ensure that any foreign entity also satisfies the English law definition of a partnership, which is a business carried on in common with a view to profit.[17] If there is a genuine partnership, this makes the structure much harder to attack, but this does make it more difficult to set up. The second note of caution is that, if these structures really are as effective as it is claimed and everyone begins using them, the Revenue is most unlikely to wait around until April 2004 before closing the loophole.

Sell shares in a company

7.32   A sale of shares in a UK company attracts stamp duty, or sometimes stamp duty reserve tax, at 0.5 per cent. Accordingly, if land is owned through a company, then the shares in that company can be sold instead. The difficulty now is getting the land into a company which can simply be sold on, often referred to as a special purpose vehicle. Section 53 FA 2003 deems a transfer of land to a connected company to take place at market value and group relief is subject to anti-avoidance rules in order to prevent its being exploited for these purposes.

---

[17]   See s. 1(1) of the Partnership Act 1890, discussed at para. 3.44 above.

7.33   The best solution is to plan for selling the land on as early as possible. If the land is held by a suitable company from the date of its acquisition, then there is no difficulty. However, this has to be balanced against other commercial and tax consequences. This idea is discussed further in the context of group relief at paragraph 7.36 below.

Get within a relief or exemption

7.34   If possible, a purchaser should try to bring himself within one of the exemptions or reliefs from SDLT.

Disadvantaged areas relief

7.35   The disadvantaged areas relief is very important in practice, especially for commercial property. However, would-be purchasers should be aware that this relief requires EU approval to continue as a state aid. Accordingly, there is a danger that it may not continue beyond 2005, with a consequent reduction in the value of commercial properties situated in a disadvantaged area. See further the discussion at paragraph 5.24 onwards above.

Group relief, reconstruction relief and acquisition relief

7.36   As has been discussed at paragraph 5.43 onwards above, these reliefs are subject to strict conditions and a three-year clawback. Nevertheless, they will undoubtedly remain a very important area for SDLT planning. The aggressive form of this planning is concerned to find ways to dispose of a land-holding company within three years of the land being transferred to it without triggering the clawback provisions. An alternative strategy may be to ensure that, if the clawback charge is triggered, tax is not charged on the full market value of the interest held by the land-holding company at the time when it leaves the group.

7.37   For group relief, the first difficulty is to ensure that all the conditions of the relief are met on an intra-group transfer. In particular, there must be no arrangement with a third party for the transferee company to be sold on. If the land is transferred with a general intention to sell the transferee company on but no third party is yet in the picture, then the relief should be available. Again, the key to successful planning is to do it early.

7.38   The next difficulty is the three-year clawback. If the land is to be disposed of outside the group, then this must be done in a way that does not attract the clawback, either because it is outside the clawback or because one of the exemptions applies. One way to achieve this is to ensure that the land-holding company does not cease to be a member of the same group as the vendor in consequence of the purchaser so ceasing under paragraph 3(4)(b) of Schedule 7 and is therefore not a relevant associated company. Alternatively, thought might be given to minimising the amount of the clawback charge, as mentioned at paragraph 7.37 above.

7.39   The conditions for reconstruction relief to apply are very strict. Not only must the complex technical requirements for a reconstruction be met, but the transaction must be for *bona fide* commercial purposes and not for the avoidance of tax. Acquisition relief is subject to much less strict conditions and there is no requirement that the transaction be entered into for *bona fide* commercial purposes. Accordingly, it is possible to use this relief for tax planning by ensuring that the consideration for the transfer consists only of shares and debt. The benefit to the vendor may be the principal for which the debt is security and which the purchaser must now pay off.

Impact of SDLT on certain types of group reorganisations, reconstructions and other corporate transactions

7.40   SDLT planning may be necessary not only when it is intended for land to be sold outside the group but also to avoid unnecessary tax charges. For example, on a group reorganisation, reconstruction or other corporate transaction where the assets which are being moved include land interests, then the SDLT provisions will clearly be relevant and account must be taken of them. The position may be quite complex, particularly where shares or other securities are also involved, since stamp duty and SDLT will be relevant as well. Moreover, there are differences in detail between the stamp duty and SDLT regimes which may have practical consequences where group or other reconstruction reliefs are in point. As a result there may be situations where, for example, group or reconstruction relief is available for either of stamp duty or SDLT purposes, but not for the other.

Surrender and regrant of lease

7.41   The relief in paragraph 14 of Schedule 4 for the surrender and regrant of a new lease is subject to strict conditions, in particular that the term and rent must be the same. This point is discussed further at paragraphs 3.29, 4.65 and 6.37 above. The Chief Secretary to the Treasury acknowledged this in the Standing Committee debates, and said that it should be possible to come within the relief provided that appropriate planning was undertaken. At least three options merit consideration. First, the terms of the existing lease might be varied before surrender. Secondly, a new overriding lease of the reversion might simply be granted, although this must take effect within twenty-one years owing to section 149(3) of the Law of Property Act 1925. Thirdly, it may be possible to give the lessee an option to extend his lease on new terms.

Sub-sale relief

7.42   Planning involving sub-sale relief was hugely important for stamp duty. Whether anything remains of such planning following the enactment of sections 44 and 45 FA 2003 remains to be seen. The key will be ensuring that the original contract is either not substantially performed, or if substantial performance does take place, that it is somehow rescinded, annulled or otherwise not carried into effect, so that tax is repayable under section 44(9).

Combining sub-sale relief and an Islamic mortgage

7.43   The possibility may exist that no SDLT is payable on the acquisition of land by an individual where the sale is structured to obtain the benefit of both sub-sale relief under section 45 and the relief in section 72 FA 2003 for Islamic mortgages. For example, A wishes to sell her house to B for £1 million. On a straightforward sale, £40,000 of tax will be payable. However, it appears that no SDLT is payable if instead B pays a deposit of £100,000 and then sells the property on to a bank for £900,000 and the bank then grants B a lease with a right for B to reacquire the freehold. No tax is chargeable on the sale between A and B because it is not substantially performed or completed. The conveyance to the bank is exempted from being a completion of the original contract under section 45(3). Both the purchase of the land by the bank and the leaseback to the individual are exempt under section 72 provided that the conditions of that section are met. However, if a purchaser deliberately enters into such an arrangement in order to avoid SDLT, there is a risk that the *Ramsay* principle may apply.

Reducing or postponing the tax charge

7.44   If SDLT must be paid, then thought might be given to deferring the tax charge or reducing the chargeable consideration.

Postponing substantial performance

7.45   Tax is now payable on the earlier of completion and substantial performance. Accordingly, if substantial performance can be deferred, then so can the charge to tax. The difficulty is that, as soon as the purchaser occupies the property, the contract will normally be substantially performed. However, there may be situations where this is not the case.

Purchase price paid by unconnected third party

7.46   Consideration paid by an unconnected third party is not chargeable consideration within the definition of paragraph 4(1) of Schedule 4. Accordingly, if such a person provides part of the purchase price, that element is not chargeable. The unconnected party must not acquire any interest in the property, other than an exempt security interest or a licence, so the money must normally be contributed as a gift because otherwise the third party will acquire an interest in the property under a resulting trust and be a purchaser himself.

7.47   The problem here is that, in practice, it will be extremely unusual to find an unconnected third party willing to give their own money as part of the purchase price. Thought might be given to trying to ensure that related parties are not connected within the meaning of section 839 ICTA 1988. However, section 839 is very widely drafted so this is much easier said than done.

7.48   However, it may be possible to combine, using, for example, a bank as an unconnected party, with other reliefs in order to mitigate SDLT or even ensure that it is not payable altogether. One idea is to take advantage of the rule that, in a sub-sale situation, where the original contract is not substantially performed then the deposit is outside the scope of SDLT provided that the original purchaser and the sub-purchaser are unconnected. Although not straightforward, it may be possible to use a structure similar to that suggested at paragraph 7.45 above.

Transactions involving debt

7.49   Where property is transferred subject to a debt and the transferee assumes liability for that debt, then SDLT is chargeable on the value of the debt.

Sale-and-build contracts

7.50   The situation where a purchaser buys a plot of land from a developer and the developer simultaneously enters into a building contract is discussed at paragraph 4.47 onwards above as part of the discussion on paragraph 10 of Schedule 4. The important point for planning purposes is that, in a sale-and-build situation, the contract for the sale of land and the building contract must be entirely separate even though they will in practice be negotiated in tandem and may be signed on the same day.

Avoiding exchanges

7.51   Section 47 provides that, where A enters into a land transaction as a purchaser wholly or partly in consideration of another land transaction where A is the vendor, the SDLT legislation will treat the arrangement as involving two separate land transactions (see further paragraph 3.26 onwards above). Although there is a limited relief for housebuilders contained in section 58 FA 2003, in general it will no longer be possible as it was for stamp duty with the appropriate drafting to structure an exchange as a sale of the more valuable property only, to avoid two charges to tax.

7.52   The double charge on an exchange under section 47 will apply even if the property which is received in exchange is derived from the original vendor and reverts back to him. Accordingly, where possible, land should be transferred subject to a vendor retaining something rather than the owner selling land to a purchaser and then buying an interest back. For example, it is better to sell a reversionary freehold to commence in ten years' time rather than to sell the freehold and then buy a ten-year lease back from the purchaser. Alternatively, it may be preferable in a sale-and-leaseback transaction for the lease to be granted to a nominee prior to the sale in order to minimise the strength of the argument that the leaseback was in consideration for the sale.

Take advantage of the lower rates for leases

7.53   Although the tax charge on a lease at a rent is much higher under SDLT than it was under stamp duty, the maximum charge is only 1 per cent of the total value of the payments that will be made under the lease. This rate is advantageous compared with the 4 per cent maximum rate on the acquisition of a freehold. One planning suggestion is that a taxpayer may consider purchasing a 999-year lease with initially very high rental payments which then decrease to a peppercorn rent. For example, instead of A buying the freehold of Blackacre for £1 million with a tax charge of £40,000, he might buy a 999-year lease with a rent of £250,000 for the first four years and a peppercorn rent payable thereafter. The maximum SDLT charge under Schedule 5 would be only 1 per cent. However, there is some doubt as to whether such a payment would be treated as rent. The Revenue would have a good argument that the payments were deferred consideration rather than rent. The better view is that rent is payment for the use of land over time and therefore must remain payable in substance throughout the lease. Conversely, the tax consequences for the vendor must be considered because rent will be taxed as income in the hands of the recipient.

7.54   A less aggressive planning suggestion is that, where possible, the purchaser should consider taking out a lease. It may be that, if the lease provides for a rent holiday, then the tax charge will be very low owing to the curious operation of paragraph 5(4) of Schedule 5 discussed at paragraph 6.21 above.

Other planning ideas

7.55   The above are just some of the planning ideas that will become relevant to SDLT. As has already been mentioned, it must be borne in mind that the best solution will increasingly depend on the individual facts as the loopholes become fewer. There may be a fact present which makes the transaction amenable to a particular relief.

7.56   Other ideas are yet to be developed. In particular, these may involve sophisticated structures involving the buying and selling of security interests and interests in foreign companies. Such arrangements are likely to be both complicated and aggressive, but they may achieve the result that the charge to SDLT is reduced.

8

Administration, compliance and appeals

Introduction

8.1   In practice, the most important change introduced by SDLT is the introduction of a new compliance regime which makes the tax directly enforceable. The purpose of this chapter is to discuss the process by which SDLT is enforced and the procedure for appealing against assessments to tax. The SDLT compliance process has been modelled on the income and corporation taxes self-assessment regime contained in the Taxes Management Act 1970. The provisions governing interest, penalties and Revenue information-gathering powers have similarly been copied, and appeals are now to the General or Special Commissioners. Practitioners who specialise in tax will be familiar with these provisions already. There are two main themes running through this chapter: one is the self-assessment regime and the other is the wider powers given to the Revenue when the normal regime proves inadequate. The Revenue has the power to obtain information, to charge interest and penalties and to make discovery assessments.

8.2   SDLT is a directly enforceable tax with its own self-assessment regime. The normal procedure is that, within thirty days of the effective date of a notifiable land transaction,[1] the purchaser must deliver a return to the Revenue stating the tax payable and accompanied by a payment of that tax. The responsibility is on the taxpayer to self-assess the correct amount of tax. The Revenue then has a nine-month window to begin an enquiry into the correctness of the return which may result in the issue of a further assessment. A return may have to be made notwithstanding that no SDLT is actually payable. Moreover, if the purchaser wishes to register his title at the appropriate Land Registry, he will either need a certificate from the Revenue confirming that a land transaction return has been submitted, or he will have to certify himself that no land transaction return is required to be made.

8.3   In order to understand the significance of these changes, it is necessary to refer back to the position under stamp duty. Stamp duty was not directly enforceable. There was no requirement to produce documents for stamping. The incentive to pay stamp duty was that documents are inadmissible in evidence or at the Land

---

[1]   A key concept for SDLT. See para. 8.6 below.

Registry unless properly stamped. Although interest and penalty regimes had been introduced for late stamping, the Revenue still had no powers to directly enforce the charge, and stamp duty was often referred to as being voluntary.

Duty to deliver land transaction return and pay tax within thirty days

8.4   There are three situations where a return is required. First, the purchaser must deliver a land transaction return to the Revenue within thirty days of the effective date of every 'notifiable transaction' under section 76(1) FA 2003. This return must include a self-assessment of any tax due and be accompanied by the payment of that tax. Responsibility for doing this is specifically given to the purchaser. Who is the purchaser is determined under the rules discussed at paragraphs 2.22 onwards above. Secondly, a return is required following the happening of a disqualifying event which triggers the clawback provisions for group relief, reconstruction or acquisition relief or charities relief under section 81 FA 2003. Thirdly, under section 80 FA 2003, a return is required where a contingency occurs or uncertain consideration within section 51 FA 2003 becomes quantifiable so that additional tax is payable or the transaction becomes notifiable.

8.5   Identifying when the duty to make a return arises is often not straightforward because of the problems in identifying the existence of a notifiable transaction and in determining the effective date. Nevertheless, the self-assessment regime is unforgiving, with a fixed £100 penalty[2] for anyone who fails either to make a return or to pay the tax on time. The Revenue will no doubt make allowances while the system beds down. Nevertheless, the SDLT regime represents a sea-change from the position under stamp duty.

Notifiable transactions

8.6   The obligation to make a return is triggered on the effective date of a notifiable transaction. Accordingly, the concept of a notifiable transaction is as important as any in SDLT. Section 77 FA 2003 determines which land transactions are notifiable transactions. For such an important provision section 77 is very poorly drafted. The SDLT code is meant to be in plain English so that it is straightforward to apply. Unfortunately, the drafting of section 77 means that it is necessary to jump all around the Act in order to determine whether a particular transaction requires a return.

8.7   All transactions on which SDLT is payable are, as would be expected, notifiable. However, if no SDLT is payable, then the transaction may still have to be notified. A very complicated set of rules must be applied to determine whether this is the case. The effect of these rules is so complicated that the draftsman has

---

[2] There is a flat-rate penalty of £100 payable if the return is delivered late which rises to £200 after three months from the filing date. See para. 2 of Sch. 10 FA 2003.

declined to provide a list of transactions which are notifiable. Instead, taxpayers are left to work out the effect of section 77 for themselves with the threat of a penalty should they fail to put in a return where one is required. While it is understandable that the Revenue needs to monitor the operation of certain reliefs, it is most unsatisfactory that the issue of when a return must be made is so unclear.

Transfers of freehold land

8.8   Section 77(3) provides that '[a]ny other acquisition of a major interest in land [other than a lease dealt with by section 77(2)] is notifiable unless it is exempt from charge under Schedule 3'. Major interests in land comprise freeholds and all leases of whatever term[3] under section 117 FA 2003.[4] Accordingly, all acquisitions of freeholds are notifiable unless exempted from charge under Schedule 3 FA 2003. For the transactions exempted under Schedule 3, see Chapter 5 above.

8.9   Accordingly, a gift of a freehold is not a notifiable transaction because there is no chargeable consideration and it therefore falls within paragraph 1 of Schedule 3. In contrast, the sale of a freehold for a nominal consideration of £1 is a notifiable transaction because chargeable consideration, however small, is given.

8.10   All acquisitions of freehold land other than those exempted under Schedule 3 are notifiable. This is so notwithstanding that no SDLT may actually be payable because of the operation of one of the reliefs outside Schedule 3. Accordingly, where, for example, such reliefs as group relief,[5] reconstruction relief[6] or relief for alternative finance transactions[7] are claimed, then the transaction remains a notifiable transaction.

8.11   The only exception to the rule that when a transfer of freehold land is relieved from the charge to SDLT under sections 57–75 FA 2003 a return must be filed is on a part-exchange of residential property under section 58 FA 2003. This is because the relief under section 58 operates to reduce the chargeable consideration to nil, and therefore brings the transaction within paragraph 1 of Schedule 3. This relief is discussed further at paragraph 5.53 above.

Transactions involving leases

8.12   The grant of a lease is notifiable[8] if the lease is either for seven years or longer and granted for chargeable consideration[9] or if it is for less than seven years and the chargeable consideration consists of either premium or rent chargeable

---

[3] In contrast to VAT, where a lease is only a major interest in land if its term exceeds twenty-one years: see s. 96 VATA 1994.
[4] The meaning of major interest is discussed at para. 4.54 above. In Scotland, until feudal reform takes effect on 28 November 2004, only the *dominium utile* interest is a major interest.
[5] Under s. 62 and Sch. 7 FA 2003.   [6] Under s. 62 and Sch. 7 FA 2003.
[7] Under ss. 72 and 73 FA 2003.   [8] Under s. 77(2)(b)(i).   [9] Under s. 77(2)(b)(i).

at the 1 per cent rate or higher. Accordingly, the grant of a ten-year lease for a nominal consideration is a notifiable transaction. The grant of a five-year lease for a £50,000 premium is not.

8.13   The grant of a lease is also notifiable where tax would have been chargeable but for a relief. The term 'relief' is not defined but must refer to those transactions exempted under sections 57–74 FA 2003 under the heading 'Reliefs' and not to transactions exempted under Schedule 3 or transactions where the chargeable consideration is reduced to nil under paragraphs 13–16 of Schedule 4 (see further the discussion at paragraph 5.23 above). Confusingly, this time the part-exchange of residential property under section 58 is notifiable because it comes under the heading 'Reliefs'.

8.14   Given that the only types of major interest are freeholds and leases and the grant of leases is dealt with by section 77(2), it seems strange that section 77(3) does not simply refer to the acquisition of a freehold. The reason is that transactions involving leases other than the initial grant, including the assignment[10] or surrender[11] of a lease, also involve the acquisition of a major interest. Confusingly, the assignment of a lease where the assignee provides a consideration is therefore always a notifiable transaction under section 77(3) even if the grant of that same lease was not notifiable under section 77(2). A reverse premium paid by the existing tenant on a surrender or an assignment does not count as chargeable consideration owing to paragraph 15 of Schedule 4. Accordingly, a surrender or assignment for a reverse premium will be for no chargeable consideration under paragraph 1 of Schedule 3 and therefore not a notifiable transaction.

Interests other than major interests in land

8.15   Finally, an acquisition of a chargeable interest other than a major interest in land is notifiable if SDLT is payable on it, or would be payable but for a relief.[12] Accordingly, the grant of an option or the sale of an easement for a nominal consideration is not a notifiable transaction, but if the chargeable consideration exceeds £60,000 then it is notifiable.

Obligation to make return where relief withdrawn

8.16   Where group relief, reconstruction or acquisition relief or charities relief is retrospectively withdrawn under the appropriate clawback provisions, then the purchaser must deliver a return within thirty days of the event under section 81. This obligation falls on the purchaser even though the purchaser may no longer own the land and may not itself have been a party to the disqualifying event. Where section 81 applies, the return must be made according to the rules contained in Schedule 10 in the normal way. For the list of what is a disqualifying event, see the discussions of the individual reliefs.

---

[10] Assignation in Scotland.   [11] Renunciation in Scotland.   [12] Under s. 77(4).

Summary of when a return is required

8.17 The effect of sections 77 and 81 is that a land transaction return must be made in the following circumstances:

1. All transactions where SDLT is payable.
2. Transfers of freehold land other than those exempted under Schedule 3.
3. The grant of a lease for over seven years and made for chargeable consideration (however small).
4. Assignments and surrenders of leases for consideration (except reverse premiums).
5. Any other transaction where SDLT would have been payable but for the operation of one of the reliefs in sections 58–74.
6. Where a disqualifying event triggers the clawback of group relief, reconstruction and acquisition relief or charities relief.
7. Where a contingency occurs, or uncertain or unascertained consideration becomes ascertained under section 80 FA 2003 so that additional tax becomes payable.[13]

Thirty-day time limit for return

8.18 A return must be made within thirty days of the effective date of a notifiable transaction under section 76(1) FA 2003. The meaning of effective date is discussed at paragraph 2.26 onwards above, and means the earlier of completion or substantial performance. Normally, the effect of section 76(1) is that a return has to be made within thirty days of completion. However, where the contract is substantially performed before it is completed, then substantial performance[14] triggers the thirty-day deadline. For example, A agrees to sell an office block to B. B is allowed to enter under a licence prior to completion to fit the premises out. The contract has been substantially performed under section 44(5)(a) because B has taken possession of the premises which are the subject-matter of the contract. Accordingly, B must file a return and pay the tax within thirty days of entering onto the premises. It does not matter that B's finance may not yet be in place.

8.19 Similarly, where a return is required under section 81 following the withdrawal of a relief, then the return must be made within thirty days of the disqualifying event.

Consequences of failure to deliver return and pay tax

8.20 Taxpayers who fail both to file a return and to pay the tax within the thirty-day period are liable to a flat-rate penalty under paragraph 3 of Schedule 10.

---

[13] See para. 4.33 above.
[14] See para. 2.30 onwards above for the meaning of 'substantial performance'.

The penalty is £100 if the return is delivered within three months of the filing date and £200 thereafter. In addition, interest begins to run from the date when the tax becomes due under section 87. Interest is calculated at the statutory rate under section 178 FA 1989. If the purchaser has not filed a return and paid the tax within twelve months of the filing date. then he becomes liable to a further penalty of up to 100 per cent of the tax payable under paragraph 4 of Schedule 10 in addition to the flat-rate penalty.

Form and contents of return

8.21   A land transaction return must be in the form prescribed by the Revenue. The form of the return is to be prescribed in regulations made by the Revenue under paragraph 1 of Schedule 10. It is understood that the Revenue's guidance notes will in certain cases require supplementary pages also to be completed and submitted – for example, if additional information is required on the purchaser or vendor, on the land, or on the transaction (including leases).

Other provisions relating to returns

8.22   If the Revenue discovers that the purchaser has not delivered a return, then it may formally direct him to do so under paragraph 5 of Schedule 10. If the purchaser fails to comply, the Revenue may apply to the Commissioners for an order seeking a further daily penalty. Such an order may specify a further penalty of £60 for each day that the return is not delivered.

8.23   A purchaser who fraudulently or negligently delivers an incorrect return or discovers that his return is incorrect and does not remedy the error is also liable to a penalty under paragraph 8(1) of Schedule 10. The penalty is the difference between the amount of tax chargeable and that declared on the return.[15] As those who specialise in tax will be well aware, one of the problems of self-assessment is that there are areas of the law where the correct interpretation is open to argument. For example, the taxpayer and the Revenue may have different views as to whether a particular transaction amounts to an arrangement so that the linked transactions rules apply.

8.24   In this situation, judgment must be exercised as to what needs to be entered on the return. For example, the taxpayer must still consider whether he needs to refer to other transactions which are in some way related, even if he has formed the view that the relevant transaction is not linked to those other transactions within the meaning of section 108 FA 2003. In practice, where there is room for doubt as to the correct interpretation of the law, then all the facts should be set out in the return including those which might support an interpretation

---

[15] Para. 8(2) of Sch. 10 FA 2003.

contrary to the taxpayer's. The taxpayer does not have to make the Revenue's arguments for it but he does have to disclose all the relevant facts in order to allow the Revenue to form its own view.

8.25   Having disclosed all the relevant facts, the taxpayer can self-assess on the basis of the law as he understands it. If the Revenue wishes to take a different view then it will have all the facts in front of it to allow it to do so. Accordingly, the taxpayer can rest assured that the penalties under paragraph 8 of Schedule 10 will not apply. In exceptional cases, it may be prudent to go even further and append a note to the return stating not only other relevant facts but also the way in which the taxpayer is interpreting the law. If the form or the additional pages do not have space to do this then this information should be provided in a covering letter.

8.26   More generally, the whole basis of self-assessment is that the taxpayer is expected to be open about the facts with the Revenue. While it is acceptable and even expected for taxpayers to interpret the law in ways favourable to them, it is essential to provide all the relevant facts to the Revenue. Taxpayers who take controversial views of the law without revealing facts that might be unfavourable to them risk having the Revenue seek penalties for fraud under paragraph 8 of Schedule 10 and even the possibility of the Revenue threatening to bring criminal charges against them.

8.27   Finally, under section 82 FA 2003, where a return which has been delivered to the Revenue is lost, destroyed or damaged so as to become useless, then the Revenue may treat it as not having been delivered. Strictly, this means that the Revenue can issue penalties and claim the tax in a situation where they have lost the return through their own error and the tax has been paid. Section 82(4) specifically makes it a defence that the taxpayer has already paid the tax! The correct interpretation of section 82 must be that the Revenue can ask for another return to be submitted where they lose the original. It cannot be right that the Revenue can recover penalties because they have lost or damaged the return. To levy a penalty in this situation would be totally unjustified and contrary to the Human Rights Act 1998.

Duty to keep records

8.28   Purchasers must keep the records needed to be able to deliver a correct return for six years after the transaction by virtue of paragraph 9 of Schedule 10. The relevant records include the contract, any supporting documents, the details of the payments made and any financial arrangements. A taxpayer who fails to keep proper records is liable to a fine of up to £3,000.[16]

---

[16] Under para. 11 of Sch. 10 FA 2003.

Revenue determination if no return delivered

8.29   If no return is delivered, then the Revenue may determine the tax chargeable to the best of their information and belief under Part 4 of Schedule 10. This supplements the Revenue's power under paragraph 4 of Schedule 10 to require the taxpayer to produce a return. A determination under paragraph 25 of Schedule 10 takes effect for enforcement purposes as if it were a self-assessment. If, following the issue of a determination, the taxpayer subsequently makes a return then that return supersedes the Part 4 determination by virtue of paragraph 27 of Schedule 10. The taxpayer's return must be made by the later of one year from the determination or six years after the original filing date in order to supersede the determination.

Procedure following submission of a return

Introduction

8.30   Following the submission of the return, the Revenue has three courses open to them. First, it can take no action, in which case the return will stand. This should be the most frequent course of events. Secondly, it can correct obvious errors or omissions on the return whether in its own favour or the taxpayer's under paragraph 7 of Schedule 10. Finally, the Revenue has a window of nine months within which to open a formal enquiry into the taxpayer's return under Part 3 of Schedule 10. As a result of this enquiry, the Revenue may determine that further tax is payable. However, special rules apply under paragraph 31(2) of Schedule 10 if there has been fraud or negligence by the taxpayer or his advisers and in this situation the Revenue has up to twenty-one years in which to issue an assessment. If the taxpayer exercises his right under paragraph 6 of Schedule 10 to amend his own return within twelve months of filing, then the nine-month window begins from the date of the amendment by virtue of paragraph 12(2)(c) of Schedule 10.

Correction of a return by the Revenue

8.31   The Revenue may amend the return to correct obvious errors or omissions during the nine-month period following the filing of the return.[17] Notice must be given to the purchaser of the correction, and the purchaser then has three months in which to reject it.[18]

Enquiry into return

Time period for opening an enquiry

8.32   Once a return has been submitted, the Revenue has nine months within which to give the taxpayer notice that it is enquiring into the return under Part 3 of

---

[17] Under para. 7 of Sch. 10.   [18] Para. 7(4) of Sch. 10.

Schedule 10. The nine-month period runs from the later of the filing date or the date on which the return was delivered. The enquiry may extend to anything contained in the return that relates to the amount of tax chargeable. A return may only be the subject of one notice of enquiry.

8.33   The purchaser has the power to amend his return within twelve months of sending it to the Revenue under paragraph 6 of Schedule 10. If the purchaser amends the return in this way, then this alters the time periods for the enquiry window. The basic rule is that the Revenue has nine months to raise an enquiry from the date of amendment under paragraph 12(2)(c) of Schedule 10. However, if the return has already been the subject of one notice of enquiry, a second enquiry may only relate to the consequences of the amendment by virtue of paragraphs 12(2) and 13(2) of Schedule 10.

The process of enquiry

8.34   The Revenue may require the purchaser to produce documents or other information which they require for the purpose of the enquiry under paragraph 14 of Schedule 10. The taxpayer cannot be compelled to produce documents relating to the conduct of any pending appeal by virtue of paragraph 14(5). To obtain information, the Revenue must give the taxpayer a written information notice under paragraph 14. The information notice must allow him at least thirty days in which to comply. The taxpayer may comply by producing copies, although the Revenue may require the originals to be produced. A taxpayer who fails to provide the information is liable to a penalty.[19]

8.35   The taxpayer has the right to appeal against an information notice under paragraph 15 of Schedule 10. Written notice of appeal must be lodged within thirty days with the Revenue officer by whom the information notice was given. Appeals against information notices are heard by the Commissioners. The Commissioners will set aside the notice to the extent that it relates to information not reasonably required for the purposes of the enquiry.

8.36   During the enquiry the purchaser can amend his own return under paragraph 6 of Schedule 10. The amendment may be taken into account in the enquiry. The Revenue can also amend the self-assessment and require the taxpayer to make good the deficiency under paragraph 17 of Schedule 10. This power can be exercised if the Revenue forms the view that, unless the assessment is amended immediately, there is likely to be a loss of tax to the Crown, in other words that the taxpayer is unlikely to pay any additional tax unless it is collected immediately. Finally, it is possible for the Revenue and the taxpayer to refer a question to the Special Commissioners during the course of the enquiry under paragraph 19 of Schedule 10. The referral must be made jointly by

---

[19] Under para. 16. The penalty is fixed at £50 with further daily penalties for every day the documents are not produced after the first penalty.

both parties. A ruling given by the Special Commissioners is binding upon the parties.

Completion of enquiry

8.37   The enquiry is brought to an end when the Revenue issues a closure notice under paragraph 23 of Schedule 10. The notice will state either that the return is correct or that an amendment of the return is required. If the amendment is in the Revenue's favour, then the taxpayer must either pay the additional tax assessed or appeal to the Commissioners within thirty days. The appeal procedure is discussed in more detail at paragraph 8.96 below. Finally, if the taxpayer believes that the Revenue is dragging its heels he may apply to the Commissioners under paragraph 24 of Schedule 10 for a direction that the Revenue complete the enquiry by a certain date.

Discovery assessments and time limits

8.38   One of the fundamental rules of self-assessment is that the Revenue has a limited nine-month window in which to open enquiries following which the self-assessment becomes final. However, the normal rule does not apply in two situations provided for under paragraph 30 of Schedule 10. The first is where there has been fraudulent or negligent conduct by the purchaser, his advisers or any of his partners.[20] The second is where the Revenue could not reasonably have been aware on the basis of the information previously available to them that the full amount of tax properly due had not been paid.[21] Where the Revenue discovers that the full amount of tax has not been paid because either the full amount has not been assessed or a relief has been overclaimed, the Revenue can issue a discovery assessment to recover the extra tax provided that either of the two exceptions contained in paragraph 30 applies.

8.39   The intention is to allow the Revenue to make discovery assessments when the return is wrong either because it contains a fraudulent or negligent mistake or because it contains an omission which meant that the Revenue could not reasonably have been expected to be able to spot the error. The Revenue clearly may make a discovery assessment when there was a failure to include a material fact which made the tax liability appear lower. However, negligent errors of law and computational errors will also permit the Revenue to make a discovery assessment. Potentially, the concept of negligence can be applied very widely in tax situations because the reasonably competent adviser is expected to have everything correct. However, in practice, only errors of a certain degree of seriousness should count as negligence. Nevertheless, an apparently trivial error, such as leaving a nought off a figure in a tax computation, can have a serious impact on the tax liability and, accordingly, is probably a negligent error.

---

[20] Under para. 30(2) of Sch. 10.   [21] Para. 30(3) of Sch. 10.

8.40   The exceptions are disapplied under paragraph 30(5) if both the loss of tax arises from a mistake in the return as to the basis on which the tax liability should have been computed and the return was made in accordance with the practice prevailing at the time. This is designed to protect taxpayers from being assessed to additional tax where the law changes and the Revenue alters its view in consequence. However, it is often the case that there is no prevailing practice in difficult areas of the law. This can produce difficulties if a decision of the courts subsequently shows the taxpayer's view to have been wrong. In this situation, the taxpayer must rely first on the defence that he was not negligent in applying the law as he did, so that paragraph 30(2) cannot apply. Secondly, he must argue that the Revenue could reasonably have been expected to be aware of the situation on the basis of the information available, so that paragraph 30(3) cannot apply. What the Revenue can reasonably have been expected to be aware of in the situation where the courts have clarified what was formerly an uncertain area of law is a more difficult question and will depend on the particular circumstances. Nevertheless, the fuller the disclosure made in the return, the harder it is for the Revenue to claim that it was unaware of something.

8.41   Paragraph 31 of Schedule 10 provides that the general time limit for SDLT assessments is six years. However, this is subject to the nine-month limitation that applies when the purchaser files a return. Where fraud or negligence is alleged, then the time limit is twenty-one years under paragraph 31(2). Accordingly, the six-year time limit has very limited application in practice. It will apply where the Revenue makes a discovery assessment under paragraph 30(3) on the basis that it could not reasonably have been aware of the outstanding tax. It also applies where the Revenue makes an assessment to recover an excessive repayment of tax under paragraph 29 of Schedule 10. If the taxpayer simply fails to submit a return, then the time limit will be twenty-one years because this will almost always be negligent.

Relief against overpayments

8.42   If a taxpayer believes he has paid too much tax owing to a mistake in his return, then he may claim repayment under paragraph 34 of Schedule 10. If less than twelve months has elapsed since the filing date, the taxpayer can amend his own return under paragraph 6 of Schedule 10. However, it appears that, to obtain a refund for overpaid tax, he must still apply under paragraph 34. The taxpayer has six years from the date of the transaction in which to claim relief under paragraph 34. Paragraph 34 does not apply if the mistake was made because it was in accordance with a practice prevailing at the time which has since been shown to be wrong; this mirrors the prohibition on the Revenue making discovery assessments contained in paragraph 30(5) of Schedule 10. Nor can the taxpayer claim repayment if the mistake is in respect of a claim or an election made in the return.

8.43   A repayment will be made with interest at the statutory rate under section 178 FA 1989 by virtue of section 89. The rate of interest for repayments of tax is significantly less than the rate for overdue tax. Interest runs from the date on which the payment was made to the Revenue until the date of repayment. Interest on a repayment of tax is deemed not to be liable to income tax in the hands of the recipient by section 89(5) FA 2003.

8.44   Finally, paragraph 33 of Schedule 10 specifically provides that the taxpayer may apply to the Revenue when he has been assessed to tax twice on the same transaction by mistake. The only practical effect of this is that, if there is a dispute, the taxpayer may choose to appeal to the Commissioners rather than commence a civil action. Otherwise, it is difficult to see why this specific provision is needed, because the taxpayer has a right to restitution from the Revenue in respect of the overpaid tax.[22]

Requirement to register land transactions and certificates of compliance

Introduction

8.45   Land transactions cannot be registered with the Land Registry (or the Registers of Scotland, or, in Northern Ireland, the Land Registry or the Registry of Deeds) unless accompanied by a certificate which states that the requirements of the SDLT regime have been met, by virtue of section 79 FA 2003. Certificates of compliance must be issued either by the Revenue to say that a return has been delivered or by the purchaser to say that no return is required.[23] The Revenue has the power to obtain details of certificates from land registries.[24]

8.46   The requirement to certify that the requirements of SDLT have been complied with before registering a land transaction is a policing mechanism to enable the Revenue to ensure that SDLT is being paid. The requirement that the documents cannot simply be sent to the Land Registry is a hangover from stamp duty. However, stamp duty was not directly enforceable and the requirement that documents could not be sent to the Land Registry unless stamped thus represented the major incentive to pay stamp duty. SDLT is directly enforceable so there is no longer any need to encourage taxpayers to pay in this way. Nevertheless, the idea is retained in the form of a certification procedure in order to promote the enforcement of SDLT.

When is a certificate required?

8.47   Certificates are, of course, only required when the purchaser wishes to register his interest. The general rule, under section 79(1) FA 2003, is that no document evidencing a land transaction can be registered by the appropriate Land

---

[22] See *Woolwich Building Society* v. *IRC* [1992] STC 657.
[23] S. 79(3) FA 2003.   [24] S. 79(6) FA 2003.

Registry unless accompanied by a certificate of compliance. The rule does not apply where the Land Registry are required to act without any application being made. Such occasions will arise only very rarely: the Revenue gives as an example certain situations under the commonhold regime. Section 79(1) also expressly states that a certificate is not required insofar as the entry on the register relates to an interest other than that acquired by the purchaser. This allows lenders and other creditors to register changes without having to concern themselves with SDLT.

8.48   More importantly, the rule is subject to two exceptions under section 79(2). The exceptions are for a contract which is to be completed by a conveyance or a transfer of rights under section 45 (a sub-sale). The policy behind this exemption is unclear because the new charge on substantial performance under section 44(3) and the restriction of sub-sale relief under section 45 are controversial new changes. Accordingly, it might have been thought that, if the purchaser wishes to register his contract in these situations, that is exactly when the Revenue might require a certificate.

Revenue certificates

8.49   Land transaction certificates may be issued either by the Revenue, known as 'Revenue certificates', or by the purchaser, called 'self-certificates'. The Revenue will issue a certificate that a land transaction return has been submitted. Section 79(4) provides for the Revenue to make regulations dealing with the form and content of certificates and the requirements to be met before one can be issued.

8.50   Under the Scottish system of conveyancing, in practice purchasers or grantees normally only have fourteen or twenty-one days from settlement to register the disposition or other deed granted in their favour (i.e. the time limit in the letter of obligation issued by the vendor's solicitors to the purchaser's solicitors). The Revenue has been made aware of concerns that delays in the production of Revenue certificates could prejudice the ability of a purchaser to submit the deed to the Registers of Scotland within the relevant time limit and it remains to be seen what (if any) arrangements the Revenue will propose to meet these concerns.

Self-certification

8.51   Purchasers wishing to register interests at the appropriate Land Registry in situations where a certificate is required but who are not required to file a return with the Revenue must self-certify that no such return is required. In practice, this means that purchasers wishing to register their interests who have gone through the statutory test under sections 76 and 77 to discover that no land transaction return is required must then consider section 79(1) and (2) to determine whether or not they need to self-certify. The form and contents of a self-certificate are to be laid down in regulations made under paragraph 2 of Schedule 11. The idea is that the purchaser will need to disclose the material facts on which he relies in claiming that there is no obligation to make a return.

8.52   If a transaction arouses the Revenue's interest, it may open an enquiry into the self-certificate to determine whether the transaction to which it relates is indeed not taxable. The Revenue has a nine-month period under paragraph 7 of Schedule 11 in which to open an enquiry. Once an enquiry is underway, the procedure is the same as that for an enquiry into a return, and Schedule 11 contains provisions virtually identical to those in Schedule 10. The taxpayer may be required to produce documents,[25] and records must again be kept for six years after the original transaction.[26] A taxpayer who fails to keep or produce records may be liable for a penalty. Questions may be referred to the Special Commissioners by the parties during the enquiry.

8.53   On completion of the enquiry, the Revenue will issue a closure notice.[27] If it believes tax is chargeable, it may issue an assessment. The time limit for issuing an assessment will be governed by the rules dealing with discovery assessments in Part 5 of Schedule 10. In other words, the Revenue has until six years after the date of the effective transaction for issue of the assessment, or twenty-one years in the case of fraud or negligence. Finally, if the taxpayer was fraudulent or negligent in issuing the self-certificate, then the Revenue may issue a penalty up to the amount of the tax chargeable under paragraph 3 of Schedule 10.

Liability to pay tax

8.54   Under SDLT, the purchaser is liable to pay the tax. This is a change from stamp duty which was only payable by any person who wanted to rely on the documents, although in practice this was almost always the purchaser. If there are joint purchasers, such as where property is bought by co-owners, then all are jointly and severally liable for the tax.[28] Similarly, if property is purchased by a partnership, then the partners are jointly and severally liable.[29]

Collection and payment

8.55   The basic rule is that tax must be paid when the land transaction return is filed.[30] If an amendment of a return results in extra tax being payable, it must be paid immediately.[31] This is subject to an agreement under section 90 to delay payment of the tax where the consideration is contingent or uncertain. Tax payable as a result of an assessment by the Revenue must be paid within thirty days.[32] Tax remains payable unless the Revenue agrees to defer payment or

---

[25] Under para. 9 of Sch. 11 FA 2003.   [26] Under para. 4 of Sch. 11 FA 2003.
[27] Under para. 16 of Sch. 11 FA 2003.   [28] See s. 103(2)(c).   [29] Sch. 15, para. 7.
[30] S. 86(1).   [31] S. 86(3).   [32] S. 86(4).

the taxpayer makes an application to the Commissioners to order the payment to be postponed.[33]

8.56   Unpaid tax is recoverable as a debt in civil proceedings under Part 2 of Schedule 12 FA 2003. If the amount due is less than £2,000, it is recoverable as a civil debt in the magistrates' court. Larger amounts are recoverable in the name of the collector in either the county court or High Court; or, in Scotland, the sheriff court or Court of Session. A certificate issued by the Revenue that tax is due and payable is sufficient evidence that it is.[34] If the taxpayer wishes to contest whether or not tax is due, the proper forum is the Commissioners.

Interest

8.57   Interest begins to run from thirty days after the 'relevant date' of the transaction under section 87(1) FA 2003, that is, the day after the land transaction return is due. The relevant date under section 87(3) is the effective date of the transaction, or, in a case where group relief, reconstruction or acquisition relief or charities relief is withdrawn, the date of the disqualifying event.[35] In the case of a deferred payment under section 90 FA 2003, the relevant date is when the deferred payment is due. Accordingly, where no return is made or the tax paid is less than the Revenue's final assessment, then interest will run from thirty days after the date triggering liability until the full amount of tax is paid. Penalties also carry interest until paid.[36]

8.58   The rate of interest is governed by section 178 FA 1989 and the Taxes (Interest Rate) Regulations 1989[37] and is greater than bank base rate. This is to incentivise taxpayers to pay their tax on time by ensuring they cannot employ that capital more profitably elsewhere. If a payment of tax is lodged with the Revenue pending an appeal then interest does not run.[38] Accordingly, a taxpayer bringing an appeal may wish to mitigate the interest payable in the event that he should lose by making a payment on account. If the taxpayer succeeds, he will be entitled to interest on the repayment at the lower repayment rate. Where the Revenue makes a repayment of tax or penalty, then interest will be payable on the repayment by virtue of section 89 FA 2003. The rate is again set under the Taxes (Interest Rate) Regulations 1989. The rate of interest on repayments is lower than the bank lending rate.[39]

Penalties

8.59   A taxpayer who fails to deliver a return on time becomes liable to a penalty under paragraphs 3 and 4 of Schedule 10, as discussed at paragraph 8.5 above. Penalties also become chargeable in other situations, in particular when a taxpayer

---

[33] Sch. 10, paras. 38–40.   [34] Sch. 12, para. 7.   [35] S. 87(3)(a).   [36] S. 90(3)(b).
[37] SI 1989 No. 1297; s. 87(7) FA 2003.   [38] S. 87(6) FA 2003.   [39] S. 89 FA 2003.

fails to produce documents.[40] The mechanics of the penalty regime are dealt with in Schedule 14 FA 2003.[41] The Revenue has a discretion in deciding whether or not to levy a penalty and in setting the amount up to the maximum provided by the relevant provision.[42] Notice of the penalty will be levied on the taxpayer and she has thirty days in which to pay it from the date of issue.[43] If the Revenue decides that the penalty is either too little or excessive then it has a discretion to either reduce or increase it as appropriate under paragraph 3 of Schedule 14.

8.60   Taxpayers wishing to appeal against a penalty have thirty days from the issue of the determination in which to lodge a notice of appeal with either the General or the Special Commissioners.[44] Appeals may be brought out of time with the agreement of either the Revenue or the Commissioners.[45] A decision of the Commissioners on penalties may be appealed upwards to the High Court, or, in Scotland, the Court of Session.[46] Penalty proceedings may be brought directly before a court where the Revenue alleges that a fraud has taken place.

8.61   The time limit for penalty determinations is three years after the final determination of the tax in cases where the penalty is tax-geared. In other cases, the time limit is six years. Finally, dying does not save taxpayers from a penalty assessment: paragraph 4 of Schedule 14 specifically provides that an assessment may be made on the taxpayer's personal representatives.

Revenue information-gathering powers

Introduction

8.62   The SDLT regime provides the Revenue with wide-ranging information-gathering powers contained in sections 93 and 94 and Schedule 13 FA 2003. These powers are in addition to the power to issue a notice for the purposes of an enquiry under paragraph 15 of Schedule 10. They are equivalent to the Revenue's powers to obtain information for other taxes and are based on sections 20–20D and section 111 of the Taxes Management Act 1970. There are, broadly, two levels of powers: ordinary information-gathering powers and those where fraud is in issue. The fraud powers are wider but have more procedural safeguards.

8.63   Tax practitioners will already be familiar with these provisions. To understand them properly it is necessary to put them in context. Historically, the tax system has respected the privacy of both the taxpayer and also the Revenue. The rule remains that there is no discovery in tax cases. However, nowadays we live in an information age and the tide has turned. In a self-assessment tax system which is based on openness, the onus is on the taxpayer to disclose all the relevant facts. The Revenue, too, is more open and publishes its internal manuals.[47] One result of this is that tax disputes are much more likely to settle before they come to court.

---

[40] See e.g. para. 16 of Sch. 10 FA 2003.   [41] Provided for by s. 99.   [42] Sch. 10, para. 2(1).
[43] Sch. 14, para. 2(4).   [44] Sch. 14, para. 5.   [45] Sch. 14, para. 5(3).
[46] Sch. 14, para. 6.   [47] Available on their website, www.inlandrevenue.gov.uk.

8.64   While the Revenue's powers can be used for a 'discovery exercise' to elicit the relevant facts, they are not simply a rule of civil procedure. Rather, as Simon Brown LJ spelt out in *R. v. IRC, ex parte Ulster Bank Ltd*,[48] they are 'essentially investigatory powers' belonging to the central government. They are of the same species as those used to investigate fraud, money-laundering and terrorism.

8.65   The introduction of self-assessment has corresponded with an increased use of the Revenue's information-gathering powers. The courts have tended to interpret the Revenue's powers widely in line with their role as government powers. However, the relevant chapter of the Revenue's internal manual is written in very sensitive and well-balanced terms. Reference is made to the assurance given in Parliament that the powers will not be used for 'fishing expeditions'.

8.66   The manual also states that the Revenue will not normally ask to see legal advice given to a taxpayer. However, the question of under what circumstances the taxpayer may be forced to disclose legal and tax advice has recently been the most controversial area of section 20 of the Taxes Management Act 1970. The House of Lords finally decided in *R. (on the application of Morgan Grenfell & Co. Ltd) v. Special Commissioner of Income Tax*[49] that taxpayers cannot be required to disclose documents protected by legal and professional privilege. However, privilege does not apply to all tax advice, for example that received from an accountant. Moreover, there may still be arguments about whether a particular document is privileged. The rules will now be discussed in more detail.

Power to require taxpayers to provide information

8.67   Part I of Schedule 13 gives an officer of the Revenue power to issue a notice requiring a taxpayer to give him documents in the taxpayer's possession which in the reasonable opinion of the officer may contain information relevant to a liability to SDLT. Before issuing such a notice, the Revenue must first obtain the consent of a General or Special Commissioner.[50] The Commissioner must be satisfied that, in all the circumstances, the officer is justified in issuing the notice. In practice, consent is most unlikely to be refused.

8.68   The notice must specify the documents or information required, and at least thirty days must be given to comply.[51] The notice must also give the reasons why the information is required unless either the Commissioners agree that the information be withheld or giving reasons might give away the identity of a Revenue informer.

8.69   There are restrictions on what information a taxpayer can be compelled to provide under Part 1. These are contained in Part 4 of Schedule 13. Personal records within the meaning of section 12 of the Police and Criminal Evidence Act 1984 (PACE), meaning health and personal counselling records, may

---

[48] [1997] STC 832.   [49] [2002] STC 786.   [50] Sch. 13, para. 2.   [51] Sch. 13, para. 3.

not be the subject of an order.[52] Nor may a party be compelled to produce journalistic material as defined in section 13 PACE. A party may not be obliged to produce documents relating to the conduct of a pending appeal by virtue of paragraph 20. This includes not only documents between the party and his lawyer but also, for example, a property valuation obtained for the purposes of an appeal. The general rule is that only documents originating within six years of the notice may be required to be produced. Documents originating more than six years before the date of the notice may only be required to be produced if the Revenue has satisfied a Commissioner that tax may have been lost owing to the fraud of a taxpayer.[53]

8.70   Although there is no express exemption for documents subject to legal and professional privilege, taxpayers cannot be compelled to produce them. This follows from the decision of the House of Lords in *R. (on the application of Morgan Grenfell & Co. Ltd)* v. *Special Commissioner of Income Tax*,[54] a case which related to the equivalent provision in the Taxes Management Act 1970, section 20(1). If Parliament wishes to override legal professional privilege it must do so expressly.[55]

Power to obtain documents from a third party

8.71   Under Part 2 of Schedule 13, the Revenue has a similar power to that contained in Part 1 of Schedule 13 to obtain documents from third parties. The documents must be in that person's possession or power. In the reasonable opinion of the issuing officer, the documents must be such as might contain information relevant to the liability to SDLT of a taxpayer. Again, the consent of the Commissioners must be obtained under paragraph 7 of Schedule 10 before a notice is issued and it must specify the documents required. A copy of the notice must be given to the taxpayer whose affairs are being investigated together with a summary of the reasons why the notice is being issued.

8.72   A special notice may be given under paragraph 11 to a third party requiring him to disclose documents relating to an unknown taxpayer or group of taxpayers. A notice under paragraph 11 must be authorised by an order of the Board of the Inland Revenue and requires the consent of a Special Commissioner. Before a notice can be issued, the Special Commissioner must be satisfied that there are reasonable grounds for believing that the unknown taxpayer (or taxpayers) has been failing to comply with the requirements of SDLT and that a serious breach of compliance or loss of tax will result.

---

[52] The definition in PACE applies in England and Wales and Scotland. In Northern Ireland, 'personal records' is defined in Art. 14 of the Police and Criminal Evidence (Northern Ireland) Order 1989.

[53] Sch. 13, para. 24.   [54] [2002] STC 786.

[55] See Lord Hoffmann at [2002] STC 786 at 796, para. 39 of his speech.

8.73   A notice under Part 2 may be issued to a taxpayer's legal advisers. However, that is not its only application: for example, a notice under paragraph 6 may be used to obtain information from a director of a company relevant to the tax liability of that company, or to obtain information from the vendor about the details of a land transaction. A paragraph 11 notice will typically be used in the situation where the Revenue finds that an adviser has acted for clients who have not been complying with their tax obligations and therefore believes that he may have other clients also in breach.

8.74   Third party notices are subject to the same restrictions on what type of information can be obliged to be disclosed as notices given to the taxpayer under Part 1. There is an express exemption for documents subject to legal privilege. In addition, auditors and tax advisers cannot be required to disclose communications made for the purpose of advising on the taxpayer's affairs. However, if the documents also contain information explaining information given in a return or identifying the identity of a taxpayer, then the adviser must provide a copy of the relevant parts of the document to the Revenue.[56]

Power to call for papers of tax accountant

8.75   Part 3 of Schedule 13 gives the Revenue a specific power to call for the papers of a tax accountant relating to any of his clients. The power can only be used when the accountant is either convicted of an offence in relation to tax or has a penalty imposed on him under section 96 for assisting in the preparation of an incorrect return. No such notice may be given while an appeal is pending.[57] The consent of a circuit judge[58] must be obtained before a notice can be issued. The restrictions under Part 4 that apply to a notice under paragraphs 1 and 2 again apply.

Power of Board to call for documents or information

8.76   The Board of the Inland Revenue has the power to make a taxpayer deliver documents containing information relevant to that person's tax liability under Part 5 of Schedule 13. No judicial consent is required for the exercise of this power. However, notice is not to be given unless the Board have reasonable grounds for believing both that the person may have failed to comply with any of the SDLT obligations and that this is likely to cause serious prejudice to the proper assessment or collection of tax. The exclusion for personal records and journalistic material again applies.

Judicial order for delivery of documents

8.77   If the Revenue believes that a serious SDLT fraud has been or is about to be committed and that documents which may be required as evidence in the

---

[56] Sch. 13, para. 27.   [57] Sch. 13, para. 14(2).
[58] In England and Wales. In Scotland, a sheriff, and, in Northern Ireland, a county court judge.

proceedings are in the power or possession of any person, then it may apply for an order compelling the production of these documents under Part 6 of Schedule 13. The order must be made by an appropriate judicial authority, meaning in England and Wales a circuit judge, in Scotland a sheriff and in Northern Ireland a county court judge. Failure to comply with an order may be dealt with by a judge as if it were a contempt of court. The person against whom the order is sought is entitled to notice of the application and to appear at the hearing of the application. However, this requirement can be waived if the judge is satisfied that this would seriously prejudice the investigation of the offence.

8.78   Legally privileged items cannot be required to be disclosed. However, paragraph 35(3) confirms the general legal rule that communications made for the purpose of furthering a criminal purpose, including a tax fraud, are not privileged. The Revenue may make regulations for the purposes of resolving disputes as to privilege.[59] The regulations will probably involve the appointment of an independent lawyer to determine the status of individual documents. The European Court of Human Rights recently affirmed that this was an acceptable procedure.[60]

8.79   A person who has been given notice of an intention to apply for an order must not dispose of or interfere with any document to which the application relates or disclose any information likely to prejudice the investigation.[61] In particular, an adviser must not alert a taxpayer that he is being investigated for fraud. Anyone who fails to comply with this obligation under paragraph 35 may be dealt with as if he had committed a contempt of court.

Entry with warrant to obtain evidence of offence

8.80   If the Revenue believes that evidence of a serious tax fraud is to be found on specified premises, then under Part 7 of Schedule 13 it may apply for a warrant to enter and search the premises. The warrant must be issued by a judge in the same way as an order under Part 6. The Revenue is only to apply for a warrant under Part 7 where it believes that using the Part 6 procedure might seriously prejudice the investigation.[62] In other words, if the Revenue believes that suspected fraudsters will destroy and tamper with the evidence, it may apply for a search warrant.

8.81   The warrant gives the Revenue power to enter the premises by force, to seize and remove things that it has reasonable cause to believe may be required as evidence and to search anyone believed to be in possession of evidence. Legally privileged items are, once again, exempt from seizure. The Revenue must provide the occupier with a copy of the warrant and a record of any items removed.[63] If a photocopy of the item will be sufficient evidence, then the items shall not be retained longer than necessary to make the photocopy.

---

[59] Para. 35(3).   [60] *Tamosius* v. *United Kingdom* [2002] STC 1307, ECHR.
[61] Sch. 13, para. 34.   [62] Sch. 13, para. 45.   [63] Paras. 47(1)(a) and 49.

Falsification and destruction of documents

8.82   Part 8 of Schedule 13 creates a new offence of falsification or destruction of documents. The offence is committed if a person falsifies, conceals or disposes of documents required or requested to be produced under Schedule 13 or causes or permits such events to happen. The maximum penalty is, on summary conviction, a fine of up to the statutory maximum, or, on conviction on indictment, up to two years in prison or a fine or both. There are exceptions, including where the person acts with the consent of the Commissioners and where two years have elapsed since the document was required to be produced.

Fraudulent evasion of tax

8.83   Section 95 creates a new offence of fraudulent evasion of SDLT. The offence is committed if a person is knowingly involved in the fraudulent evasion of tax by himself or another. A person found guilty is liable on summary conviction to imprisonment for up to six months or a fine of up to the statutory maximum or both. A person found guilty on indictment is liable on conviction to imprisonment of up to seven years or a fine or both.

Application of SDLT to special categories of taxpayer

Introduction

8.84   Sections 100–107 FA 2003 determine how SDLT applies to certain categories of taxpayer and in particular who is responsible for notifying and paying tax. The purpose of this section is to discuss the procedural aspects of these provisions. The substantive rules for trusts and partnerships have been dealt with in Chapter 3 above.

Companies

8.85   The responsibility for a company's compliance with SDLT is placed upon the proper officer of the company by section 100 FA 2003. The proper officer is the company secretary or the person acting as such. Alternatively, the company may act through any other person entitled to act on its behalf. A company is defined as any body corporate or unincorporated association but does not include a partnership or LLP. If the company is in liquidation or administration, then the liquidator or administrator is the proper officer.

Unit trusts and open-ended investment companies

8.86   A unit trust[64] is treated for SDLT compliance purposes as if it were a company. In the case of an umbrella scheme involving separate contributions paid, then each

---

[64] As defined in the Financial Services and Markets Act 2000.

pool is treated as a separate unit trust. If an umbrella fund buys land, then the individual pools will be joint purchasers and so only one return is necessary under section 103. Unit trusts are not deemed to be companies for the purposes of either the section 53 FA 2003 market value rule for transfers to connected companies or for the purposes of group relief, reconstruction relief and acquisition relief under Schedule 7. Stamp duty reserve tax will continue to apply to issues, surrenders and assignments of interests in unit trusts, for example interests under unit trust schemes. Section 102 FA 2003 gives the Revenue power to make regulations to treat open-ended investment companies[65] in the same way as unit trusts.

Joint purchasers

8.87   Section 103 FA 2003 sets out the responsibilities of joint purchasers other than partners or trustees. Most frequently, section 103 will apply in relation to co-owners. The general approach to joint purchasers is that the compliance and payment obligations fall jointly and severally on each purchaser, but that any purchaser may take responsibility for fulfilling those obligations. Joint purchasers need only make one land transaction return. However, the declaration that the return is complete must be made by all of them, as must a declaration on a self-certificate that no SDLT is payable. The joint purchasers are jointly liable to pay the tax.

8.88   If the Revenue enquires into a return, it must give notice separately to each purchaser. The powers to require the production of documents are exercisable separately in relation to each purchaser. A Revenue determination or assessment must be made against all the purchasers and notice given to each. Finally, each joint purchaser has a right to appeal and appeals can only be settled with the agreement of all the purchasers. A decision on an appeal, unsurprisingly, binds all the joint purchasers whether or not they appear.

Partnerships

8.89   Schedule 15 FA 2003 contains the SDLT provisions dealing with partnerships. Part 1 of Schedule 15 defines when a partnership exists for SDLT purposes (this includes an LLP) and provides that it is to be treated as transparent for tax purposes. Part 2 of Schedule 15 deals with the liability and compliance responsibilities when a purchaser purchases land. Part 3 of Schedule 13 is concerned with transfers of land into and out of a partnership by the partners and transfer of partnership interests, which transactions remain outside the scope of SDLT. Parts 1 and 3 are discussed at paragraph 3.44 onwards above. This section is concerned with the compliance consequences of a straightforward purchase of land by a partnership under Part 2 of Schedule 15. However, in some cases, it will be necessary to actively consider whether a partnership exists before considering anything else.

---

[65] As defined in s. 236 of the Financial Services and Markets Act 2000.

An ordinary purchase of land by a partnership falls within the SDLT regime under Part 2 of Schedule 15. The chargeable interest is treated as held by or on behalf of all the partners. The responsible partners are jointly and severally liable to pay tax and to comply with the requirements of SDLT. The responsible partners are those persons who were partners at the effective date of the transaction and any person who becomes a member after that date. However, the partnership may nominate a representative partner to act as the representative of the partnership for SDLT purposes.

Trusts

8.90   The application of SDLT to trusts is set out in Schedule 16. The substantive application of SDLT to trusts is discussed at paragraph 3.35 onwards above. Schedule 16 draws a distinction between 'bare trusts' and other settlements. Where the trustees of a bare trust acquire land, the beneficiary is treated as the purchaser under paragraph 3 of Schedule 16. If the trust is not a bare trust, the trustees are themselves treated as the purchasers. Under paragraph 1(2) of Schedule 16, a bare trust is one where the trustee holds the trust property for one or more persons who are absolutely entitled as against the trustee, or who would be so entitled but for being a minor or a person under a disability. If a person holds property as the nominee of another trust, this is also a bare trust. A person is absolutely entitled against the trustee under paragraph 1(3) where, subject only to satisfying the outstanding liabilities of the trustee, he has the right to direct how the property is to be dealt with. Accordingly, a beneficiary who can exercise his *Saunders* v. *Vautier*[66] rights to determine the trust is absolutely entitled against the trustee.[67]

8.91   Where a person acquires a chargeable interest as bare trustee, the acquisition is attributed to the beneficiary, who is treated as the purchaser. Accordingly, if a trustee buys land on behalf of the beneficiary, it is the beneficiary who must file a return and pay SDLT. While treating bare trusts as transparent for other taxes makes sense, this treatment is questionable for SDLT because often the reason for using a trustee to make a purchase is so that the trustee handles all the responsibilities that arise in connection with it. It does not make sense for a beneficiary to have to complete an SDLT return and pay tax if the whole point of using a trust is so that the beneficiary is not troubled by these sorts of things. However, if the beneficiary is, for example, a minor, then the person who acts as his representative is the taxpayer by virtue of section 106 FA 2003 (discussed at paragraph 8.93 below).

8.92   In contrast, where trustees of a settlement which is not a bare trust acquire land, they are treated as the purchasers. In this situation, the trustees must pay the

---

[66] (1841) 4 Beav 115.
[67] If there are two or more beneficiaries: *Kidson* v. *MacDonald* [1974] Ch 339 and *Stephenson* v. *Barclays Bank Trust Co. Ltd* [1975] 5 TC 151.

SDLT and file the return. The Revenue may recover any payment, including interest and penalties, from any of the responsible trustees. The responsible trustees are the persons who were trustees at the effective date and anyone who subsequently becomes a trustee. The Revenue must issue notices and assessments to each of the relevant trustees.

Persons acting in a representative capacity

8.93   Section 106 deals with four specific categories of persons acting in a representative capacity. Each is made responsible for discharging the SDLT obligations of the person whom he represents. The first category is a person who has responsibility for the management and control of the property of an incapacitated person. The second is parents and guardians of a minor. The third is personal representatives of a purchaser. The fourth is receivers appointed by the court.

The Crown

8.94   A land transaction where the purchaser is a Minister of the Crown, the Scottish Minister or a Northern Ireland department is exempt from charge under section 107(2) FA 2003. Transactions entered into by listed parliamentary bodies are also exempt. This section is incongruously located within the Act because it properly belongs with the other exemptions and reliefs.

8.95   Section 107(1) states that the general rule is that SDLT applies to public offices and departments of the Crown. However, SDLT is not chargeable if SDLT would ultimately be borne by the Crown. Accordingly, a purchase of land by an NHS trust will not be chargeable to SDLT. However, apparently, a purchase by a local council will be chargeable, because local councils are funded partly by council tax. This section is not very satisfactory. Section 107 does not exempt the Crown from having to file a land transaction return, although the implication is it need not do so.

Appeals

8.96   SDLT appeals will now be heard by the General or Special Commissioners. This is in line with other taxes and is a change from the stamp duty position where appeals are heard by the High Court or the Court of Session.

8.97   Schedule 17 gives the Lord Chancellor the power to make regulations concerning appeals to the Commissioners. Almost certainly, those regulations will be the same as those for other taxes. The costs of a successful appeal will therefore be irrecoverable other than in exceptional circumstances. Stamp duty appeals were few and far between, and SDLT will certainly result in an increased amount of litigation.

9

Commencement, transitional provisions and future developments

Introduction

9.1 The SDLT regime will commence on 1 December 2003.[1] The general rule is that SDLT will apply to all land transactions from that date onwards and stamp duty will be abolished except for transfers of stock and marketable securities.[2] However, putting this idea into practice is not straightforward and the result is a lengthy and complicated set of provisions.

9.2 First, many transactions will straddle the commencement of the SDLT regime: most simply, a contract entered into before 1 December 2003 may be completed after that date. Accordingly, special rules are needed to deal with these situations. Where the transactions involve more complex situations, such as sub-sales and option agreements, more complicated rules are required.

9.3 Secondly, not all the provisions of the new regime are ready to commence on 1 December 2003. In particular, the SDLT rules governing the transfer of land into and out of a partnership by a partner and sales of partnership interests are not ready to be implemented, so the old stamp duty rules continue to apply to such transactions (see paragraph 3.44 above). Other provisions will be introduced or possibly amended before commencement using the Treasury's various powers to vary the Act by making regulations.

9.4 This chapter will first discuss when SDLT commences and the transitional rules for transactions which straddle the introduction of SDLT. The second part of the chapter will consider the areas where the SDLT code is incomplete at the time of going to press, when these outstanding issues are scheduled to be dealt with and what other developments are likely to happen in the near future.

---

[1] The implementation date for the new regime is to be appointed by Treasury order under para. 2 of Sch. 19. The Revenue has announced that this date will be 1 December 2003 and has resisted all pressure to postpone it.

[2] S. 125(1) FA 2003.

Commencement and transitional provisions

General rule: a land transaction whose effective date is on or after 1 December 2003 is an SDLT transaction

9.5   The SDLT regime takes effect from the implementation date, 1 December 2003. However, subject to Schedule 19, the SDLT provisions came into force when the Finance Act 2003 received Royal Assent on 10 July 2003. SDLT was brought immediately into force in this way in order to allow the Revenue to exercise the various powers contained in the legislation to make regulations.

9.6   The commencement and transitional provisions are contained in Schedule 19 FA 2003. The key provision is paragraph 2(1) of Schedule 19 which provides that 'a transaction is not an SDLT transaction unless the effective date of the transaction is on or after the implementation date'. The implementation date is the date appointed by the Treasury for the SDLT regime to commence under Schedule 19(2). The implementation date has been announced as 1 December 2003 and the overwhelming likelihood is that SDLT will indeed commence on this date.

9.7   The effective date of a land transaction is the date of completion or substantial performance, whichever is the earlier.[3] The meaning of substantial performance is discussed at paragraph 2.30 above. Accordingly, a land transaction the effective date of which falls on or after 1 December 2003 will usually be an SDLT transaction. However, the rule in paragraph 2 of Schedule 19 is subject to an exception, an extension and a special set of rules which governs sub-sales and options.

Exception: a transaction is not an SDLT transaction if the contract is entered into before 11 July 2003

9.8   First, under paragraph 3 of Schedule 19, a transaction is not an SDLT transaction if it is effected in pursuance of a contract entered into before 11 July 2003 even if that contract is not substantially performed or completed until after that date. 11 July 2003 is the day after the passing of the Finance Act 2003 and is known as the 'first relevant date'.[4] For example, A agrees to sell Blackacre to B by a contract dated 10 July 2003. The contract is completed on 5 December 2003. This transaction is entirely outside the scope of SDLT. *Ad valorem* stamp duty is payable on completion under the old stamp duty regime.

9.9   However, the exception under paragraph 3 does not apply in three cases where the original contract is not simply carried into effect. The first situation is where there is a variation of the contract or an assignment of rights after 10 July 2003.[5] The second situation is where the land transaction is effected in

---

[3] Ss. 119 and 44 FA 2003.   [4] Para. 3(2) of Sch. 19 FA 2003.
[5] Para. 3(3)(a) of Sch. 19 FA 2003.

consequence of the exercise of an option after 10 July 2003.[6] The third situation is where the purchaser is a different person to the purchaser under the original contract because of a further contract made after 10 July 2003.[7] These rules are primarily designed to deal with sub-sales and options and are discussed further at paragraph 9.12 onwards below.

Extension: a transaction entered into after 10 July 2003 and completed on or after 1 December 2003 is an SDLT transaction (even if substantially performed before 1 December 2003)

9.10   The extension to paragraph 2 is contained in paragraph 4 of Schedule 19 which provides that, where a transaction is completed by a conveyance on or after 1 December 2003 then it is an SDLT transaction even if it was substantially performed before that date. The rule in paragraph 4 does not apply either to contracts entered into before 11 July 2003 and kept within the stamp duty regime by paragraph 3 of Schedule 19 or to contracts substantially performed before 11 July 2003. In other words, where a contract for a land transaction is entered into after 10 July 2003, then it must be both substantially performed and completed before 1 December 2003 in order for it not to be an SDLT transaction. The purpose of this rule is to ensure that a transaction which is provided for by a contract after 10 July 2003 and substantially performed but not completed before 1 December 2003 does not fall outside the charge to both stamp duty and SDLT.

Summary of basic transitional provisions

9.11   Provided that the contract is simply carried into effect so that the rules in paragraph 3(3) of Schedule 19 do not apply, then the effect of the transitional provisions in practice is as follows:

1. A contract made on or after 1 December 2003, whether or not it is completed by a separate conveyance, is an SDLT transaction.
2. Where the contract for a land transaction is made after 10 July 2003, then SDLT applies unless it is both substantially performed and completed before 1 December 2003 (relief will be given for any stamp duty paid where the contract was made before 1 December 2003 and the consideration exceeded £10 million[8]).
3. Where the contract for a land transaction is made before 11 July 2003, then SDLT will not apply. This is so even if completion takes place after 1 December 2003. However, if the contract is varied or there is a sub-sale then SDLT may apply under the rules discussed below.

---

[6] Para. 3(3)(b) of Sch. 19 FA 2003.   [7] Para. 3(3)(c) of Sch. 19 FA 2003.
[8] See para. 5 of Sch. 19 FA 2003 and the discussion at para. 9.34 below.

Transitional rules in situations where the original contract not simply given effect to (including sub-sales)

9.12   This section is concerned with how the transitional rules apply in the situation where the original contract is not simply carried into effect. The rules apply not only to sub-sales but also to options and the situation where a contract is varied after 10 July 2003. Owing to the importance of resting on contract and sub-sales as stamp duty planning techniques, these rules have been of huge importance in practice as taxpayers have sought to take advantage of the stamp duty regime before its abolition.

9.13   The provision which governs this area is paragraph 3(3) of Schedule 19, as discussed at paragraph 9.9 above. Paragraph 3(3) provides that the rule that a land transaction made in pursuance of a contract made before 11 July 2003 is outside the scope of SDLT does not apply in the following three situations:

1. if there is any variation of the contract or assignment of rights under the contract on or after that date;
2. if the transaction is effected in consequence of the exercise after that date of any option, right of pre-emption or similar right; or
3. where the purchaser under the transaction is a person other than the purchaser under the contract because of a further contract made on or after that date.

9.14   Importantly, a land transaction within paragraph 3(3) is not automatically within SDLT. The effect of paragraph 3(3) is only to disapply the rule in paragraph 3(1). Accordingly, the next step is to consider the rules in paragraphs 2 and 4 of Schedule 19 to decide whether SDLT applies. In other words, for SDLT to apply to the original contract, either the effective date of the land transaction must be after 1 December 2003, so that it is an SDLT transaction under paragraph 2(1) of Schedule 19, or it must be substantially performed before 1 December 2003 but completed afterwards, so that it is an SDLT transaction by virtue of paragraph 4(3) of Schedule 19. For the original contract to be chargeable to SDLT, the completion or substantial performance must take place otherwise than as part of the completion of the sub-sale, owing to the operation of section 45(3) FA 2003.

9.15   The situations governed by paragraph 3(3) will now be discussed with reference to examples.

Variation of original contract

9.16   Paragraph 3(3)(a) applies where an original contract made before 11 July 2003 is varied. Paragraph 3(3) applies where there has been any variation, however small. For example, it applies where the purchase price is varied between contract and completion or where a purchase of land from a local authority is made subject to a section 106 agreement which is incorporated into the contract. It also applies to the variation of a lease made before 11 July 2003. For example, A agrees to sell Blackacre to B by a contract dated 1 July 2003. A survey discovers a small defect and the purchase price is agreed to be reduced by 5 per cent on 1 August 2003. If the conveyance takes place after 1 December 2003, then SDLT will apply to the sale by virtue of paragraph 4(3) of Schedule 19.

Assignment of rights under original contract and sub-sales

9.17   The application of the transitional provisions to sub-sales and assignments of rights is of enormous ongoing importance. This is because of the huge amount of stamp duty planning which involved resting on contract, the result of which is that many taxpayers, and, in particular, large corporate entities, have split-title[9] structures currently in place. When these structures were established, it was expected that sub-sale relief would be available on a sale to a third party on the winding up of the structure so that stamp duty would only be chargeable on consideration given by the third party. The abolition of sub-sale relief as originally drafted in the Finance Bill 2003 raised the possibility that such a sub-sale could complete both transactions and trigger a double charge to SDLT on both the sub-sale and the original contract. In response to these concerns, the provisions which are now sections 44 and 45 were amended so that it is now clear that SDLT will not apply to contracts where a sub-sale takes place afterwards provided that the original contract is substantially performed before 1 December 2003.

9.18   Assignments and sub-sales are two ways to achieve the same end result. Paragraph 3(3)(a) applies to assignments and paragraph 3(3)(c) to sub-sales. However, nothing turns on that and each is treated in the same way as the other, and for convenience the term 'sub-sale' will be used throughout the following discussion to refer to either. For the meaning of sub-sale and a detailed discussion of the general SDLT rules on sub-sales contained in section 45 FA 2003, see paragraph 3.2 above. In a sub-sale situation, the tax treatment of the original contract and the sub-sale must be considered separately.

Original contract made before 1 December 2003

9.19   If the original contract is made on or after 1 December 2003, then the normal SDLT rules described at paragraph 3.2 above apply. Accordingly, the transitional rules are only concerned with situations where the original contract is made before 1 December 2003. As mentioned above, the effect of paragraph 3(3) of Schedule 19 is that it disapplies paragraph 3(1). Accordingly, where a contract is made before 11 July 2003 and a sub-sale takes place on or after that date, then the original contract is treated in the same way as one made after 10 July 2003.

---

[9]   Where the beneficial owner of the property has not received the legal title in order to avoid paying stamp duty.

9.20   The application of the transitional rules to the original contract in a sub-sale situation requires some difficult analysis. Nevertheless, the result is easy enough to state. The original contract will not be chargeable to SDLT provided that it is substantially performed before 1 December 2003 or never substantially performed apart from on completion of the sub-sale. If the original contract is substantially performed on or after 1 December 2003 apart from on completion of the sub-sale, then it will be chargeable to SDLT.

9.21   The analysis required to reach this conclusion is less straightforward. The statutory position is that, if a sub-sale takes place after 10 July 2003, then paragraph 3(3) of Schedule 19 operates to displace the rule in paragraph 3(1). Accordingly, if the sub-sale agreement was entered into before 11 July 2003, then the original contract remains outside SDLT. If the sub-sale was made after 11 July 2003, then it is necessary to consider the rules in paragraphs 2 and 4 of Schedule 19.

9.22   Paragraph 2(1) of Schedule 19 provides that a transaction is not an SDLT transaction unless its effective date is on or after 1 December 2003. Paragraph 4(2) provides that a transaction is not within SDLT if it was substantially performed before 11 July 2003. Paragraph 4(3) provides that, in any case apart from where the contract was substantially performed before 11 July 2003, the fact that the transaction is substantially performed before 1 December 2003 does not affect the matter of whether the transaction is an SDLT transaction. The effective date of the original contract is the earlier of substantial performance or completion under section 119 FA 2003. The completion of the original contract takes place on completion of the sub-sale because the conveyance to the ultimate purchaser completes both the original contract and the sub-sale.

9.23   However, section 45(3) FA 2003 provides that substantial performance or completion of the original contract at the time of the completion of the sub-sale is to be disregarded. Accordingly, the effective date for the purposes of paragraph 2(1) of Schedule 19 is the date when the contract is substantially performed apart from in connection with the completion of the sub-sale. Whether the original contract is chargeable to SDLT depends upon whether such substantial performance takes place before 1 December 2003.[10]

9.24   For example, A agrees to sell Blackacre to B on 1 July 2003. B goes into possession on 1 August 2003, before completion, and agrees to sub-sell Blackacre to C on 1 October 2003. If the sub-sale is completed after 1 December 2003, then the original contract between A and B is not chargeable to SDLT because the effective date is 1 August 2003, the date of substantial performance.[11]

---

[10] This interpretation is contrary to the statement made by the Chief Secretary to the Treasury in Standing Committee (before the legislation was amended).

[11] See para. 2(1), Sch. 19 and s. 45(3), and the Stamp Office Customer newsletter, issue 3.

9.25   A sub-sale must be considered separately from the original contract, and the rules in paragraphs 2–4 of Schedule 19 apply to determine whether it is within the SDLT regime. If a contract for a sub-sale is made before 11 July 2003, then it is outside the scope of SDLT under paragraph 3(1) of Schedule 19. If a contract for a sub-sale is made after 10 July 2003, then it will be an SDLT transaction unless it is both substantially performed and completed before 1 December 2003,[12] in the same way as any other contract, by virtue of paragraphs 2 and 4 of Schedule 19.

9.26   For example, A agrees to sell Blackacre to B for £100,000 on 1 August 2003 and B pays a £10,000 deposit. On 2 September 2003, B, before completion of the original contract has taken place, agrees to sell Blackacre to C for £120,000. Completion of both contracts takes place on 1 November 2003 when C pays £120,000 to B and B pays the remaining £90,000 to A and B directs A to make a conveyance directly to C. These transactions are outside the scope of SDLT entirely. *Ad valorem* stamp duty is payable on the £120,000 paid by C for the sub-sale.

9.27   A contract for a sub-sale or an assignment of rights made after 1 December 2003 is chargeable to SDLT in the normal way. Accordingly, tax becomes payable on the chargeable consideration given by the sub-purchaser on the effective date of the transaction.

9.28   For example, A agrees to sell Blackacre to B for £1 million on 1 October 2003. B pays a deposit of £100,000 and completion is fixed for 1 January 2004. On 20 December 2003, B assigns her rights to C for £1.2 million. Completion only takes place on 1 January 2004 when C pays £900,000 to A and £300,000 to B and A makes a conveyance to C.

9.29   The assignment is chargeable to SDLT under section 45 on the £1.2 million given by C. Whether the original contract between A and B is also chargeable will depend on whether it is substantially performed after 1 December 2003 apart from in connection with the completion of the sub-sale.

Options

9.30   The third situation covered by paragraph 3(3) of Schedule 19 is the exercise of an option. The effect of paragraph 3(3)(b) is to confirm that the land transaction arising from the exercise of an option is within SDLT if it is either substantially performed or completed after 1 December 2003 under the rules contained in paragraphs 2(1) and 4 of Schedule 19. Paragraph 3(3)(b) does not itself

---

[12]   Unless it is never carried into effect.

affect the position of the original grant. However, paragraph 9 of Schedule 19 contains a much tougher rule, the effect of which is that consideration given for the grant of an option made on or after 17 April 2003 and exercised on or after 1 December 2003 is chargeable to SDLT.

9.31   Paragraph 9 of Schedule 19 contains a special rule for options and rights of pre-emption granted before 1 December 2003 but exercised after that date. Paragraph 9(4) of Schedule 19 provides that, in this case, the acquisition of the option is treated as automatically linked with the exercise of the option. Any stamp duty paid on grant is credited against the SDLT chargeable on exercise under paragraph 9(5). This rule is overly harsh and more strict than the SDLT rule itself because a genuine option not acquired for tax purposes would arguably not be linked with the exercise of it, as discussed at paragraph 3.22 onwards above.

9.32   Moreover, if the option was granted or varied on or after 17 April 2003, then the consideration for the grant or variation is not only aggregated for the purposes of the linked transactions rules but actually deemed to be part of the consideration for the exercise by virtue of paragraph 9(2) and (3). Again, credit is given for stamp duty paid on the acquisition of the option. The intention behind paragraph 9 is to ensure that consideration given for the grant of an option after 16 April 2003 is chargeable to stamp duty or SDLT. However, its effect is wider because options where the grant is genuinely separate from the exercise are also deemed to be linked transactions.

Interaction between SDLT and stamp duty

9.33   From 1 December 2003 stamp duty is only chargeable on instruments relating to stock or marketable securities, by virtue of section 125(1) FA 2003.[13] In addition, stamp duty also continues to apply as a temporary measure to transactions involving transfers of land to and from a partnership by a partner and to the acquisition and disposal of interests in partnerships under section 125(8) and Schedule 13 as discussed at paragraph 9.3 above. Section 125(5) expressly provides that stamp duty is only abolished for land transactions that are SDLT transactions or would be but for an exemption or relief from SDLT.

9.34   Where *ad valorem* stamp duty is paid on a contract entered into before the implementation day and SDLT subsequently becomes payable, the stamp duty is credited against the SDLT payable under paragraph 5 of Schedule 19. This will be the case, for example, where the contract is chargeable itself under section 115 FA 2002 because the consideration exceeds £10 million. It should be noted, however, that, where there are a number of such contracts in the

---

[13] S. 125(1).

period prior to 1 December 2003 with a number of such stamp duty charges arising, then the credit will be inadequate because the stamp duty charge under section 115 is limited to the profit element under each contract. The credit will therefore not equal the full amount of SDLT due and there will be an excess to pay. Conversely, where SDLT is chargeable on a conveyance under a contract made before the implementation date, then that contract is deemed to be duly stamped for stamp duty purposes under paragraph 6(1) of Schedule 19.

9.35   Paragraph 7 of Schedule 19 deals with the situation where, in applying the linked transactions rules for SDLT, one or more of the earlier transactions was chargeable to stamp duty. In this situation, the consideration on which *ad valorem* stamp duty was paid is included in the aggregation for SDLT purposes.

9.36   Paragraph 8 of Schedule 19 makes a provision corresponding to section 240 FA 1994 for the transitional period between stamp duty and SDLT. It provides that, where an agreement for a lease is entered into before the implementation date and a lease giving effect to the agreement is executed after the implementation date, then the stamp duty interest and penalty provisions do not apply, provided the lease and agreement are presented for stamping together and any stamp duty is paid.

Likely future developments

9.37   The introduction of SDLT as enacted in the FA 2003 is a huge change, but the development of SDLT is only beginning. There are a number of gaps in the SDLT regime, such as the treatment of partnership transactions, that need to be filled by new legislation, and the Treasury has a number of specific powers to amend the statute. Other areas, notably the tax treatment of rental leases, are subject to ongoing consultation. It is also worth looking ahead to consider what the effect of the new tax is likely to be in practice and in particular how the new compliance regime is going to operate.

Implementation date

9.38   Most important of all, the Treasury must make an order to appoint the implementation date under paragraph 2(2) of Schedule 19 FA 2003. The government has announced that 1 December 2003 will be that date and has steadfastly resisted pressure to delay.

The charge to SDLT on rental leases

9.39   As discussed in Chapter 6 above, although section 56 and Schedule 5 FA 2003 have been enacted, these provisions are subject to an ongoing consultation and the Treasury has an express power to amend the legislation under section 112(1) FA 2003. The power under section 112 must be exercised by the implementation date, so any change must be announced by 1 December 2003.

It is highly likely that there will be some change to Schedule 5, although in practice the benefit to taxpayers is unlikely to be great. The possible changes are discussed in Chapter 6 above. The Revenue is also likely to clarify how it will interpret the requirement under section 51(2) FA 2003 to provide a reasonable estimate of uncertain rents in the particular case where the rent is determined by reference to turnover or profits.

Partnerships

9.40   Land transactions relating to partnerships are currently excluded from SDLT by Part 3 of Schedule 15, as discussed in at paragraph 3.44 onwards above. New rules governing transactions involving partnerships are due to be introduced in 2004 following consultation on published draft clauses, which are currently awaited. The government's intention is to prevent perceived avoidance in this area, and its proposals are likely to be challenged during the consultation on the basis that they penalise commercial rather than tax-driven structures. Those with partnership interests are likely to feel aggrieved if they see their structures treated more harshly than the corporate vehicles which were not attacked by the SDLT provisions despite the government's stated intention in its April 2002 consultative document to charge all land-rich vehicles within the new tax.

Corporate finance transactions

9.41   Security interests such as ordinary mortgage arrangements are excluded from SDLT under section 48 FA 2003. Individuals, but not companies, can benefit from the reliefs for other types of finance transaction under sections 72 and 73 FA 2003. Accordingly, it would seem right in principle that corporate finance transactions connected with land should only be charged to the extent that a net interest in land is transferred. The Revenue is clearly concerned that a general relief for securitisations of land and sale-and-leaseback arrangements would be susceptible to abuse. Nevertheless, taxpayers will lobby hard for such a relief and continued skirmishing is to be expected here.

Complex commercial transactions

9.42   Special provisions dealing with complex commercial transactions may also be enacted in the near future, possibly as part of the Finance Act 2004. Areas of particular interest are internal transactions within large property developments and PFI deals. Chapter 3 contains a discussion of the particular problems that SDLT may pose for PFI. The Finance Act 2003 does not contain any special treatment for land transactions in this area, though the relief for situations where tax would be borne by the Crown under section 107 FA 2003 may be relevant for pre-PFI restructuring. It is possible that special provisions for sale-and-leaseback arrangements as part of PFI transactions will be enacted.

Minor amendments

9.43 Missing reliefs and consequential changes to other statutes also fall to be implemented as a tidying-up exercise. The significant reliefs to be reinstated are those for land transactions in connection with reorganisations and mergers of friendly societies and building societies.

Statements of Practice and Revenue guidance

9.44 The Revenue's interpretation of the SDLT provisions will be made known by a range of measures including the publication of a new internal administrative manual, formal Statements of Practice, leaflets and newsletters. Only one publication from the stamp duty era directly applies to SDLT – SP 1/2003 on the disadvantaged areas relief. Other information is urgently needed but, realistically, will emerge over an extended period. Areas of greatest interest include the tests for group relief (to replace SP 3/98) and the treatment of building contracts when land is acquired (to replace SP 8/93). Guidance on how the Revenue will apply the new linked transactions rule in section 108 FA 2003 would also be useful but it is likely that the Revenue's interpretation will be contested by some taxpayers and appeals may be brought before the Commissioners. Revenue guidance, including Customer newsletters is available via the Stamp Taxes website, www.inlandrevenue.gov.uk/so/. There is also a Revenue Enquiry Line, 0845 6030135.

Case law

9.45 Disputes are bound to arise over the many uncertain and contentious areas in the legislation which will fall to be settled in the courts. This will in due course build up SDLT-specific case law. Now that appeals are to the Commissioners rather than direct to the High Court, it is thought that the parties may be more willing to proceed to a hearing as cost should be less of a deterrent.

Administration

9.46 The administration of SDLT is unlikely to be static, even when all the sets of administrative regulations are in place. The land transaction return will be amended from time to time and, in the longer term, the land registries will embark on e-conveyancing (initially for residential property) which will incorporate the collection of SDLT. In the meantime, processing of land transaction returns will be centralised at Netherton and some of the existing Stamp Offices will take on specialised roles. There will be a Risk Identification Assessment Team (RIAT) based in Bristol, which will be responsible for the criteria used to select cases for enquiries. The Complex Commercial Unit will be based in Manchester to review larger land transactions, and Worthing will be the general Customer Service Unit. Other Stamp Offices will be standard compliance offices.

Compliance under the SDLT regime

9.47   The work in reforming stamp duty on land has thus far been carried out by the Revenue, its helpers from industry and the professions who have participated in the consultations, parliamentary draughtsmen, and legislators. But implementation of SDLT draws in the individuals and businesses who will pay the new tax and their advisers on individual transactions. The new compliance regime in particular creates significant and onerous obligations of making returns, paying the tax on time, monitoring the position on an ongoing basis and maintaining records. In particular, those liable will be required to self-assess, pay and file within thirty days of the 'effective date' of the land transaction. Further, if land registration is required, they will have to produce a Revenue certificate that the return has been received or a self-certificate that the land transaction is not a notifiable one.

9.48   Any businesses such as property investment companies, banks that finance property transactions, retail outlets, hotels, pubs, shops and all companies where property is an enabling asset need to be prepared to tackle the new compliance issues that will arise. Companies need to review all their systems to be able to record and identify all those events that will be classified as land transactions under the new regime and make sure they are set up to retain all land conveyancing files for the required six years.

9.49   Companies will therefore need to adopt systems to alert themselves to the SDLT triggers and to identify, report and pay the tax due. These systems will need to cater for subsequent adjustments where paper is not involved and will need to be capable of handling complex calculations on occasions. They will also need to be capable of spotting and applying reliefs such as that for disadvantaged areas. They should also be capable of picking up clawback situations. Many companies may therefore think it expedient to look at developing arrangements for electronic systems for the secure transmission of returns and payment as well as for the safe storage of data.

9.50   Revenue enforcement may at first be geared towards taxpayer education. But we can be sure that over time the direct enquiry powers will come to be used more and more, and these will be backed up by the use of penalties for those who fail to comply to the Revenue's satisfaction. SDLT was largely enacted to counter perceived avoidance of a voluntary duty. Undoubtedly, the Revenue officials who administer the new tax will see the enforcement of the mandatory tax as a key priority.

Future development of the law

9.51   Finally, SDLT is a modern tax replete with anti-avoidance provisions and backed up by a self-assessment regime. Accordingly, it is expected that its development will follow that of other taxes. Annual amendments will be made in the Finance Act and many of these will be designed to put an end to the latest planning as well as filling the gaps in the SDLT code. Moreover, section 109 FA 2003 gives the Revenue a general power to amend the legislation (other than the rates of tax) by making regulations; any regulations must first be approved by the House of Commons under section 110 FA 2003. From a constitutional perspective, this is an alarming power. However, from a tax perspective, it is quite normal because the Revenue will often announce that the law will be changed retrospectively to alter the tax treatment with effect from the date of the press release. It is anticipated that section 109 will be used in order to counter tax planning that the Revenue regards as avoidance.

Appendix 1   Practitioner checklist

Shown below are the key questions that a practitioner or potential taxpayer needs to consider when a transaction might have an SDLT consequence. Terms shown in bold are listed in the Glossary with cross-references to the relevant chapters of this book. The checklist is intended to remind the reader about the relevant concepts and is neither exhaustive nor a substitute for a full analysis.

1. **Is the transaction potentially subject to SDLT?**
   (a) Is there a **land transaction**?
       - must be an **acquisition** of a **chargeable interest** in **land**
       - UK **land** must be involved in the transaction
       - **exchanges** are treated as two land transactions
   (b) Is there a **chargeable interest**?
       - either an interest in UK **land**
       - or the benefit of a condition, etc. affecting the value of an interest
       - **exempt interests** not chargeable (e.g. **licences, security interests**)
   (c) What is an **acquisition**?
       - A transfer of an existing interest
       - a grant of a new lease
       - a creation of a new interest
       - the surrender or release of an interest
       - the variation of an interest

2. **Who is the taxpayer?**
   The **purchaser** in a land transaction must deliver a return and pay any SDLT on the **chargeable consideration** within thirty days of the **effective date**.
   Who is the **purchaser**?
       - transferee of an existing interest
       - person entitled to a new interest
       - person whose interest benefits from a surrender, release or variation
       - in each case a person must either give consideration or be a party to the transaction to be treated as a purchaser

3. **On what date is the SDLT payable?**
   (a) What is the **effective date** of the transaction?
       - normally **completion**

- if the contract is **substantially performed** then the date of substantial performance is the effective date
- for options it is the date on which the option is acquired

(b) When is a contract **substantially performed**?

- when the **purchaser** takes possession of the whole or substantially the whole of the land; or
- the **purchaser** becomes entitled to receive the rents or profits; or
- a substantial amount of the consideration is paid or provided; or
- in the case of a lease, the first payment of rent is made

4. **What is the amount on which SDLT is payable?**

(a) Is there any **chargeable consideration** for the transaction? The general rules include the following when given as consideration:

- money or money's worth given directly or indirectly by the purchaser or a person connected with him
- VAT chargeable in respect of the transaction
- existing debt assumed by the purchaser (including transfer of land between parties subject to an existing mortgage and transferee takes over mortgage payments)
- the release of debt due to the purchaser or owed by the vendor
- the value of **building works** (though not where the works are carried out after the **effective date** on land held by the purchaser or a person connected with him and it is not a condition of the transaction that the works are carried out by the vendor or a person connected with him)
- the value of the **provision of services**
- the **net present value** of rent under special rules for leases

(b) When do special rules operate in calculating **chargeable consideration**?

- consideration attributable to more than one matter is apportioned on a just and reasonable basis
- **postponed** consideration is included without a discount
- special rules for **contingent**, **uncertain** or **unascertainable** consideration
- special rule for **partitions** of joint entitlements
- special rule for employee benefits
- contingent consideration ignored in **right-to-buy** transactions
- **annuities** etc. limited to twelve years' payments
- **market value** rule applies to exchanges
- deemed **market value** may apply if the **purchaser** is a **connected company** or if part of the consideration is shares in a **connected company**

5. **When is there no SDLT to pay?**

- land is outside the UK
- exempt interest including **licences** and **security interests**
- chargeable consideration below the threshold – threshold is lower for property which is entirely **residential**

- **exemptions** including where there is no consideration
- **reliefs** including
  - **disadvantaged areas relief**
  - **group relief**
  - **reconstruction relief**
  - **acquisition relief**
  - **charities relief**

6. **How much SDLT is payable?**
   (a) How is SDLT calculated (other than on rent)? As a percentage of the **chargeable consideration**:
   - the **percentage rate of tax** depends on the band of **relevant consideration**
   - the lowest band is different for **residential** property
   - the 0 per cent band does not apply for the premium for the grant of a lease if **average annual rent** exceeds £600
   - for **linked transactions** the total consideration determines the rate of tax
   - a fraction of the consideration determines the rate of tax for **collective enfranchisement** and **crofting community right to buy**
   (b) What is the SDLT charge on a lease where rent is payable?
   - the premium for the lease is charged in the normal way
   - calculate the **net present value** of the rent over the period of the lease
   - apply the charging formula to the calculated **net present value**

7. **What are the compliance responsibilities?**
   (a) Which land transactions must be notified to the Revenue?
   - grants of leases for at least seven years if there is chargeable consideration
   - grants of leases under seven years if they are chargeable to SDLT or if they would be chargeable but for a **relief**
   - other acquisitions of **major interests** unless **exempt** under Schedule 3
   - acquisitions of other interests if they are chargeable to SDLT or if they would be chargeable but for a **relief**
   (b) How does SDLT affect land registration?
   - **certificate** required for registering or evidencing land transactions except for contracts to be completed by a conveyance and transfers of rights under such contracts
   - **Revenue certificate** if the land transaction is **notifiable**
   - **self-certificate** otherwise
   (c) What are the ongoing concerns and obligations?
   - records to be preserved for at least six years after the **effective date** of a **land transaction**
   - some reliefs subject to three-year **clawback**
   - duty to submit further **land transaction returns** once **contingent, uncertain** or **unascertained** consideration becomes known

8. **Is it stamp duty or SDLT for a transaction spanning 1 December 2003?**

Depends on timing of:
- executing the contract
- substantially performing the contract
- exercising any option
- any variation, assignment or sub-sale
- completing the contract with a conveyance

In relation to:
- Royal Assent (10 July 2003)
- implementation date (1 December 2003)

Check the Revenue transitional flowchart (www.inlandrevenue.gov.uk/so/sdlt_flowchart .pdf) to see if you have an SDLT transaction.

Appendix 2   Table of exemptions and reliefs

Exempt land transactions (under Schedule 3)

	Description	Paragraph of this book	FA 2003	Corresponding stamp duty exemption
Transactions where there is no chargeable consideration	Transactions for no chargeable consideration, including gifts and transfers of property into and out of trusts, are exempt.	5.5	section 50, Schedule 3, paragraph 1	Category L of Regulation 4 to the Schedule to the Stamp Duty (Exempt Instruments) Regulations 1987 (SI 1987 No. 516)
Certain grants of leases by registered social landlords	A limited range of leases granted by registered social landlords to individuals are exempt.	5.13	Schedule 3, paragraph 2	FA 2003, section 128
Transactions in contemplation of or in connection with divorce or separation	Land transactions between the parties to a marriage in connection with or in contemplation of divorce or judicial separation are exempt.	5.8	Schedule 3, paragraph 3	Category H of Regulation 4 to the Schedule to the Stamp Duty (Exempt Instruments) Regulations 1987 (SI 1987 No. 516)
Variation of testamentary dispositions, etc.	A transaction within two years of a person's death that varies a disposition of property for no monetary consideration is exempt.	5.11	Schedule 3, paragraph 4	Category M of Regulation 4 to the Schedule to the Stamp Duty (Exempt Instruments) Regulations 1987 (SI 1987 No. 516)

Reliefs

	Description	Paragraph of this book	FA 2003	Corresponding stamp duty exemption
Acquisition by bodies established for national purposes	The National Heritage Memorial Fund, the Historic Buildings and Monuments Commission for England, the Trustees of the British Museum and the Trustees of the Natural History Museum are exempt.	5.98	section 69	FA 1982, section 129(1)
Acquisition relief	Reduces SDLT rate to 0.5 per cent when a purchaser company acquires land as part of the undertaking of the vendor company in return for shares. There is a clawback of the relief if certain events affecting the control of the purchasing company occur within three years.	5.79	section 62 Schedule 7, Part 2, paragraphs 8–13	FA 1986, section 86
Alternative property finance	Relief is available for financing arrangements, including 'Islamic mortgages', where an individual sells land to a financial institution which leases it back or resells it to him.	5.101	sections 72 and 73	Not applicable
Charities relief	Purchases of land made by charities are exempt subject to charitable use of the land and subject to clawback in the event of a disqualifying event within three years.	5.93	section 68, Schedule 8	FA 1982, section 129

(Cont.)

	Description	Paragraph of this book	FA 2003	Corresponding stamp duty exemption
Collective enfranchisement by leaseholders	Rate of SDLT determined by reference to fraction of consideration. Effectively, SDLT is charged as if leaseholders acquired their shares of the freehold separately.	5.110	section 74	Not applicable
Compliance with planning obligations	Land transactions which transfer land to a public authority in order to comply with a planning obligation are exempt from charge.	5.89	section 61	Not applicable
Compulsory purchase facilitating development	Prevents a double charge to SDLT where the person acquiring the property is not the ultimate developer, for example a local planning authority.	5.88	section 60	Not applicable
Crofting community right to buy	Rate of SDLT determined by reference to the total consideration divided by the number of crofts. Effectively, SDLT is payable as if each crofter were to purchase his land separately.	5.111	section 75	Not applicable
Demutualisation of building society	A land transaction on the demutualisation of a building society effected under section 97 of the Building Societies Act 1966 is exempt from charge.	5.108	section 64	Building Societies Act 1986, section 109
Demutualisation of insurance company	When land is transferred as part of the demutualisation of an insurance company, that transfer is exempt from charge, subject to a number of conditions.	5.106	section 63	FA 1987, section 96(5)
Disadvantaged areas	All acquisitions of non-residential property in the designated areas are exempt, as are purchases of residential property up to £150,000.	5.24	section 57, Schedule 6	FA 2001, section 92 and Schedule 30, as amended

	Description	Paragraph of this book	FA 2003	Corresponding stamp duty exemption
Exchanges of residential property involving housebuilders	Relief where a housebuilding company acquires an individual's main residence in part-exchange for a new dwelling.	5.35	section 58	Not applicable, although note Stamp Act 1891, section 58(4)
Group relief	Group relief is available for transfers of land between companies in a 75 per cent group subject to conditions about arrangements for de-grouping the purchaser and the provision of external finance. There is a clawback of the relief in the event that the purchaser de-groups within three years.	5.46	sections 62, Schedule 7, Part 1	FA 1930, section 42, and FA 1995, section 151
Incorporation of limited liability partnership	Transfers of land to a limited liability partnership in connection with its incorporation are exempt from charge, subject to three conditions.	5.99	section 65	Limited Liability Partnerships Act 2000, section 12
Parliamentary constituency reorganisation	Transfers of land by a local constituency organisation to its successor which occur as a result of a boundary change to parliamentary constituencies are exempt from charge.	5.112	section 67	Finance (No. 2) Act 1983, section 7
Purchases by the Crown	Purchases by government ministers, departments, Parliament, etc. are exempt.	5.2	section 107	FA 1987, section 55(1)
Reconstruction relief	Total exemption from charge when a purchaser company acquires land as part of the undertaking of the vendor company in return for shares and detailed conditions are met. There is a clawback of the relief if certain events affecting the control of the purchasing company occur within three years.	5.73	section 62, Schedule 7, Part 2, paragraphs 7 and 9–13	FA 1986, section 75

(Cont.)

	Description	Paragraph of this book	FA 2003	Corresponding stamp duty exemption
Registered social landlords	Registered social landlords are exempted from charge when they are tenant-controlled, when they purchase from other RSLs or certain public bodies, or the purchase benefits from a public subsidy.	5.14	section 71	FA 2000, section 130
Relocation relief	Relief when an employer or specialist relocation company purchases an employee's main residence when the employee has to move home due to job relocation.	5.40	section 59	Not applicable
Right-to-buy transactions, shared-ownership leases, etc.	Certain transactions involving purchases at a discount from public sector bodies or registered social landlords have special rules to charge the consideration paid after allowing for the discount, without taking account of contingent consideration.	5.16	section 70, Schedule 9	FA 1980, section 97
Statutory reorganisation of public bodies	A land transaction is exempt from charge if both vendor and purchaser are public bodies and the reorganisation is effected under a statutory provision.	5.91	section 66	Not applicable

Appendix 3   Analysis of Scottish property deeds

Scottish conveyancing procedure admits a wide range of documents for different purposes. Some will give effect to a 'land transaction' as defined in sections 43 and 48 FA 2003, and of those some will relate to a 'major interest' as defined in section 117 FA 2003. This will be relevant in determining whether a transaction is notifiable so that a land transaction return is required to be submitted to the Revenue (see paragraph 8.6 onwards above) and, accordingly, whether a Revenue certificate or a self-certificate is required to be submitted to the Registers of Scotland under section 79 (see paragraph 8.47 onwards above).

There follows a list of common Scottish property deeds and a note of whether it is considered these give effect to a land transaction, and, if so, whether they relate to a major interest. Remember that available exemptions may also affect whether a return is required, for example if the land transaction to which the document gives effect is entered into for no chargeable consideration.

Document	Effects a land transaction?	Major interest?	Comments
Assignation of lease	Yes	Yes	
Assignation of standard security	No	N/A	Exempt – security interest
Assumption and conveyance, deed of	Yes	Yes	Transfers title to new trustees of beneficial interest
Charter of novodamus	Yes	Yes	
Compulsory purchase order	Yes	Yes	Exempt but notifiable – section 60
Consolidation, minute of	Yes	Yes (unless it only consolidates superiority and mid-superiority interests)	
Deed of conditions	Yes	No	

(*Cont.*)

175

Document	Effects a land transaction?	Major interest?	Comments
Deed of gift by QLTR	Yes	Yes if relating to *dominium utile*	Exempt – no consideration
Discharge of real burdens	Yes	No	
Discharge of standard security	No	N/A	Exempt – security interest
Disposition	Yes	Yes (unless of a superiority)	
Disposition *ad perpetuam remanentiam*	Yes	Yes (if grantee is owner of *dominium utile*)	
Excambion, contract of	Yes	Yes (unless it relates only to superiority interests)	
Feu disposition	Yes	Yes	
Forestry dedication agreement	Yes	No	
General vesting declaration	Yes	Yes	
Lease	Yes	Yes	
Lease, minute of extension of	Yes	Yes	
Lease, minute of variation of	Yes	Depends on nature of variation	
Memorandum of allocation of feu duty	Yes	No	Exempt – no consideration
Missives of let	Yes	Yes	
Notice of title	Yes	Yes (unless only relating to superiority interests)	
Partnership agreement	No	N/A	
Partnership, minute of dissolution of	No	N/A	Might have the effect of transferring beneficial ownership of land from partnership to former partners, but this would be excluded from SDLT under paragraph 12 of Schedule 15.

Document	Effects a land transaction?	Major interest?	Comments
Ranking agreement	No	N/A	Exempt – security interest
Renunciation of lease	Yes	Yes	
Resignation of liferent	Yes	No	
Servitude, grant of	Yes	No	
Servitude, discharge of	Yes	No	
Standard security	No	N/A	Exempt – security interest
Statutory conveyance	Yes	Yes	May be exempt under section 107
Sublease	Yes	Yes	
Trust, declaration of	Possibly	Possibly	May have effect equivalent to creation of a beneficial interest in land
Wayleave agreement	Yes	No	

Index